Mr Sadler is Principal Lecturer in Education at the City of Birmingham College of Education and was formerly Senior Lecturer in Education at the Nigerian College in Northern Nigeria. He is author of a successful textbook for African students, A *West African Teachers Guide* and, with Mr A. N. Gillett, part-author of the well-known book *Training for Teaching: A Three Year Course.*

J. A. COMENIUS AND THE CONCEPT
OF UNIVERSAL EDUCATION

by the same author

WEST AFRICAN TEACHER'S GUIDE

TRAINING FOR TEACHING
(part-author)

1. Family Teaching in The Czech Brethren

J. A. COMENIUS AND THE CONCEPT OF UNIVERSAL EDUCATION

BY

JOHN EDWARD SADLER

M.A.

Principal Lecturer in Education
City of Birmingham College of Education

London
GEORGE ALLEN & UNWIN LTD
RUSKIN HOUSE MUSEUM STREET

FIRST PUBLISHED IN 1966

*This book is copyright under the Berne Convention.
Apart from any fair dealing for the purposes of
private study, research, criticism or review, as per-
mitted under the Copyright Act, 1956, no portion
may be reproduced by any process without written
permission. Inquiries should be addressed to the
publishers.*

© George Allen and Unwin Ltd, 1966

PRINTED IN GREAT BRITAIN
in 11 point Juliana type
BY EAST MIDLAND PRINTING CO LTD
BURY ST EDMUNDS

PREFACE

THIS study of the work of John Amos Comenius arose from a suggestion by the Czech artist, Kokoschka, to Sir Stanley Unwin from which I was able to profit. I am very grateful to Sir Stanley Unwin for his interest in the project and for his support in carrying it out.

It became clear that a visit to Czechoslovakia was essential and through the good offices of the British Council I became the guest of the Czech Ministry of Education in Prague. I was able to attach myself to the Comenius Research Group of the Pedagogical Institute and the members gave me generously of their time and knowledge. I was able to visit places in Moravia associated with Comenius and gained much assistance from those I met at Brno, Fulnek, Uherský Brod and Přerov. Since returning to England I have maintained my contacts with Czech scholars who have given me unfailing kindness.

In England I have been helped and encouraged by Professor M. V. C. Jeffreys and Dr P. Platt of the Birmingham Institute of Education.

I owe a very deep debt of gratitude to Dr Dagmar Čapkova who has read through my manuscript and given me the benefit of her unique knowledge of Comenius.

I have chosen to concentrate my attention upon the theme of universal education as it appears in the work of Comenius and for which he found a ready response in England. It might well serve as a point of common interest between the peoples of Great Britain and Czechoslovakia at the present day.

ABBREVIATIONS

ODO   J. A. Comenii *Opera Didactica Omnia*. 4 Vols. Amsterdam 1657.

Labyrinth   *The Labyrinth of the World and the Paradise of the Heart* (First Czech Edition Leszno 1631).

Janua   *Janua Linguarum Reserata* (First Edition 1633).

Physica   *Physicae ad Lumen Divinum Reformatae Synopsis* (1633)

Methodus   *Methodus Linguarum Novissima* (First Edition Leszno 1648).

Continuatio   *Continuatio admonitionis fraternae ad S. Maresium* (First Edition Amsterdam 1669).

Consultatio   *De Rerum Humanarum Emendatione Consultatio Catholica* (Seven Parts).

VSJAK   *Veškeré spisy Jana Amosa Komenského* (Brno 1910-1929).

CONTENTS

ILLUSTRATIONS

CHAPTER 1

INTRODUCTION

SINCE 1829 when František Palacký drew the attention of his countrymen to the greatness of John Amos Comenius (Komenský) numerous biographies have been written and it would be superfluous to add to their number. The most detailed account in Czech is that of J. V. Novák and Josef Hendrich in 1932. There is an excellent study in French by Anna Heyberger in 1928 but the best English biography is entitled *That Incomparable Moravian* by Matthew Spinka of Chicago in 1934. There is a wealth of material in the collections of Correspondence of A. Patera in 1892 and of Jan Kvačala in 1897 and 1902 and also in the papers of Samuel Hartlib used by G. H. Turnbull in 1947. Comenius wrote an autobiographical defence against the attacks of one Samuel Maresius in 1669 (*Continuatio admonitionis*) parts of which have been translated into English by R. F. Young in 1932 (*Comenius in England*). Following the Prague Conference of 1957 on the 300th anniversary of the publication of the *Collected Works* of Comenius (*Opera Didactica Omnia*) a popular account was written by František Kožík and this has been translated into English (*Sorrowful and Heroic Life of John Amos Comenius*) in 1958 and two novels in Czech have aroused much interest in his story.[1] Nevertheless it is necessary to give a survey of the biographical, historical and bibliographical background to the development of ideas concerning universal education.

BIOGRAPHICAL

A strong sense of vocation is the key to the life of Comenius in that it lifted him above circumstances, above his critics, even above his own defects and limitations. An essentially humble man, his lips had been touched with a live coal from the altar and this gave him a consciousness of power which would otherwise have indicated presumption. Thus it was in keeping that he should compare himself to Moses – 'since my wish, so like to that of Moses (of desiring that all people should be prophets) became known, I have found so many opponents, that I cannot keep silent'[2] and the comparison might well form a basis for an analysis of his life.

John Comenius was born on March 28, 1592, though, like Moses, in obscurity. There were three girls and himself in the family of Martin and Anna Komenský and they came from the village of Komna in South East Moravia. A few miles away is the town of Uherský Brod where the father became a respected member of the religious body known as the Unity of Brethren and where Comenius grew up. In the seventeenth century it was a place of some importance though it had declined since the Middle Ages. The print of 1704[3] shows four gates in the wall that surrounded it but it was evidently not impregnable for one sector is on fire and this was not the first time for it was partially destroyed in 1683. Some distance away and nearer to the pine and birch-clad slopes of the White Carpathians is the smaller town of Nivnice, confidently claimed by many as the actual birth-place. The mill is pointed out, beside a quietly-flowing stream, which local inhabitants are convinced marks the site of his original home and where he spent some of his childhood years.

At the age of twelve John Comenius lost father, mother and two sisters, probably from pestilence. They were buried in the cemetery of Uherský Brod[4] and an uneasy period followed for the orphan. For a short time he was at Strážnice nearer to the Hungarian border in the charge of an improvident aunt and unhappy at school. Then he came back until, at the age of sixteen, he was sent by his Church to the Grammar School of Přerov, and it was here that his fortune changed. He proved to be an apt scholar and was accepted into the household of the Rector, Bishop Lanecký, as an acolyte in training for the ministry. From the bishop he received the name of Amos, meaning Loving, and was accepted almost as a son. Through the Bishop he was brought to the favourable notice of the leading nobleman protector of the Brethren, Charles Žerotín, and thus a few days after his nineteenth birthday he matriculated at the Calvinist Academy of Herborn in Nassau. In his studies he had an intense sense of purpose and excellent teachers and, in a remarkably short time, laid the foundations of a scholarship which, if not profound, was adequate for his needs. After a brief visit to Amsterdam he went for a year to the University of Heidelberg where he received inspiration from his teachers and interest from the wedding of the young Elector Palatine, Frederick, to Princess Elizabeth of England.

His studies finished, he returned to Přerov as a teacher until, at the age of twenty-four, he was ordained as a Minister of the Brethren at a Synod held at Zeravice in Moravia. For the next two years he acted as assistant to Bishop Lanecký and his first pastoral appointment was to the church at Fulnek in Northern Moravia. He was held in high esteem and had a very considerable responsibility with a mixed congregation of Czechs and Germans and the direction of a school. The Church buildings were considerable as is obvious from the reconstruction work now being carried out by Professor Menel. The minister's house had accommodation for servants and young men preparing for the service of the Church and when he went to Fulnek Comenius took with him as wife the stepdaughter of the Burgomaster of Přerov, Magdalena Vizovská. Within the year he was comfortably settled in, a child was born, he had a library and a reasonable expectation of useful service. He might have considered himself a prince in Egypt.

Almost immediately there fell upon him the plagues of Pharaoh, Pharaoh being in this case the Emperor Ferdinand II and the plagues the Spanish soldiery who over-ran the land and the pestilence that followed in their wake. For seven years Comenius was a refugee in his own land sheltering wherever noblemen were able to afford him shelter. His young wife, being just delivered of a second child, died of the pestilence and with her the babies. He fled, perhaps to Třebíč where he was with a Pastor Paul Cyrillus, then to Brandýs in the most beautiful valley of the Orlice River (now called Komenský Valley). In this place Charles Žerotín had power to give him safety for a time but the most secure refuge was in the remote fastnesses of the Giant Mountains. At the age of thirty-two he married again, this time to Dorothy, daughter of Pastor Cyrillus, and maintained an uneasy life at Třemešna (North-east of Dvůr Králové) on the estates of George Sadovský of Sloupno.

These seven years were without doubt filled with anxiety and pain. He was constantly aware of the destruction of his land and the persecution of his Church. He had to live in secret hiding-places. Matthew Spinka speaks of his 'formidable exterior' in the face of his personal tragedies but this seems less than just. The 'little book' which he sent to his wife left behind in Fulnek may seem to us stiff and theological but the letter which accompanied it was a cry from the heart – 'I am forced to leave you and cannot be by your side and I know the sorrow and distress in your heart of which I am not exempt'.[5] As a minister he had to keep faith and hope alive in others and for this purpose the words of Scripture came to him most naturally and there is every indication that he was helpful in his ministrations to distraught women such as his own mother-in-law, Madam Cyrillová, to whom he sent a tract: 'The Name of the Lord is a high Tower'. It was from a young girl of sixteen, Christina Poniatowska, driven crazy by terror that he himself derived a support for his faith through her prophecies of ultimate deliverance. Surely God, who had opened up a way through the Red Sea, could deliver his faithful Church in Bohemia.

It was, therefore, in confident hope of eventual salvation that in 1628 Comenius and a considerable band of the Brethren crossed the mountains and found a temporary home for themselves at Leszno in Poland. There they joined the descendants of an earlier band of exiles who had fled in the previous century and found relative security under the local lord, Rafael Leszczyński. It was, however, to be their home intermittently for twenty-eight years and for Comenius it was a wilderness experience. However sanguine their hopes the exiles had to adjust themselves to their Polish neighbours. Leszno had a school, which had become a gymnasium in 1624, in which Comenius was soon involved and, when the printing press from Kralice was set up, it became the publishing centre for the Brethren. In all the activities of his Church Comenius took an active part especially after he became Secretary. He was an indefatigable correspondent and he was always ready to defend or advance

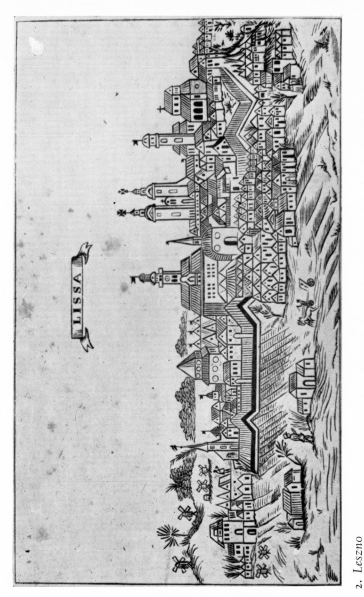

2. *Leszno*

the cause of the Brethren with his pen. In addition, he had the cares of his aged parents-in-law and a young child and did what he could to fulfil the duties of citizenship when special need arose as, for instance, when pestilence threatened the city.[6]

Of all the dark years experienced by the Leszno community none was blacker than 1632. In that year Gustavus Adolphus of Sweden, whom they had thought invincible if not immortal, was killed at Lützen; Frederick of the Palatinate, the ill-fated Winter King of Bohemia, from whom so many summers had been expected, died a few days afterwards a wanderer and an outcast. Earlier in the year Landgraf Moritz of Hesse-Cassel, perhaps the most enlightened of the German Protestant princes, had died. Comenius wrote a funeral poem bewailing these losses – the removing of the very pillars of the Protestant cause[7]. How could he continue to believe in prophecy when the foretellings of Christina Poniatowska and Christopher Kotter were thus proved false? It was not the first crisis of faith but Comenius turned increasingly to a concept which he believed would make possible the reform of all men. This he called Pansophy through which 'men, seeing in a clear light the ends of all things, and the means to those ends, and the correct use of those means, might be able to direct all that they have to good ends'.[8] Henceforth to realize this concept universally became the burning passion of his life and the vocation to which he dedicated himself. First he had to persuade his Church for, without their support, he could not go forward and one of the Brethren – a Polish noble, named Jerome Broniewski – feared that there was a danger 'in the admixture of divine things with human'. Might Pansophy be, not the Promised Land, but the Golden Calf? However, after two enquiries by the Bishops and then the whole body of the clergy Comenius was given full support to go on.

For fifteen years from the age of forty-nine to sixty-four Comenius tried in one way or another, in one place or another to spy out the land to which he believed mankind was destined. His wanderings took him far from his native land or his adopted home. In the Baltic he was buffeted by gales that drove him a hundred miles back from his course. In England he stayed less than a year because the Civil War broke out and turned men's minds to other things than Pansophy. In Sweden he found superficial approval but ultimate scepticism from the Chancellor, Axel Oxenstierna and bound himself to a contract for which he had neither aptitude nor liking. In West Prussia he laboured for nearly six years to fulfil that contract and at the same time to fulfil his mission. The return 'home' (for that was how he thought of Leszno) brought fresh sorrows and fresh disappointments – the death of his wife, Dorothy, the abandonment of Bohemia by the signatories of the Treaty of Osnabrück, his election to be Senior Bishop of a Church on the verge of extinction. Only a profound sense of vocation could have energized him to embark upon a new project in Hungary – after he had provided for his younger children by marrying a third wife, Jane Gajus. The immediate objective was to reform the Grammar School of Saros Patak but for him it was a means to an end. He was resolved, as the Rector of the School wrote to Samuel Hartlib, 'to devote himself wholly to pansophical studies.'[9] There was no reason why he should not have combined the two, but before he could do so he was recalled to Leszno by threatening dangers. On April 26, 1656, the final disaster of Leszno fell upon him, he being then just over sixty-four years of age. On that day Polish soldiers, having occupied the city, proceeded to destroy it with senseless brutality. Comenius managed to bury his manuscripts and books and escape with his family into Silesia. The city of Leszno burned for three days and with it Comenius had every reason to think that his writings were irretrievably lost. After great hardships he eventually reached Amsterdam where he was received with hospitality and kindness. There he stayed for the rest of his life and thus ended his wanderings in the wilderness. But the Promised Land was still beyond Jordan.

In some ways the last fourteen years were the most remarkable. Superficially they were years of frustration, feebleness and failure. The dreams of the restoration of Bohemia were – only dreams. The prophecies on which he staked his reputation were – only delusions. The Millenium was a mirage; Pansophy a discarded slogan. One after another his contemporaries and intimate associates preceded him to the grave – Samuel Hartlib, Laurence de Geer, Peter Figulus and the wife of his old age, Jane.

But yet something of greatness remained. Of course, he should have conceded the victory to fate but he refused to accept defeat. Within a year of the destruction of his manuscripts he was feverishly preparing for the press a new edition of 1,000 odd pages of his surviving didactic works – the *Opera Didactica Omnia* of 1657. Though the Church of the Brethren was scattered and disorganized he proceeded to raise and administer very considerable funds for their relief. His closing years derived their strength from his indomitable resolve to bequeath to posterity the pansophic wisdom rejected by his contemporaries and to that end to urge solemnly upon his son, Daniel, and his most intimate assistant, Christian Nigrinus, the duty of publishing his great collection of Pansophic works on the reform of human affairs. He never feared but rather welcomed death and seemed in face of it to breathe a more rarefied air than earth could afford. He would not have thought it inappropriate to quote, 'And Moses went up from the plains of Moab unto the mountain of Nebo, to the top of Pisgah . . . and the Lord showed him all the land' (Deut: 34).

Comenius died on November 13, 1670, and was buried at the French Reformed Church of Naarden on the Zuyder Zee. Only the figure 8 was on his tomb and the place of it was forgotten. Born in obscurity he was buried in oblivion.

HISTORICAL

The circumstances of his life forced Comenius into politics; the conditions of his times gave a revolutionary slant to his outlook; his own inclination gave to his point of view a religious and internationalist flavour. He saw history in terms of a series of challenges to which man must make an adequate response although in the end it was only God who could bring the slow process of time to a culmination in which good would triumph over evil. Specifically he believed that this final conclusion of history was at hand. Perhaps because of this he did not appreciate the real changes which were taking place around him – mercantilism, rationalism and the other movements which were the real revolution of the seventeenth century.

One of the outstanding features of life in the seventeenth century was that it took war for granted. G. N. Clark estimates that there were only seven complete calendar years in which there was no war between European states.[10] Between war and peace there was no sharp demarcation nor could there be until states could maintain standing armies and conduct their hostilities with some regard to international law. In Comenius' day most wars were waged between loose alliances, there was no supra-national authority, and although, theoretically there were feudal service and militia, in fact, armies consisted of mercenaries engaged for a campaigning season and then paid off. The professional soldier was willing to hire himself to the best leader or the highest payer and mutinies and desertions were frequent. The supply of arms, ammunition, provisions and clothing was very irregular and generally the soldier was expected to live off the land. Campaigns were decided by pitched battles in which solidly massed bodies of infantrymen opposed each other with long pikes and matchlocks while the cavalry fought on the wings. When the battle was over the victors were able to seize the booty and advance rapidly into the country behind. Soldiers were more inspired by the personality of their leaders than by national feeling though sometimes religious fervour played an important part in promoting valour. Gradually the advantage of good organization as a basis for the military art became obvious and victory went to those who used more scientific methods but particularly to those who used business methods to keep their armies intact. Since states were generally unable to do this themselves they employed 'entrepreneurs' like Wallenstein, or they called in capitalists to organize their supplies, like de Geer. The brutality and destructiveness of war were intensified by religious fanaticism and reached a high peak during the Thirty Years' War. Although contemporary witnesses were often unreliable there is universal agreement that Germany suffered atrociously and the statement of one of them will suffice, 'I would not have believed a land could have been so despoiled had I not seen it with my own eyes'.[11] In Bohemia there was less excuse than in Germany because there was relatively little actual fighting there but yet the most sober historians are surprised at what happened. Seton Watson estimates that between 1620 and 1648 the population of Bohemia and Moravia fell from about four and a half million to just over one million[12] and the account given by Ernest Denis of the destruction of property is stagger-ing.[13] The aspect of war which appalled Comenius even more than its devastation was the callous selfishness which it en-gendered. In this respect there was little to choose between one side and the other. Maximilian of Bavaria went on with the war when it could have been stopped to gain more lands from the Palatinate but the rest of the Protestant princes only banded to-gether when they saw their ecclesiastical property threatened by Ferdinand II's ill-advised Edict of Restitution of 1629. For Comenius the crowning example of the ignobility of war was that between England and Holland between 1664 and 1667 over a clash of commercial interests.

A brief survey of the impact of war upon the life of Comenius will suffice to show that it was a constant background. He was born at a time when Protestantism was beginning to look victorious. England had warded off the Spanish threat, with the death of Parma (1592) the Dutch felt a little more secure, Henry of Navarre was fighting for his crown (assisted incidentally by Charles Žerotín) and the Protestant princes of Germany had successfully infiltrated into the lands of monasteries and bishops. Always there was the threat of the Turks which may be illus-trated by the killing of 65,000 Christians in Croatia in the year of Comenius' birth. Always, too, there was the threat of marauding bands of which he had first-hand experience as a boy in the destruction of Strážnice.

He took a sufficiently active part in the events leading up to the battle of the White Mountain to be one of the first to be proscribed by the Government of Ferdinand. While in hiding the devastation of war was his constant preoccupation whether it was the destruction of his Church at Fulnek or the dispersal of his old teachers in Nassau or the Palatinate. When he went to Poland he was electrified with excitement by the news of the Battle of Breitenfeld in 1631 because it became a symbol of ultimate victory. There was a certain genuineness about the way in which Gustavus Adolphus combined piety and valour that made Comenius accept him without hesitation as a modern Joshua. All the greater was his consternation when a year later his hero fell at Lützen covered with wounds. The war dragged on for another sixteen years and at the end there was a peace which solved nothing, left a legacy of degradation and despair and did nothing but demonstrate the futility of war as an expression of ideals. It was a lesson which Comenius never completely learnt and he did not cease to invoke prophecy as a means of building up new Protestant alliances in the belief that in certain circumstances war could be justified. He drew a sharp distinction between a war of retribution upon the Hapsburgs when all other means had failed and a war undertaken for commercial ends as seemed to him to be the case in the Anglo-Dutch War of 1664.

The opposition between idealism and power politics, between the physical nature of man and the spiritual, between pacifism and the defence of legitimate self-interest seems to find its ultimate expression in war but it is manifestly expressed in many other ways and it is perhaps the most intractable problem in all human affairs. It may be illustrated by reference to the experience of one of the leading members of the Unity of Brethren to whom Comenius was deeply indebted – Charles Žerotín. Žerotín belonged to a powerful family, owning extensive lands in Bohemia and Moravia, and he was an influential member of the Upper House of the Bohemian Parliament or Diet. Although there were three estates – nobles, knights and burgesses – who had to be unanimous in their decisions, real power lay with the nobles. Since 1526 the crown of Bohemia had become in fact hereditary to the Austrian House of Hapsburg although in theory the estates had the right to elect their king. Žerotín was a deeply religious man with an inclination towards Calvinism through his education at Strasburg, Basel and Geneva. He was also a legally-minded man anxious to avoid an open struggle between Catholics and Protestants. But it was Václav Budovec, another leading nobleman member of the Unity of Brethren, who forced from the Emperor, Rudolph II, the celebrated Letter of Majesty of 1609 which virtually gave freedom of conscience and recognition to the National Protestant Confession. The Letter of Majesty said, 'No decree of any kind shall be issued by us or by our heirs against the above peace' but Žerotín had in mind an ideal of government in which there should be religious toleration, a united nation with a common culture, and a gradual raising of the status of serfs. Unfortunately he found his fellow nobles keen only to defend their own rights and privileges and so he withdrew from politics. He has been much criticized for this. He might have injected some very necessary resolution into the Estates when they yielded to King Matthias in 1617 and elected Ferdinand of Styria to succeed him. He might have prevented the fatal quarrellings which ruined the Protestant cause when they deposed Ferdinand and elected Frederick of the Palatinate in his place. His counsel might well have been decisive before the Battle of the White Mountain and certainly the support of his Moravian followers might have brought victory instead of defeat. His reasons for standing aside were complex but amongst them was a determination to rely on law rather than force and non-violent resistance to the oppressor coupled with justice to the oppressed. Experience seemed to prove him wrong. He had not estimated correctly the nature of Ferdinand or the inflexibility of the Jesuits. Tyrants make law an instrument of tyranny. Ideological warfare is in some ways more potent than physical force and the Jesuits set themselves to destroy even the Czech language as well as the religious traditions of the Czech people. Comenius did not condemn Žerotín but said that he alone 'dared to oppose cruelty and expostulated with the Emperor and, like Obadiah of old, sustained many in caves with bread and water'. What was surprising – and disconcerting – was that the descendants of Hus and Žiška should have submitted so tamely. Ernest Denis suggests that if people like Žerotín had led a resistance movement instead of preaching submission they would not only have saved religious freedom but also the freedom of the common people.[14]

Comenius realized the truth of the dictum that violence breeds violence and in general he took the pacifist line but he believed very much in another dictum that unity is strength. He was appalled to find that the 'wicked' were able to unite while the 'good' fell apart. The Protestant Union of German states was formed in 1608 and the Catholic League in the following year but of the two it was the Protestant Union that was ineffectual and dissolved itself in 1621 just when it should have concerted its efforts to save Bohemia. As the Jesuits were the most disciplined and militant section of the Catholics so were the Calvinists of the Protestants but the difference was that Calvinists hated Lutherans almost as much as Catholics. In addition Calvinists were not so successful in maintaining their missionary efforts because they had no central organization behind them. The difference may be illustrated in the case of Poland. During the sixteenth century the Polish nobles turned towards Calvinism partly because they saw in it a means for establishing a national church independent of Rome and without too much influence from German Lutheranism. Men of great influence like Radziwill 'the Black' or of great intellectual power like Jan Laski caused Calvinism to become the dominant religion in Lithuania while Lutheranism was stronger in Prussia and Great Poland. Following their expulsion from Bohemia in 1548 the Brethren also established themselves and expanded in southern Poland. All realized that their disunity was a source of weakness and in 1570 they made an agreement (the Consensus of Sandomierz) of mutual toleration. It was not, however, an organic union and was unable to withstand the full flood of the Counter-Reformation led by the Jesuits. One after another of the Polish nobles returned to the Catholic fold including one who had been Comenius' pupil and later his protector – Boguslaw Leszczyński of Leszno. Between 1606 and 1620 it is estimated that the Polish Protestants lost two-thirds of their churches. In Hungary Lutheranism spread rapidly in the early part of the sixteenth century especially in the German areas of Slovakia and Transylvania but later there was a movement towards Calvinism because it seemed more free from the influence of priests. The Lutherans were stronger in the towns and the Calvinists in the country and possibly because they were evenly balanced they accepted the principle of toleration and made their country a home for refugees from Germany – Alsted and Bisterfeld are examples. Strangely enough Hungary was the only country in Central Europe in which Protestantism survived the Counter-Reformation. In Germany the antagonisms between Catholic, Lutheran and Calvinist remained but the Thirty Years' War left the princes as the only power to whom the demoralized people could turn and so it was the prince who determined the religion of the people. Thus religion became an arm of the state and, since there were some three hundred states, there was no united voice of religion. The position was even worse than before, since Calvinism had the same legal standing as Lutheranism. Church lands seized by the Catholics since 1624 were restored to the Protestants who had seized them from the Catholics since 1555. The princes seemed, indeed, for the most part, indifferent to religion itself and their churches became mere preaching institutions. Of course, there was plenty of religious enthusiasm but not all of it very healthy. Theologians tended to be rigid, dogmatic and offensive. People believed in witchcraft, demon-possession and magic. It was not mutual tolerance which reduced sectarian antagonism but retreat into quietism.

It is remarkable that men still had a feeling of the unity of Europe, despite all the religious and political differences. Of course, the Holy Roman Empire had long since ceased to unite Europe. In fact, since the Emperor was identified in the minds of Protestants with Catholicism the idea of Christendom had lost its appeal. But yet in institutions, in beliefs and in culture, there was a unity binding together the peoples of Western and Central Europe. People knew of the vast lands across the Atlantic and of the great land masses in Africa and Asia but they tended to think of the people who lived there as 'barbarians', inferior in technical skill and in cultural tradition. European settlements beyond the sea were looked upon as interesting adjuncts of the main civilization which might bring economic advantage but ought to bring to benighted savages some knowledge of a higher way of life. There were certain exceptions to this. For the Turks there was a mixture of fear and respect and a tacit acknowledgment that they were more or less impervious to European influence. Intercourse with the East brought the knowledge that there were other forms of civilization than the European and the great trading companies of England and Holland brought back not only goods but ideas as well.

BIBLIOGRAPHICAL AND CRITICAL

Comenius attempted to write over two hundred books and it is certain that a large number (probably about fifty) have been irretrievably lost although over the past hundred years there have been some remarkable 'finds' of manuscripts, presumed lost. The most authoritative collection of the works of Comenius is that of the Czech scholars, J. V. Novák and Josef Hendrich (*Veškeré Spisy J.A.K.* – hereafter called VSJAK). This was begun in 1911 and it was intended that the full works should be included in thirty volumes but since 1930 this ambitious plan has been halted. The best list of published editions is that made in 1959 by the Czechoslovak State Pedagogical Publishing House (*Soupis Děl J.A.K.*). In 1957 an International Conference was held in Prague to celebrate the three-hundredth anniversary of the collection made in Amsterdam (*Opera Didactica Omnia* – hereafter called ODO) and as a result the Research Group of the Pedagogical Institute was commissioned to edit and publish the works of Comenius discovered in 1935 (hereafter called the *Consultation*) and some progress has been made in this great task.

Since about 1850 a large body of literature about Comenius has been produced and a survey made in 1911 gave no less than 13,300 items (Čeněk Zíbrt: *Bibliography of Czech History*). Since then many more books have been added and Jelínek, writing in 1951, calls it an 'uncatalogued mass'.[15] The scientific study of Comenius is now centred in Prague and the Research Group already referred to acts as a clearing house through its journal, the *Acta Comeniana*.

The international fame of Comenius began in 1633 with the publication of his famous text-book, the *Gateway of Languages Unlocked* (generally known as the *Janua*) but this brought him to the notice of a group of social reformers throughout Europe headed by Samuel Hartlib. This group recognized that behind the *Janua* was a concept of universal wisdom, which Comenius called Pansophy, and they encouraged him to develop it. For some years while he was at Elbing (1642-1648) Comenius tried to express this idea but particularly in a series of works which he called the *General Consultation concerning the Improvement of Human Affairs* (the *Consultation*). It is impossible to say how much was completed during this period and how much in the last years of his life, but Dr Brambora suggests that some parts at least were written and destroyed in the Leszno fire and that he re-wrote them at Amsterdam from recovered fragments.[16] At any rate a Dedication and the first two parts were printed in a Folio Edition in 1657 and in Octavo in 1662. If he had completed the rest why did he not print it all together? The answer is probably that he sent manuscript copies to various people for comment and was deterred by the hostile comments of a Huguenot divine at Groningen, Samuel Maresius.[17] His dying request that his pansophic works should be published was never carried out but even if they had been it may be doubted whether they would have had much effect. His reputation was already under a cloud and with it his dream of universal reformation. For this several reasons may be given. Historically his outlook on affairs was discredited and even some of his co-religionists felt they had been duped. There was no liberation for Bohemia, no union of Protestant states, no millenium. His literary and didactic influence was not really enhanced by the 1657 Edition of his works for it was small in number, inordinate in length, and cluttered with text-book material already well-known. All his books were in Czech or Latin and therefore available to a diminishing circle of readers for Czech books were proscribed or destroyed in Bohemia and Latin was being replaced by national languages throughout Europe.

The manuscripts of the *Consultation* were copied out (probably by Nigrinus) but not published despite the support of Comenius' benefactor, Laurence de Geer, for such a project. Instead they were entrusted to the Pietists, a religious group at Halle founded by A. H. Francke. Francke commissioned one of the group, Justus Docemius, to publish them but, apart from a reprint of the first part, the Panegersia, in 1702 by Buddaeus, nothing was done. The manuscripts found their way to the library of the orphanage at Halle together with a number of printed fragments which must have been printed during Comenius' life-time. There they remained for over two hundred years unknown and unnoticed.

In the English-speaking world the fame of Comenius rested entirely on his text-books which continued to be popular after his death. Robert Boyle was certainly well acquainted with him and through his connection with the Royal Society and the Corporation for the Propagation of the Gospel in New England he must have kept alive the ideas of Comenius until his death in 1691.[18] There is no direct evidence for the influence of Comenius on John Locke, but Locke was acquainted with Samuel

Hartlib as a young man (Hartlib died when he was thirty), knew Boyle, and lived in Holland for six years shortly after Comenius' death, and it is possible to believe that he had read the *Great Didactic*.

In Germany two men, at least, held Comenius in great admiration and consciously tried to make use of his ideas. One was A. H. Francke and the other G. W. Leibniz. The whole educational system established by Francke at Halle between 1694 and 1733 was an attempt to realize the Comenian programme while Leibniz as the first President of the Berlin Royal Society of Science in 1700 tried to realize the proposals of Comenius for the advancement of knowledge. Leibniz firmly believed that there would be a revival of Comenius' influence and, indeed, wrote a poem to this effect in 1671.[19] Nor must we omit the grandsons of Comenius, Daniel and John Jablonsky. Daniel was the one whom Comenius made Bishop of the Unity of Brethren and it was partly at his instigation that the Berlin Royal Society was initiated, while John became its first Secretary.[20]

However, most people at the beginning of the eighteenth century accepted the judgment of Pierre Bayle, the French exile in Rotterdam, that he was an impractical visionary, if not a dangerous fanatic which was in effect the charge of Maresius.[21] Apart from the text-books which continued the memory of his name there was little direct influence of Comenius for over a hundred years.

One line of communication was through the revival of the Unity of Brethren founded in 1724 on the estates of Count Zinzendorf at Herrnhut in Saxony close to the Bohemian border. Zinzendorf was moved to this by reading Comenius' Latin version of the old Brethrens Order of Discipline (*Ratio Disciplinae*) and the first Bishop of the Revived Church, David Nitschmann, was consecrated in 1727 by Daniel Jablonsky.[22] In 1738 John Wesley visited the little religious settlement and it is evident from his *Journal* that he was greatly impressed. From the first the little community gave their attention to education and they were clearly influenced by Comenius in this respect. They had boarding establishments at which children were educated in a strongly religious atmosphere at the Church's expense. Their approach influenced in turn the educational ideas of Wesley and of the American settlements of the Brethren or Moravians as they came to be called.

Most of the great German and French educational writers of the eighteenth century echo what Comenius said in the seventeenth but only in a few cases is there direct evidence of inspiration. Perhaps the strongest links are in the cases of Basedow and Herder. Basedow's *Elementary Work* of 1774 has so much in common with the *Orbis Pictus* and the *Janua* that it is hard not to suspect a connection. Herder does make a reference to Comenius as a peace reformer[23] which makes it easy to find parallels in his ideas about man, nature and the universe. Goethe certainly knew and appreciated the *Orbis Pictus* as 'the only book of its kind' which came into his hands.[24] Nevertheless it does not seem that the immense projects for universal reform by which Comenius set such store had much influence on the Age of Enlightenment or the Romantic Movement.[25]

During the eighteenth century there was little opportunity for any interest in Comenius to develop in Bohemia or Moravia: this was not so true in Slovakia which, through its connection with Hungary, enjoyed greater freedom though slower economic development. Thus the Protestant tradition was stronger and members of the more enlightened middle classes, though few in number, knew and appreciated the works of Comenius. Some of them went to the universities of Halle or Jena for their education where the memory of Comenius was kept alive. Foremost among Slovak educational thinkers influenced in this way was Daniel Lehocky (1759-1840) and the very close parallel between his ideas and those of Comenius, particularly in the field of infant education, shows direct inspiration.[26] The works of Comenius were known in Slovakia many years before they influenced the national revival in Bohemia.[27]

A number of factors brought about an awareness of the significance of Comenius during the early nineteenth century. First there was the movement towards popular education in the early nineteenth century brought about by a combination of forces – the explosive idealism of the French Revolution, the hopes and fears engendered by the Industrial Revolution, but particularly the upsurge of nationalist feeling in Prussia following the humiliation of the defeat of Jena in 1806. Fichte's

Addresses to the German People, published while the French were still in possession of Berlin, were an impassioned plea for national regeneration through education. It had very much in common with Comenius although Fichte and many others went to Pestalozzi for their inspiration. But mass education required a philosophical basis for its pedagogy and it was doubtful whether Pestalozzi could supply this. Von Raumer, who also went to Pestalozzi at Yverdun, wrote a book on the *History of Pedagogy* in 1842 in which he seemed to single out Comenius as the real founder of the science of education and German pedagogues began to explore what Von Raumer described as the 'inexhaustible treasure' of his work. Both the leading German educationalists of the period, Johann Herbart and Friedrich Froebel, were influenced by him. Herbart indeed, died just before Von Raumer's book appeared but his theory of ideas and of essences has more in common with Comenius than with Pestalozzi. In the case of Froebel there is a direct link. Karl Krause drew his attention to Comenius' book, *The School of Infancy*, and this strongly influenced him in devising a form of education for young children as a garden in which they should be brought into a mystical union with nature and the universe. At that time *The School of Infancy* was only available in the Latin version of ODO but in 1858 Daniel Benham, a member of the Moravian Church in England, published an English translation and in the same year the original Czech version was published in Prague following the discovery of the manuscript by Antonin Gindely at Leszno two years previously.

The second factor was the Czech nationalist revival. In this movement the re-discovery of Comenius as a great Czech patriot played an important part. The biography of Comenius written by František Palacký and published in 1829 was the first detailed study to be made. It is interesting to remember that although an edition of the *Labyrinth* was published in 1782 at Prague it was felt to be sufficiently dangerous to be banned by the Austrian Government in 1809. But it continued to exert an influence on Czech culture through the Slovak poet and educationalist, John Kollár (1793-1852), who was a friend of Palacký.[28] Because of his efforts to preserve the Czech language and his mastery of it Comenius held a high place in the estimation of philologists, such as Josef Jungmann,[29] and among Czech patriots. A search began for his lost manuscripts and, through the initiative of the famous biologist, J. E. Purkyně, the Czech version of the Great Didactic (Didaktika Velika) was discovered at Leszno in 1841.

The attention given to Comenius over the last hundred years may be said to compensate for previous neglect though, until quite recently, it was concentrated on a narrow interpretation of his pedagogy which belittled his pansophic theory. In the second half of the nineteenth century Germany led the way in pedagogical study and, through the influence of Karl von Raumer, Comenius was widely accepted as having laid the foundations of a science of education. A considerable number of books and dissertations followed and two societies were formed to stimulate interest and research – the Leipzig Comenius-Stiftung of 1871 and the Berlin Comenius-Gesellschaft of 1892.[30] At Leipzig a pedagogical library was formed which, by the end of the century, included some 70,000 works and it continued to operate until 1935 but was largely destroyed during the war of 1939 to 1945. The Berlin Gesellschaft was led by Ludwig Keller and it helped to maintain the interest of teachers in Comenius through its journal – the Monatshefte – which continued under various names until 1914.

The emergence of education as an academic subject in England and America led to a considerable interest in the history of educational ideas and Comenius was given an honoured place by R. H. Quick in a book on Educational Reformers of 1868 (Ch. X). In 1892 the tercentenary of the birth of Comenius was commemorated at the New York Teachers' College by the President, Nicholas Murray Butler, and an article on the text-books of Comenius was written by W. H. Maxwell and, to mark the occasion, there was published the New York Educational Review. Soon after, Will S. Monroe (Massachusetts Professor of Pedagogy) wrote a series of books and translations. In Britain three names will suffice for this period – Matthew Keatinge who translated the Great Didactic and wrote an excellent Introduction, S. S. Laurie, who first introduced Comenius to English readers, and J. W. Adamson whose book, Pioneers of Modern Education 1600-1700, linked him with his background. In

France interest was stimulated by Michelet's *Nos Fils* of 1869 and Gabriel Compayré's *History of Pedagogy* of 1886.

In addition to this strong interest in Comenian pedagogy there was considerable research during the nineteenth century into its historical background. The origins of the Unity of Brethren were carefully studied by Antonin Gindely, Ernest Denis, Jaroslav Goll, Edmund de Schweinitz, J. T. Müller and others. A number of biographies of Comenius were written, notably by Gindely, Fr. Zoubek and Jan Kvačala. Studies were made of the history of Bohemia before 1620 of which those of Ernest Denis are of special interest. In addition there continued to be discoveries of lost works and Jan Kvačala and Patera made collections of the voluminous correspondence of Comenius. Thus J. T. Müller, the historian of the Moravian Church, found a manuscript of *Haggaeus Redivivus* in 1893 at Zittau, near to their headquarters at Herrnhut. A fragment of one of Comenius' major works, the twenty-eight volume *Theatrum Universitatis Rerum*, was found at Holešov in Moravia in 1893 and a further fragment in 1919. Of special interest was the discovery of the autobiographical defence which Comenius made in 1669 (the *Continuatio Admonitionis Fraternae*). It was found by Jan Kvačala in the Leningrad Public Library in 1913.

We must briefly consider the development of Comeniology during the last thirty years. First of all some attempt has been made to bring into order the great bulk of literature dealing with Comenius through the bibliographical notes of the *Acta Comeniana* since 1957. Klaus Schaller has made very full bibliographies in his books particularly the *Pedagogy of Comenius* (*Die Paedagogik des J.A.C.* 1962) and Dr Brambora has classified the post-war literature,[31] while Dr Čisařová-Kolarova has given an account of recent Russian literature.[32] Secondly there has been a shift of interest in Comenius from Western Europe towards the East. With a few exceptions students in the West have tended to be connected by birth or marriage with Czechoslovakia – Matthew Spinka, Vladimir Jelínek and Otokar Odložilík in America, Anna Heyberger in France, Giuliana Limiti in Italy. There is less attention in the English-speaking world than sixty years ago, though the work of G. H. Turnbull, the late Professor of Education at Sheffield, is a most important contribution to Comenian study. Mention must also be made of the group of German scholars associated with the Münster Comenius Institute – Dimitrij Čyževskij, Klaus Schaller and Heinrich Geissler. Thirdly there has been a re-orientation of approach. In the eighteenth century Comenius was thought of as a writer of text-books, in the nineteenth as a forerunner of pedagogy. The tacit assumption was that he was interesting in the history of education but that the application of scientific psychology had made him out of date. Now there is available the full range of his thought, even though individual works have been lost, and consequently it is possible to make a reappraisal of the educational philosophy of Comenius. Emphasis has moved from methodology to sociology and from the school to the whole of life. Historical research can now be motivated by social purpose rather than by antiquarian interest.

The most important factor in bringing these changes about was the discovery of the 'lost' manuscripts of the *Consultation* at Halle. It is remarkable that these manuscripts remained hidden for so long for it was known that they had been put in the care of the Pietist group at Halle and their contents were known from the 1702 Edition of the *Panegersia*. Following information from the Herrnhut community Jan Kvačala did make a search but in vain. They were known by scholars as the 'lost' pansophical works[33] and it was by coincidence that they were at last brought to light by Dimitrij Čyževskij in 1934 while he was looking for documents connected with Slavonic history. The *Consultation* consisted of seven Parts and the missing five were thus recovered together with a Lexicon of concepts (*Lexicon Reale Pansophicum*). Čyževskij sent a typed copy to Josef Hendrich in Prague but in 1945 the East German Republic sent the original manuscript to Charles University and Hendrich translated two parts into Czech (*Pampaedia* 1948 *Panorthosia* 1950) and the Comenius Institute has now prepared the whole Latin text for publication.[34] Already in 1958 Čyževskij in collaboration with Schaller and Geissler had published the Latin text together with a German translation of the *Pampaedia* and many years before, in 1888, Šmaha made a Czech translation of the first two parts, *Panegersia* and *Panaugia*.

Although the discovery of the *Consultation* was the chief

stimulus for research on Comenius there were at least two others. In 1931 S. Souček found a number of manuscripts at Leningrad which he believed to be adaptations for school use of parts of Comenius' great encyclopaedia – *The Theatre of the Universe* – two of them in Czech and four in Latin. Unfortunately he died in 1935 before they could be published, but considerable sections are now available.[35] In 1951 G. H. Turnbull discovered among the papers of Samuel Hartlib two manuscripts which he believed to be pansophical works of Comenius and these were published in Prague.[36]

Nevertheless this new material would not in itself have provoked more than a scholarly interest if it had not been that certain governments and international organizations saw in Comenius a possible focus for their aspirations. Thus Unesco took the tercentenary of the publication in Amsterdam of his *Collected Works* (ODO) as an opportunity for producing a volume of excerpts with an introduction by Jean Piaget. The Czechoslovak Government used the same occasion for organizing a conference of scholars from all parts of the world and authorizing a reprint of the Amsterdam Edition of 1657 and a series of editions of the complete works of Comenius over a period of years (1957-1970). Their point of view is expressed thus in the Foreword to the new ODO Edition:

'After three centuries there arise the conditions that will make possible the realization of even his most daring schemes. The socialist society realizes the unified school system from primary school up to the highest standard as Comenius proposed: in the socialist society all children are given a general education without any discrimination of sex, social origin or property.'

The social motivation behind Comenian studies in Communist countries since 1950 explains, though it does not invalidate, the interpretation given. Comenius has been presented as a great radical thinker affirming the possibility that human nature could be changed by education. He has been linked with social reformers or revolutionaries – for instance in England with John Lilburne the Leveller, John Bellers the Quaker and Robert Owen the Socialist. His educational methodology is seen as an expression of his educational philosophy and as something which could be detached without great loss from its religious framework. This theme has been presented with enthusiasm and conviction by men such as A. A. Krasnovskij in the Soviet Union (J. A. *Komensky*, 1953), Robert Alt, Professor at the East German Humboldt University (*The Progressive Character of Comenian Pedagogy*, 1953), B. Suchodolski of Warsaw University (*Commentary on the Great Didactic*, 1956), and in Czechoslovakia itself by Jirina Popelová (*The Significance of Komensky for World Culture and the Peace Movement*, 1956). Many other names could be given but these will suffice to indicate the basic approach of this new movement.

NOTES

(a) *Biographical*
1. Miroslav Hanuš: Pt. 1. *Osud národa* (The Fate of the Nation).
       Pt. 2. *Poutník v Amsterdam* (Wanderer in Amsterdam).
    Leontina Mašinová: Pt. 1. *Mladá Léta* (The Years of Youth).
       Pt. 2. *Do Labyrintu Světa* (Labyrinth of the World).
       Pt. 3. *Planouci pochodeň* (The Flaming Torch).
2. Pampaedia II.1.
3. D. Čapková and J. Kyrášek: Život a Dilo J.A.K. (1963) No. 27.
4. J. V. Novák: J.A.K. Jeho Život a Spisy (1920) p. 5.
5. M. Spinka: That Incomparable Moravian p. 37 cf A. Heyberger: J.A.C. Sa Vie et Son Oeuvre d'Éducateur p. 31.
6. Tractate: Concerning the Pestilence (1631).
7. Trans. by L. W. Forster: Slavonic Review Vol. XXXIX 1960 p. 24-30.
8. Via Lucia XVI.5.
9. G. H. Turnbull: Hartlib, Dury and Comenius p. 373.
(b) *Historical*
10. G. N. Clark: The Seventeenth Century p. 98.
11. General Mortaigne quoted by C. V. Wedgwood: Thirty Years War p. 448.
12. Seton Watson: History of Czechs and Slovaks p. 130.
13. E. Denis: La Bohême depuis le Montagne Blanc (1903).
14. E. Denis: 'Fin de L'Indépendence de Bohême' – quoted by P. Brock: Political and Social Doctrines of Unity of Czech Brethren p. 339.
(c) *Bibliographical and Critical*
15. Jelínek: Analytical Didactic of Comenius p. XVI cf. J. Patočka: 'Present State of Comenian Studies' (Historica) p. 197.
16. J. Brambora: Informacní Bulletin (1963) p. 26.
17. S. Maresius: Antirrheticus (1669).
18. J. B. Čapek: Comenius and Boyle (Archiv pro Badani XXI 1962).
19. Leibniz (1671) 'Tempus erit quo te, Comeni, turba bonorum
       Factaque, spesque tuas vota quoque ipsa colet'.

20. R. F. Young: *Comenius in England* p. 21.
21. Pierre Bayle: *Dictionnaire Historique et Critique* (1695) p. 882-7.
22. J. E. Hutton: *History of the Moravian Church* p. 171, p. 209.
23. J. G. Herder: *Über den Menschen freundichen, Comenius* (1795).
24. Goethe: *Dichtung und Wahrheit.*
25. cf W. S. Monroe: *Comenius* pp. 146-58 cf Jelínek: *Op Cit.* pp. 179, 181.
    cf *Monatshefte* (1906): Comenius u. die Philanthropisten s. 174.
26. *Acta Comeniana* (1958.2) pp. 226-250 and (1960.1) pp. 21-39.
27. *Acta Comeniana* (1963) pp. 83-143.
28. *Acta Comeniana* (1958.2) pp. 251-273.
29. cf J. Jungmann: *Slovesnost* (1825).
30. cf W. S. Monroe: *Comenius* pp. 178-179.
31. *Pedagogika* (1955) pp. 231-240.
32. *Pedagogika* (1953) p. 428.
33. cf. Prof. Drtina: *Vyznam pansophiskych snah J.A.K.* (1907).
34. A full account of Čyževskij's discovery is given in Patočka's *Present State of Comenian Studies* pp. 204-207.
35. *Acta Comeniana*: 1963 pp. 191-222.
36. G. H. Turnbull: *Two Pansophical Works* (Prague 1951).

PART I

SOURCES AND DEVELOPMENT

CHAPTER 2

THE CONCEPT OF THE
GOOD MAN

IN the view of Comenius the fundamental aim of universal education was to make every human being 'good' by which he meant 'made in the image of God'. This concept was, however, a complex one for which he took inspiration from a number of sources but it was essential to his purpose that the different strands should be woven into a harmonical unity with no one of them emphasized at the expense of another. First he had to bring into harmony the inner life of the soul of man and the outward expression of goodness in the social life, that is mystic experience and practical virtue. Thus he says, 'there are two parts of celestial wisdom . . . the one is a clear and true knowledge of God; the other is prudence to regulate carefully and wisely one's self and all external and internal actions that pertain both to this life and to future life'.[1] Secondly he had to integrate faith and reason. The good man was he who, accepting his limitations, looked to God for wisdom and depended upon God for everything. At the end of his life he came to think of faith as the one thing necessary but for him faith was never blind. Without the exercise of reason it would become only superstition and therefore the good man was one who cultivated all his own powers to the fullest extent and became wise by striving for wisdom. Thus a fully-rounded personality was a universal objective to be obtained through right education.

THE MAN OF MYSTIC EXPERIENCE

Throughout his life Comenius turned to mystic experience both for himself and for others when he needed solace from trouble. To his wife and mother-in-law he brought messages of comfort in the inner life of the spirit.[2] To the persecuted flock of the Brethren he showed a way of escape from anxiety[3] and for all who felt lost in the labyrinth of the world he offered the paradise of the heart. When faith, hope and reason faltered then the only thing still open to man was self-abandonment to the love of God. In 1625 he wrote a book called the *Centre of Security* (*Centrum Securitatis*) in which mysticism is taken a little further than resignation and he seems to approach the thought of God as 'the depth of our being' rather than as an external, if loving, Father. Thus he says, 'God is the wheel, the centre of which is everywhere and the periphery nowhere'.[4] In the second period just before his death he went through a similar experience of bereavement and despair and again he turned from the world of sense to the inner world of the spirit. The one thing necessary was to stop struggling and relax. Man must learn to be receptive and make use of the intuitive faculty to appreciate the transcendent nature of God.

Comenius was strongly imbued with the view of the Church Fathers that the world was wholly bad but that God had provided a way of escape for the Christian. Ultimately this escape could only be realized in the hereafter but even in this life man could give his allegiance to the Other World. It was not simply that the world was in a state of anarchy since the anarchy came from the false ideas in men's minds. The world of the seventeenth century was in the same state as the world of the fifth and the causes were the same. It was 'the flooding of Pagan ideas under the rule of Constantine' that had made St Augustine seek for peace in the City of God[5] and this was also the theme of Comenius' allegory, the *Labyrinth*. The true Christians do not try to reform the world. Each one 'remains in his own dwelling, within his own heart, opening it to the Lord God above, and obtaining full peace of mind'.[6] There are two arguments for withdrawing from the world – first it is full of 'vanity and glittering misery',[7] second it is full of violence, 'wild beasts should settle their differences thus, not men'.[8] The Paradise of the Heart to which the Christian could escape owes something to St Augustine's City of God but something to an allegory written by one of his most-loved teachers, John Valentine Andreae, the Christianopolis of 1619. The inhabitants of this ideal city show that mystic retreat is not just to escape from pain and cruelty. It is the better part of life to turn away from all contact with the physical world and the happy man is he who 'returns to himself and shakes off the dust of the earth'.[9] This concept of mysticism as a higher form of activity than physical motion and of the superiority of the life of contemplation came into Christianity through Plotinus' interpretation of Plato in the third century A.D. and Comenius was much influenced by it. There was, of course, the practical difficulty of finding an opportunity for contemplation in a turbulent world and therefore Comenius was afraid of being mixed up with divisions and debates. Those who lived in the Paradise of the Heart 'said they had no concern with strife: they walked silently and quietly as though looking heavenward' and the Pilgrim, that is Comenius, adds sadly, 'I overlooked this spot and missed here the centre of heaven and earth.'[10]

There were many people in the seventeenth century who were looking for what might be called an 'upper room Christianity'. Such 'seekers' belonged to different sects – Anabaptists, Waldensians, Brownists and others – but they had in common a desire to leave all 'man-made notions' and institutions. Eventually they found a leader in George Fox who was a contemporary of Comenius. Fox mentions the 'Bohemian exiles' in his *Journal* but there is no evidence of direct contact with Comenius. Both were affected by the same influences. According to both men the true Christian was the one 'who lived in the virtue that took away the occasion of war'.[11] Unfortunately it was not always a protection against violence. The history of the Anabaptists, for instance, is a grim enough fulfilment of the words of one of their number, Grebel, who said, 'Christians are sheep in the midst of wolves, sheep ready for the slaughter.'[12]

Comenius gives in the second part of the *Labyrinth* an account of his ideal: 'he was a man with venerable grey hair. When he spoke his speech was full of a kindly severity and it was clear in every way that he was God's ambassador. For he was in no way tainted with the smell of the world.'[13] From this it is clear that mystic experience is not immediately or instantly available because it is concerned with a mystery. God has 'concealed himself as with a curtain'.[14] To penetrate this mystery was out of the course of the mind's normal action and therefore an abnormal experience, but not on that account to be despised or feared. From the fourteenth century there had been those who claimed to have had such experiences, either in the form of a trance or of an intense release of energy and feeling. Whether they were in William James' words 'healthy-minded or sick-minded varieties of religious experience' is not relevant to the fact that they were dramatic escapes of the spirit into the light which illuminates everything. If they were psychical dissociations they were none the less valid experiences. That, at least, was the view of Comenius and he was acquainted with their writings, and had personal relationships with a number of the great mystics. Thus there was Nicholas of Cusa (1401-1464) who said, 'I love my life because Thou, O God, art the sweetness of my life', and Paracelsus (1493-1541) for whom the mystical experience

Rather consists in opening out a way
Whence the imprisoned splendour may escape,
Than in effecting entry for a light
Supposed to be without.
(Browning: *Paracelsus* Bk.1.)

At the time when Comenius was passing through Silesia on his way to Leszno there was living a mystic whom he must have known – Jacob Boehme, the shoemaker of Gorlitz – and of whom there are many echoes in the *Centre of Security*. Boehme had experiences of intense ecstasy in which he felt 'the entire Bible lying within him' and complete harmony between himself and the universe. 'As you find man to be,' he says, 'just so is eternity.' All tensions are resolved and the wheel of life moves towards motionless calm.[15] Comenius himself claimed to have known such times as when he says, 'looking at this light, I beheld wondrous things more than I dare tell.'[16] Even though mysticism was abnormal there was, in Comenius' view, no reason why it should not be cultivated so that the devout person might 'have wings on which to rise swiftly above the machine of this world' whenever he might please.[17] Without doubt Comenius believed in supra-sensory powers. Thus he says, 'The heart of the godly often feels that which has befallen elsewhere. They can by means of dreams and visions imagine what has befallen or will befall. It is this which often causes the astonishment of all worldly-wise men when they see how some plain little fellow speaks wondrous mysteries and prophesies future changes in the world as if he saw them before his eyes.'[18] Belief of this kind was not uncommon at that time. There was Divine Magic as well as Black Magic and Comenius believed with Paraclesus, 'Hidden things which cannot be perceived by the physical senses may be found through the sidereal body, through whose organism we may look into nature in the same way as the sun shines through a glass.'[19] Comenius, unfortunately, was not able to distinguish the genuine from the spurious in this respect. His correspondence with the Flemish mystic, Antoinette Bourignon (1616-1670) was a source of comfort and inspiration[20] but the prophecies of Nicholas Drabík too often led him into the shadows and not out of them. We can hardly blame him for a credulity common to his age. Maybe the time will come when science will accept the validity of religious experience outside the range of objective verification and help us to find other 'Doors of Perception' than the sensory ones.[21]

The real justification for Comenius' belief in mysticism is very much the same as that given by Plato and continued by the Church Fathers that there is something of God in the human soul. Thus Comenius quotes Plato's words (from the *Timaeus*) 'God is the highest good, elevated above all existence and above nature, towards which all creation strives'.[22] This 'striving' after God is clear evidence that there is something of the same nature as God within creation. Tertullian puts it thus, 'The corruption of nature is another nature . . . and yet there remains an original good of the soul which is divine and akin to it and in the true sense natural. For that which is from God is not so much extinguished as obscured. It can be obscured because it is not God: it cannot be extinguished because it is from God.'[23] The figure of darkness and light is continually in Comenius' mind but it is because man has something within that he is capable of responding to the light and that is why he can emerge from the shadows of the cave into the brightness. In the fifth chapter of the *Great Didactic* Comenius develops this theme quoting from Plato and Aristotle, Seneca and Vives but the argument is that man has an inner light to lead him to God. 'Does not this teach us,' he says, 'that, in very truth, all things exist in man; that the lamp, the oil, the tinder, and all the appliances are there, and that if only he be sufficiently skilled to strike sparks, to catch them and to kindle the lamp, he can forthwith reap the fullest enjoyment of the marvellous treasures of God's wisdom.'[24] The way of the mystic is the way of light (*Via Lucis*) but to enjoy it man must turn himself as Plato puts it:

'The faculty by which man learns is like an eye which cannot be turned from darkness to light unless the whole body is turned; in the same way the mind as a whole must be turned away from the world of change until it can bear to look straight at reality, and at the brightest of realities which is what we call the Good.'[25]

THE MAN OF VIRTUE

Comenius was aware of the temptations facing the man of mystic experience. While life continued there could be no complete contracting out from earthly living. Withdrawal from the world was necessary but only in order to gain strength for the life of virtue. This was the 'other part' of celestial wisdom. The mountain of transfiguration must be followed by the healing of the lunatic son – and the world was in a state of lunacy against which the Christian must witness by a blameless life. The problem was to discover the nature of virtue, and in his search for an answer Comenius went through the experiences of his own Church – the Unity of Brethren.

The movement began in the fifteenth century as an attempt to realize the ethics of the Sermon on the Mount and thus had spiritual affinities with the Cathars and Waldensians. Peter Chelčický (1419-1450), who gave the first inspiration, believed that there was an inevitable conflict between authority and love in which the Christian had no choice but to repudiate authority. Thus he says: 'Authority cannot exist without cruelty. If it ceases to be cruel it will at once perish of itself since none will fear it. Therefore authority is far removed from love.'[26] The problem is how far to take the implications of non-aggression but Chelčický was prepared to go to the ultimate limits. He accepted that pacifism meant the avoidance of any way of life which might be a temptation to others. It meant extreme simplicity, manual toil and minimum contact with money. The trader had on him 'the mark of the beast' and town-life was reckoned harmful to the soul.

There were times when Comenius was much drawn to this ideal as he shows by his picture of the 'holy ones' who escaped from the labyrinth of the world into the paradise of the heart – 'external things which the world calls riches they considered as a burden yet they used them for the necessities of life – for the necessities only, I say'. Simplicity was not only the way of holiness, it gave health and contentment as well – 'for as the human body can certainly be sustained by little and very simple food . . . it is clear that but small and simple labours are required for this purpose, as was indeed the case in ancient times'. Happiness did not depend on self-gratification for 'if all that was useless, unnecessary and sinful had been taken away the larger part of men's trade would sink to the ground'.[27] It was an ideal of frugality without asceticism, renunciation of the world without withdrawal from it, labour without soul-destroying drudgery.

But was it possible? The history of the Church of the Unity seems to indicate that it could not be maintained for long. The little company of Brothers who formed a community in the valley of Kunvald about 1457 under the leadership of Řehoř took their inspiration from the writings of Chelčický and from the Bible and their subsequent development was very similar to that of other such communities. Their simplicity did not protect them from persecution but when they survived they attracted others to join them. By the end of the century they were growing in numbers and influence but this very success brought problems of adjustment to the austerity of Chelčický and Řehoř. A more widely spread community could not so easily isolate itself into a paradise of the heart which was in danger of becoming an island of make-believe. The attitude of Lukáš of Prague, the new leader, was that the things of the world only became evil through misuse and through the capital sins of Pride, Envy, Avarice, Anger, Sloth, Gluttony and Lust. By the end of the century there was a schism in the Church and in 1494 a synod was held at which the majority rejected the idealistic teachings of Chelčický. There was to be no loosening of standards but more flexibility in applying them and Lukáš sternly condemned any change of attitude: 'This eating, this drinking, this self-indulgence, this marrying, this living in the world – what a poor preparation it is for men who are leaving Babylon.'[28] Preachers have always been prone to exaggerate moral decline and the frequent injunctions against finery and modishness in dress give evidence of concern about such temptations.[29] The Papal Nuncio, Carlo Caraffa, speaks of 'some degree of luxury in their habits of life' but the evidence shows that the Brethren fulfilled the high standards they imposed upon themselves. Thus the Dominican, Lielenstein, after charging them with heresy, concludes: 'I grant that in regard to morals they are good, in speech truthful and in brotherly love of one kind', and Camerarius says: 'No ambition will be found amongst them, no aiming at superiority. There is no quarrelling, no malevolence or strife.'[30] Whenever there was some accommodation to expediency it was accompanied by an effort to safeguard spiritual values. Of special interest is the attitude towards voluntary poverty. Thus in 1512 there was long discussion arising from the case of a widow who had extensive estates round Brandýs (Johanka z Krajku). Two principles were put forward – first that the wealth must not have been acquired by sinful means and second that it must not be used for luxurious living. Provided wealth was used as a trust and the duty of alms-giving was observed it was justified. A synod in 1591 at Lipnik condemned lords selling their estates and living on the proceeds and said: 'Lords should remain lords and on no account give up their calling.'[31] If wealth was allowed (and indeed the Puritan virtues tend to promote it) then some extension beyond subsistence occupations had to be allowed but the Brethren insisted that they must be of social and moral benefit. Dicing, gaming, juggling, fortune-telling, usury, pimping, and prostitution were forbidden and even music and painting were frowned upon because of their connection with village merry-making and church decoration. The majority of the Brethren continued to be of the peasant class and there was always a witness against all money-making for its own sake but nevertheless it was agreed that wealth could be used for the glory of God. The greatest care was taken to preserve standards of sexual morality and marriage was only allowed with the permission of the Church.

Although Comenius was much influenced by the ideals of Chelčický and Řehoř he does not refer to them and his general attitude approximated to that of Lukáš. The paradise of the heart could not be obtained by outward observance or social segregation but by the constant subjection of the will to the image of God. Thus: 'None other universal remedy can be found but that man should learn to place before his will, like the clearest torch, none other than God, things and the senses rightly formed and guided.'[32] He was not behind Lukáš in condemning the 'wantonness' of the Brethren – their tendency to 'show off wit and sagacity', to strive for 'priority of seats and ranks' their 'coveteousness to be well provided for'.[33]

Despite these strictures the Church of the Brethren was one of the most successful experiments in holy living ever made but Comenius tended to come closer to stoic philosophy than to the Sermon on the Mount. He quotes very frequently from Seneca with approval though he is not uncritical: 'Seneca praised poverty while surrounded by tons of gold.'[34] Nevertheless he speaks of Seneca's 'perfect wisdom' in saying 'As a young man I have considered how to live well; but having become an old man I am considering how to die well'. Seneca's Epistles expressed Comenius' approach to virtue almost perfectly – 'This is wisdom, to return to nature, and to the position from which universal error has driven us. . . . Man is not good but becomes so, as mindful of his origin, he strives towards equality with God.'[35]

Generally Comenius' treatment of morality is pedestrian, practical and earth-bound. The cardinal virtues are prudence, temperance, fortitude and justice and 'a sound judgment on matters of fact is the foundation of all virtue'.[36] In the Orbis Pictus morality is dealt with in seven chapters covering Diligence, Temperance, Fortitude, Patience, Humanity, Justice and Liberality and taking the Golden Mean as the ideal of safety.[37] The general argument is that action becomes moral when duty is preferred to inclination and since the will is often too weak to restrain inclination a man should constantly occupy himself with work. Comenius finds support from the words of Seneca:

'It is toil that nourishes noble minds.'[38] By guarding his health, avoiding the vices of fear, envy and avarice, by moderation in all things and a prudent preparation for life after death, a man would both conserve body and soul and acquire excellence. Yet Comenius had in mind a nobler ideal than self-preservation and a more practical one than philosophical speculation. To be 'in the image of God' meant to do good to others and here again it is Seneca who gives the right word: 'Let others begin strife, you begin the reconciliation.'[39]

If Seneca was the favourite classical author of Comenius, his most favoured book of the Bible was the Proverbs of Solomon. Here he found an inexhaustible mine of wisdom in which comfort to the poor was happily mixed with advice to the prosperous.

In his own life Comenius exemplified the virtues he recommended. He neither despised the small patrimony left him as a boy nor neglected to provide for his wife, Dorothy, in the marriage contract of 1624. From his best-selling text-books he made little profit and from his indefatigable labours for de Geer he reaped but a paltry reward, being most concerned that his needy friends at Leszno should be provided for. Though he was doubtful whether marriage would be necessary in paradise, since there would be 'far truer joy in Christ' and that on earth 'even at its best sweet mingles with bitter',[40] yet he was a good family man, enjoying the affection of his wives and children.

THE MAN OF FAITH

To say that the morality of Comenius was earth-bound does not mean that his faith was not heaven-directed. He believed there was nothing more dangerous than to transform into learned knowledge something which should be put into practice but for him morality and faith were inseparable. The 'man of virtue' must have a frame of reference in which to work; that is, he must also be a 'man of faith'. Works without faith or faith without works – each was dead without the other.

When, in the fifth century, St Augustine postulated the City of God he proposed a theological foundation for it and thus he established the system of thought which dominated the Middle Ages and was accepted by most Christians up to the time of Comenius. It was not intended as final and unalterable since, as Comenius says:

'In his old age, the holy father Augustine, having learnt and found out much about the things of God . . . retracted, corrected and explained many things he had taught before . . . and the pious do not consider it to be their blame but their honour . . . that they gladly correct whenever they find a thing can be said better.'[41]

But there could be no doubting the basic truth that, in a ruined world, God had ordained a mysterious instrument of grace, the Catholic Church, through which the mercy of God could be mediated and by which man's tendency towards depravity could be held in check. The Church was the means by which the two great tendencies of religious history could be kept in balance – the necessity for permanence and certainty and the urge towards spontaneity and immediacy. The religion of mysticism was only possible within the framework of the religion of authority.

Comenius did not object to the theology of the Catholic Church nor to its claim to universality. His objection was to Rome and Papal power which had so far betrayed its trust it must be destroyed 'as a filthy harlot'. The Church of Rome had been the Mother of Christians but had become 'a step-mother, yea, even a wild she-bear'[42] and the Pope was 'the Antichrist, the man of sin, the son of perdition and the most dangerous seducer'.[43]

Comenius was not satisfied that the Reformation had radically changed the situation. It was simply the first act of the healing of the blind man by Christ (Mark 8). It had purified 'some parts of religion and removed the reign of the Pope' but 'locally and diversely and not with any universal idea'. For individual Reformers he had great respect – John Hus, the forerunner of them all – Martin Luther, who 'came in the spirit and might of Elijah – John Calvin, whom he regarded as the greatest of all, but he wrote to his old friend and mentor, J. V. Andreae, who was a Lutheran minister: 'On earth I do not reverence anybody as my master, the one in heaven is enough for me.'[44] He was bitterly

D
49

disappointed that the different sections of the Reformed Church had split on questions of dogma. The Lutherans had been 'more absorbed in excited dispute than in establishing discipline and a truly Christian, quiet life'. The Calvinists had been so concerned with theological disputation that they had caused some of the sons of the Church to be for ever 'searching for novelties' and this had resulted in the multiplication of sects. Sectarians were 'insects'. He writes to Andreae: 'Perhaps you remember, my good man, that in the very beginning I proclaimed that I was no sectarian and that, together with thee, I condemned all sects as the work of Satan. . . . May God have mercy upon us that we may be at last liberated from our dizziness.' Comenius never had much taste for dogmatic subtleties, especially if they led to dissension. Rather than that he would prefer to say: 'It is not clear; I am adjourning the matter; the beginning of reform must be made by halting and silence.'[45] No issue of theology – not even predestination or transubstantiation – was worth fighting over – 'It is better to overlook than to cut everything to pieces in exaggerated zeal' – and in any case truth would be advanced by considering both sides of every disagreement.

However much men might misuse it the Church remained the divinely ordained means of salvation and to Comenius the Bible had the same validity. Men might neglect it, misquote it, misunderstand it, but the Scriptures remained as a divinely-inspired revelation. His early up-bringing in the family of an Elder of the Brethren would have made him thoroughly acquainted with it and it would have formed the centre of his studies at school, in the home of Bishop Lanecký and at Herborn and Heidelberg. Of his teachers at Herborn John Henry Alsted was the author of *Triumphus Biblicus*, a brave attempt to harmonize verbal inspiration with mystical interpretation, and Piscator whose monumental *Concordance* must have been a gold-mine for preachers. At Heidelberg his interest in prophecy and the Revelation of St John was heightened by the teaching of David Pareus and Henry Alting. Pareus' *Irenicum* was published during his year of study (1614) and he was convinced that the thousand years' reign of Christ on earth was an immediate possibility. During the sad years when he was a fugitive Comenius was specially drawn to the Psalms and Prophets and in 1626 he made a translation into Czech of the Psalms from which his persecuted brethren might draw some consolation. He himself recorded many years after how much he owed to Scripture when he was depressed: 'Springing from my bed I seized the Bible and prayed to God not to abandon me; immediately I came upon Isaiah and, feeling my distress vanishing as I read, I took my pen.'[46]

A literal acceptance of Scripture inevitably raises problems when the text conflicts with fact or reason and seventeenth century philosophers dealt with such difficulties by assuming that truth was not all of one order. There was truth of faith and truth of fact and the two could be harmonized by assuming an allegorical meaning for all statements.[47] Even Isaac Newton was able to keep these two kinds of truth separately but it was not without some danger to mental honesty. The Cambridge Platonists boldly took the line: 'To follow reason is to follow God.' The Quakers relied on the 'inner light'. But there were many who, in the words of Thomas Hobbes, 'took the bare words but not the scope of the writer . . . and cast atoms of Scripture as dust before men's eyes'.[48] Despite his frequent use of Scripture Comenius took a rational view and always maintained that it could not conflict with reality or reason. There were mysteries which could not be solved while men see 'through a glass darkly' and meanwhile he found comfort because 'God does not call us to heaven asking us smart questions. It is more profitable to know things humbly than to know them proudly'.[49] Fundamentally his attitude is undogmatic – 'Since the all-wise God is the author of nature and of Scripture too, the truth which is imprinted upon things cannot possibly fail to harmonize with the truth expressed in words though here and there it may be difficult to understand. In individual passages of Scripture mysteries are offered to us under a veil'.[50] The 'harmonic drawing' of truth out of Scripture must be 'through the Scripture itself, by the light of reason and through illustrative experience and selected examples' – this was the task which he assigned to the supreme council of the Church.[51] Fortunately there were many parts of the Bible where he found no mystery and no conflict between earthly and divine wisdom and from these he quotes with happy confidence. Above all he found inspiration in Solomon who was given 'largeness of heart, even as the sand that is on the sea-shore so that he could expound all things in nature from the cedar tree even to the hyssop' (1 Kings, IV. 29). In Proverbs, Ecclesiastes, the Book of Wisdom and the Song, Comenius found a wealth of metaphors, aphorisms and illustrations combining homely wisdom with piety. Where, in the Bible, there was mystery or contradiction Comenius was content to let the words be their own witness.

The 'good man' was the 'man of faith' of Hebrews 11 who derived his strength of mind from the constant exercise of piety, the offices of the Church and the inspiration of Scripture.

Only faith could sustain men exposed to the extremity of evil and it was to increase their faith that Comenius wrote of the sufferings of his co-religionists – 'Woe is to us on all sides . . . a cruel bloody sword is destroying my dear homeland . . . and most painful of all is that the truth of God is oppressed and the pure services of God are stopped'.[52] In these circumstances it is necessary to recall the promises of God, to remember that suffering is a refining process, and to repent of sin which had brought down chastisement. In the second book of *The Afflicted* (Truchlivý) he faces the problem of undeserved pain where reason can find 'no hope left'. Then only faith can give constancy and constancy became the highest virtue.[53] In the labyrinth of the world the good man 'does not allow himself to be disturbed in the peace of his mind by the nations of the world . . . many things displease him but he does not therefore grieve . . . the world, it is true, is going from bad to worse but by fretting shall we improve it?'[54]

Nevertheless the constancy of faith is more than exercise of the will and greater than any ideology. Comenius speaks of the 'sainted Luther' because for him *'Glaube'* was a dynamic, inward experience resulting in a personal discovery of God: 'No one,' said Luther, 'can understand God or God's word unless he has had it revealed immediately by the Holy Ghost . . . in experience the Holy Ghost teaches us.'[55] Practice of good only comes through knowledge of it and this can only be acquired by faith – that is awareness of God, readiness to co-operate in His purposes, preparation for the moment of departure into His immediate presence. For Comenius the supreme struggle was against pride and self-will within man's mind and it was the 'Lamb's War between God and the Devil'. The culmination of life much to be desired is thus expressed in the last words of the English Quaker, James Nayler: 'There is a spirit which I feel that delights to do no evil, nor to revenge any wrong, but delights to endure all things, in hope to enjoy its own in the end.'

From time to time Comenius was accused of heresy because he was not rigid in dogma. His theology was like Luther's – a medieval phenomenon[56] and he was not attracted to the more logically irresistible 'plan of salvation' of Calvin because it seemed to lead to dissension for which no creed was worth while. The man of faith 'has no concern with this strife . . . he walks on silently and quietly as if in thought, looking heavenward'.[57] The only thing about which there must be unity was in love towards God. In things 'instrumental', such as 'the Word, the Keys and the Sacraments', and in things accidental, such as local customs, there could be toleration of differences and true unity could be achieved 'by allowing the whole garden of the Church to blossom with voluntary piety without coercion, that is without the keys of priestly discipline'.[58]

THE MAN OF WISDOM

When the Church of the Unity of Brethren rejected the highest ideals of Chelčický in 1494 they still retained the tradition of simplicity but tried to adapt it to their growing numbers and influence. Increasingly the leaders were drawn from the upper ranks of society, both from the nobility and from substantial townsmen. After the death of Lukáš in 1528 interest in social radicalism was less strongly marked and the Brethren began to appear as respectable and loyal members of society. Persecution continued but it was intermittent and never so severe as after 1620. When the situation was very black it was a nobleman, Konrad Krajek, who went to Vienna to plead with King Ferdinand I and he took with him a Confession signed by twelve lords and thirty-three knights. The policy of accommodation, where possible, led to further departure from the primitive simplicity represented by Bishop Augusta to a more liberal attitude represented by Jan Blahoslav. It was Blahoslav who, by his writings from 1550 until his death, reconciled the Unity to Humanism and brought in what has been called a 'Golden Age' culminating in full recognition of their right to exist by the Letter of Majesty of 1609. The old traditions remained but the Brethren looked for leadership to a new type of man – the scholarly Blahoslav, the energetic man of affairs Václav Budovec, the cultured man of the world, Charles Žerotín.

The change of point of view was profound though subtle. There was less emphasis on human depravity and more on human potentiality, a less claustrophobic view of the Unity's place in the world and renewed hope of Protestant, if not universal, unity. There were many among the Brethren who were willing to take an active part in the life of the nation and to accept the wider duties and opportunities open to them. In the education of their children they were ready to accept the literature of the Ancient world as worthy of some attention and to cultivate the learning of the Humanists.

Comenius was never able to go the whole way with the Humanists. He condemned the reverence paid to Aristotle[59] but he also regarded the classical poets as sirens luring men to destruction. He always had a deep suspicion of Italian Humanists because of their tendency towards atheism[60] and he showed almost no appreciation of Renaissance art.[61] On the other hand he was painfully aware of the evils of Christendom which made a mockery of religion and a justification for atheism – the coat of mail over the priest's surplice struck him as 'monstrous'.[62] But this was the prostitution of human nature, not its inherent character. In man himself he did not find the 'positive inclination to evil' so much emphasized by Luther,[63] nor could he agree with Calvin's grim conclusion:

'The mind of man is so entirely alienated from the righteousness of God that he cannot conceive, desire, or design anything but what is wicked, distorted, impure and iniquitous; his heart is so thoroughly envenomed by sin that it cannot breathe anything but corruption and rottenness.'[64]

That, Comenius found insulting to God and man. He frequently quotes Ludovicus Vives with approval as, for instance, in the fundamental fifth chapter of the *Great Didactic*: 'What else is a Christian but a man restored to his own nature, and as it were brought back to the starting-point from which the Devil has thrown him.'[65] Certainly all men (being of Adam's brood) have been thus thrown back, but he adds: 'If we wish to find a remedy for the defects of nature, it is in nature herself that we must look, for it is certain that art can do nothing unless it imitate nature.' This approach to the salvation of man Comenius found almost exactly echoed in Seneca: 'We must keep to the road indicated by nature.'[66]

Comenius was also with the Humanists in their refusal to accept the Augustinian cleavage between the sacred and the secular though here he was more cautious. Generally he followed Erasmus in the view that religion consists of two things – knowledge through reason of what is necessary for salvation (*Veras habere opiniones*) and performance in thought, word and deed of what is known (*Bene agere*). But this is also wisdom and the two are identical – to know virtue and to practise it[67] and therefore says Erasmus: 'It would be well for us if we made less of dogmatic subtleties and more of the Gospel.'[68] The words of the Bible are for guidance not for argument and should be left to make their own witness and 'in this', says Comenius, 'Erasmus gave a good example in his *Compendia Theologiae*'.[69]

There is a subtle but important difference between Augustine's sentence: 'We love good in so far as we know it and hate evil in so far as we understand it', and the words of Vives: 'True wisdom consists in judging things correctly, so that we estimate a thing at its true worth, and do not esteem something vile as though it were precious, nor condemn what should be praised'.[70] To Augustine knowledge of goodness came through faith and by revelation. To Vives (and following him, Comenius) it comes also through judgment, reason or wisdom. Comenius shows his thinking by quoting Cardanus whom he calls the 'Christian philosopher': 'God has equipped man with three tools: mind, with which to invent what is necessary: words, as a helper: hands, with which to carry out all that he has either thought out with his mind or learned from the words of others.'[71] This is very similar to what Comenius calls the 'proper functions of humanity' – Reason (*Ratio*), Speech (*Oratio*) and Action (*Operatio*).

Comenius took over from the Renaissance much of the confusion of thought that hid the complete re-orientation from the Middle Ages. He kept the old language but gave it a secular application. His ideal of the 'man of wisdom' was still profoundly Christian but the emphasis was on civic virtues no longer arising from revelation. From time to time the old ideal of orientation towards heaven reasserted itself as can be clearly seen in his last work *The One Thing Necessary* (*Unum Necessarium*). But the illustration which he chose as frontispiece for the *Collected Works* was not of a man with a Bible in his hand and his eyes looking upward but of a man with a pen in his hand and a globe in front of him pointing towards scenes of human in-industry and activity. Negatively, the 'man of wisdom' was one who avoided or, at least, moderated all the passions. Positively, he was one who took a full part in the life of the community, made sound judgments and acted with strict probity. Even preparation for the after-life was given a prudential slant because it motivated a man towards a present life of virtue. The logical conclusion was well put by Cardanus, 'To affirm the soul immortal is not only pious and prudent but blameless as well and the cause of a multitude of goods.'[72] Had Comenius read the autobiography of Cardanus, which was published with his *Works* in 1663, he might have been shocked to learn that Cardanus was extravagant and tormented in his sexual life.[73]

Comenius shows clearly the influence of the Renaissance concept of human dignity as that quality which makes a man complete, an adept in the art of living and a perfect citizen – the 'perfect governour', 'magnanimous in all the arts of peace and war'. Such a man would value posthumous fame (that last infirmity of noble minds) more than temporal advantage. He would scorn to persecute others and Comenius quotes the 'admirable saying' of Cicero: 'It is unworthy of the dignity of a wise man to believe what is false or to defend anything accepted without investigation'.[74] Even the theologians should consider their 'honour' when deciding what is holy. It was the ideal towards which many of the leaders of the Unity of Brethren from the time of Blahoslav onwards set themselves and it was probably because he was so disgusted with the lack of such virtue in the ruling class of Bohemia that Žerotín turned away from politics at a crucial moment.

It was, however, essentially an aristocratic ideal and it is at this point that Comenius differs most profoundly from the Humanists. He agreed with them in the belief that man is potentially capable of moral virtue but took a far more optimistic and universal view of the possibilities. Thus he objects to the 'piecemeal explanation' of Cicero concerning the condition of man and put the position thus: 'The seeds of virtue are native in our souls, and if they are allowed to grow, nature herself would bring us to a life of blessedness. But now, the moment we see the light we live in the midst of constant wickedness. We seem to suck error with our nurse's milk and nature gives way before obstinate conviction'.[75] The remedy, to be effective, must be universal. It is a dilemma applicable to the twentieth century as much as to the seventeenth thus expressed by a modern philosopher, Carl Jung:

'A spiritual goal that points beyond the purely natural man and his worldly existence is an absolute necessity for the health of his soul. It is the Archimedean point from which alone it is possible to lift the world off its hinges and to transform the natural state into a cultural one.'[76]

Comenius believed he had found that 'Archimedean point' by which no man should degenerate into not being a man, that is not being 'in the image of God'. And his advice, 'one of the most universal rules of practical wisdom', is applicable to everyone: 'Do in your deeds what you would wish to see in the hour of your death'.[77]

CONCLUSION

There are in Comenius different interpretations of human goodness. Sometimes he treats it as a kind of esoteric experience by which man can elevate himself above the world. Then he treats it as the pearl of great price for successful living on earth. Quickly he returns to the concept of goodness imputed by God's grace and mercy. And there are times when he transforms it into civic virtue and personal dignity. It is many-sided enough to be considered universal.

J. A. COMENIUS

The special contribution of Comenius to the concept of the 'good man' lies in his continual effort to realize the parallelism between each of the components. He tried to think of them existing together and, at the same time, constantly overcoming contradictory elements and combining harmoniously.

NOTES

(a) *The Man of Mystic Experience*
1. *School of Infancy* Ch. II.
2. *Reflections on Christian Perfection* (1662) and '*The Name of the Lord is a High Tower*' (1662) VSJAK Tome XV.
3. *Truchlivý I.* (1623) *Truchlivý II.* (1624).
4. VSJAK Tome XV 378.
5. *Panorthosia* XVIII.16.
6. *Labyrinth* Ch. XLII.
7. *Labyrinth* Ch. XIX.12.
8. *Labyrinth* Ch. XX.5.
9. J. V. Andreae: *Reipublica Christianopolitanae Descriptio* Ch. XVII.
10. *Labyrinth* Ch. XVIII.
11. George Fox: *Journal* (1657).
12. Quoted by Rufus Jones: *Mystical Religion* p. 387.
13. *Labyrinth* Ch. L.
14. *Great Didactic* XXXIII.19.
15. Jacob Boehme: 'Mysterium Magnum' Quoted by Rufus Jones: *Mystical Religion* p. 169-170.
16. *Labyrinth* Ch. XLII.
17. *Pampaedia* III.27.
18. *Labyrinth* Ch. XLII.
19. Franz Hartmann: *Life of Paracelsus* (1896) p. 53.
20. Kvačala: *Korres.* II. 149.
21. cf. Aldous Huxley: *Doors of Perception* p. 117-122. cf. Louisa Rhine: *Hidden Channels of the Mind* (1964) Duke Univ.
22. *Great Didactic* V.20.
23. Quoted by Victor Gollancz: *From Darkness unto Light* p. 208.
24. *Great Didactic* V.8.
25. *Republic* VII. 518c.
(b) *The Man of Virtue*
26. Peter Chelčický: *O Trojím Lidu* p. 44.
27. *Labyrinth* Ch. IX.
28. Quoted by J. E. Hutton: *History of the Moravian Church* p. 69.
29. Quoted by P. Brock: *Political and Social Doctrines of Unity of Czech Brethren* p. 268.
30. Ranke: *History of the Popes* Bk. VII.Ch. II Quoted by J. E. Hutton p. 154. Seifferth: *Church Constitution of Moravian Brethren* p. 11. Camerarius: *Historica Narratio* p. 48.
31. P. Brock: *Op Cit.* p. 264. 270.
32. *Pampaedia* III.20.
33. *Haggaeus Redivivus*: p. 34. (Ed. B. Souček 1952).

34. *Labyrinth*: Ch. XI.
35. Seneca: *Epistles* 93.
36. *Great Didactic*: XXIII.5.
37. *Orbis Pictus*: Ch. CXI.
38. *Great Didactic*: XXIII. 11.
39. *Panorthosia* VIII.
40. *Labyrinth*: XXXIX.
The Man of Faith
41. *Retuňk proti Antikristu*: p. 236 (Ed. B. Souček 1924).
42. *Bequest of Dying Mother*: XVII.
43. *Retuňk proti Antikristu*: p. 150.
44. Kvačala: *Korres.* 102.
45. *Panorthosia* VIII.16.
46. Patera: *Korres.* 235 (Letter to Montanus).
47. Basil Willey: *Seventeenth Century Background* p. 59.
48. T. Hobbes: *Leviathan* XLIII.
49. Conclusion to *History of Lasitius*: p.293 (Ed. L. B. Kaspar (1869)).
50. *Via Lucis* XIV.8.
51. *Panorthosia* XVIII.6.
52. *Truchlivý*: VSJAK Tome XV.
53. cf. *Via Lucis* IV.1.
54. *Labyrinth* XLVIII.
55. Preface to *Magnificat* (1521).
56. Harnack: *History of Dogma* VII.169.
57. *Labyrinth* XVIII.
58. *Panorthosia* XVIII.8.
The Man of Wisdom
59. cf. *Physica*: Preface p. 161 'In Christianorum scholis Aristotelem tam-
   quam unum solum philosophiae magistrum tolerari non debere'.
60. cf. *Great Didactic* XXV.12 'What is it that in these days leads so many
   Italians towards atheism'.
61. cf. *Labyrinth* XI 'I perceived that these dear admonishers took no
   greater interest in the beautiful pictures than the ugly . . . some indeed
   approached the ugly ones with great pleasure'.
62. *Labyrinth* XX.1.
63. Eugene F. Rice Jr.: *The Renaissance Idea of Wisdom* p. 125.
64. E. M. W. Tillyard: *The English Renaissance – Fact or Fiction* p. 23.
65. L. Vives: *De Concordia et Discordia* I of *Great Didactic* V.1.
66. *Pampaedia* VII.29.
67. E. F. Rice: *Op. cit.* p. 160-161.
68. Erasmus: *Epistle* DLXXXVII Quoted by Rufus Jones: *Spiritual Reformers* p. 3.
69. *Panorthosia*: XVIII.11.
70. L. Vives: *Introductio ad Sapientiam* (Opera II.70).
71. *Pampaedia* II.7 Cardanus: *De Subtilitate* XI cf. Methodus Ch. I.
72. Cardanus: *De Sapientia* 520.2. Quoted by E. F. Rice: *Op. cit.* p. 172.
73. E. F. Rice: *Op. cit.* p. 165 Cardanus died in 1576 but his works were
   published posthumously.
74. *Panorthosia* XV.1.
75. *Pampaedia* IV.11.
76. C. G. Jung: *Development of Personality* (1954) p. 86.
77. *Pampaedia* XIII.5.

CHAPTER 3

THE CONCEPT OF ENCYCLOPAEDIC KNOWLEDGE

ALTHOUGH Comenius always insisted that man's 'true work' was concerned with goodness he was certainly not an anti-intellectual. The virtue of the poor and humble showed the power of divine grace but it was no excuse for ignorance. Certainly Comenius was suspicious of the men of learning. Their superficiality, contentiousness and pomposity grieved him 'to tears' and he found nought for his comfort in their pretensions. His great aim was to make knowledge the possession of every man, not the specialism of the few, and he condemned any attempt to turn learning into a mystique. He himself was not a profound scholar in any particular department although he was well read and interested in a great many subjects. He took the universe for his text-book and in that sense he was an encyclopaedist for he believed that every single aspect was in some way related to the whole. The object of knowledge was to understand the unity of all things not to amass facts and for this purpose Comenius believed that the means were all ready to hand – the physical universe, 'open to be read in every clime and in every age by all men' – the 'universal notions' of the human mind 'the same for man and woman, for the child and the old man, for the religious and the irreligious' – and finally the divine revelation 'for ever unveiling more mysteries' (*Via Lucis* IV). Thus encyclopaedic knowledge is not knowledge of every particular thing but a unified understanding of the universe, the self and of all the practical activities of God and man.

KNOWLEDGE OF THE UNIVERSE

Comenius was keenly interested in the 'noble science of

astronomy and knew of the work of Tycho Brahe and Kepler though not without doubts: 'I began to catch strenuously at the stars but I clearly saw that the stars by no means danced in accordance with the fiddles of these men.[1] He went to Amsterdam in 1613 only five years after Hans Lipperscheim had presented the first real telescope to the Dutch Estates General and through Bacon he knew of the 'wonderful exertions of Galileo in perfecting this instrument.[2] Amongst the manuscripts discovered by S. Souček in 1931 is one on astronomy written in the 1630's.

He found the Copernican theory 'indifferently supported by the phenomena'.[3] Mersenne, the French mathematician with whom Comenius had some correspondence, published a book in 1623 demonstrating the weakness of the Copernican hypothesis. Even Galileo did not repudiate the Ptolemaic system until 1632 when he published the *Dialogues on the Two Chief Systems of the World* and was called before the Inquisition to answer for his heresy that Holy Scripture must be wrong. The Jesuits, who were the leading astronomers of the time, and Pope Urban VIII were content to view the Copernican Theory as a 'working hypothesis'. This seems to have been the attitude of Comenius. There is a footnote in Chapter IV of the *Janua* noting that 'according to Copernicus' modern system the earth revolves round the sun' but the likelihood is that (with many others) he came to favour the compromise theory of Tycho Brahe that the planets revolved round the sun and the whole solar system moved round a fixed and stationary earth.[4] In fact the transition from one point of view to the other was just beginning to gain ground and 'traditional science so far revealed astonishing resilience and the new had not yet acquired an outlook positive enough to take its place'.[5] Herbert Butterfield says about this transition: 'Many of us have gone too far perhaps in imagining a cast-iron Ptolemaic system'[6] and Copernicus really left the traditional celestial machinery intact nor could this be disturbed until the telescope could be made more effective and this took about twenty years before there was any impact on scientific observation.[7]

It was not simply the conflict with Scripture that made Comenius hesitate about the Copernican hypothesis nor simply the diminishing of the importance of the earth in relation to the universe. It seemed rather to threaten his whole framework of presuppositions. It seemed to deny that the universe had any centre at all – as the posthumous editor of Copernicus said: 'You could regard any point as the centre'.[8] Comenius would have shared the uneasiness of John Donne:

> The new philosophy calls all in doubt;
> The sun is lost and the earth and no man's wit
> Can well direct him where to look for it.

The universe that Comenius could understand was one where everything had its nature and 'its capacity for keeping its appointed place'[9] and the stars, as 'lamps' for man, moved in continual harmony. The picture of the Heavens as drawn in the *Orbis Pictus* is essentially the same as that of Dante with the globe of heaven 'wheeled about' or 'turned on an axle tree' and the sun as the fountain of light. Comenius was prepared to accept new discoveries of men 'shrewdly investigating the secrets of nature' and he speaks of 'stars which because of their smallness send forth slender rays which cannot be seen except with the astronomer's instruments'.[10] He did reject astrology although it was on the increase in popularity but he could not emancipate himself from the medieval cosmogony. Without some understanding of magnetism and gravity how could he visualize a force capable of putting the earth mass into orbit and keeping it under control?

He had really only the Genesis story interpreted by classical physics to delineate an 'accurate anatomie of the universe, dissecting the veins and limbs in all things in such a way that each part shall appear in its place and without confusion'.[11] The *Physicae Synopsis* which he wrote in 1633 was a 'Naturall Philosophie reformed by Divine Light' interpreting Aristotelian physics according to the motto which he took from Vives 'By the Torch of Christ'. He took the same line in the text-books dividing the material world into the four medieval elements, explaining thunder as 'a brimstone-like vapour breaking out of a cloud' and explaining the presence of sea-shells 'even in Midland countries' by reference to the Flood.[12]

He had the same lyrical reverence for the sun as Copernicus[13] and speaks of the 'certainty that the heaven is really one all through and turns with the same motion'.[14] He dismisses the idea of a fifth element, incorruptible and separate from the universe, since 'everything in earth or heaven has a source of energy within itself as well as its external source which is God' though this was the heresy for which Bruno was burnt at the stake in 1600. The Russian writer, Krasnovskij says: 'In trying to retain Christianity Comenius was led from clean theism to pantheism and near to Spinozism'[15] to which Comenius has an answer: 'The more clearly nature is revealed the more clearly and fully will the majesty of the Creator of Nature shine forth'.[16]

The seventeenth century was a time of transition between the medieval view of independent forces working on each other and the modern view of mechanistic causation. Aristotelian physics presupposed that some things had a principle of 'motion' which enabled them to fulfil their own 'nature'. The universe as a whole was kept in motion by the interaction of certain independent elements – earth, air, water and fire – and a supreme force which was itself unmovable. This system made magic reasonable and miracles consistent with nature. Opposed to it was the modern mechanistic system of 'laws' inherent in every particle of matter which produced movement through attraction or repulsion and stability through a balance of forces about a pole. It became the foundation of Newtonian physics and, as Hobbes demonstrated, could be applied to human relationships.

Comenius alternated between the two systems. He speaks of the 'brightly lit theatre in which we can watch the course of all things . . . the continual struggle between the forms of nature and matter'.[17] He could not accept the idea of a simple struggle between opposing forces such as Alsted suggested in earth and heaven or Campanella in heat and cold but imagined a third force which he called 'spirit' to mediate between them and bring eventual stability[18] thus returning to the astral, terrestrial and spiritual forces that Paracelsus spoke of as Man's 'Mothers'.[19] For Comenius there was no irreverence in supposing a mathematical symbol to represent God but of all numbers 'three' was for him most significant and he tended to use triplets for every purpose 'like a host of troikas driving towards the land of Beulah'.[20]

On the other hand he frequently took a mechanistic view. Comenius thought of the great clocks which were being made in the seventeenth century, such as the one in the Prague Old Town Hall, with reverent awe – 'Is it not a truly marvellous thing that a machine, a soulless thing, can move in such a life-like, continuous and regular manner.'[21] Then he goes on to ask what is the force behind the clock, and, by inference, behind creation: 'What is the hidden power that brings all this to pass? Nothing but the all-ruling force of order; that is to say, the force derived from arranging all the parts concerned according to their number, size and importance.' This enthusiasm for the mystical patterns of mathematics, which was common enough at that time, did not, of course, make him a mathematician. In the *Labyrinth* he admits his limitations with disarming candour – 'When they showed me the deepest of all, which was algebra, I saw such a heap of weird and crooked writings that giddiness nearly overcame me.' The arithmeticians claimed that no knowledge was more certain than theirs and the poor man admits: 'These things I but dimly understood'. His situation is indicated thus: 'there was much talk about geometry being more wondrous than any other subtlety in the whole world. It was not sufficient to have the spectacles of dialectics but the view must also be made clear by an eye-salve composed of physics and mathematics'. Comenius continued to use the spectacles but never managed to get hold of the eye-salve. Nevertheless he was feeling his way towards the ideal enunciated by Galileo:

'Philosophy is written in that vast book which stands ever open before our eyes, I mean the universe; but it cannot be read until we have learnt the language and become familiar with the characters in which it is written. It is written in mathematical language, and the letters are triangles, circles and other geometrical figures, without which means it is humanly impossible to comprehend a single word.'[22]

For Comenius there was always the danger of 'a most ready precipice into error' if sense, reason and scripture were not used to correct each other. Each of them unaided by the others was weak and fallible – 'Philosophy is lame without divine revelation' but an uncritical acceptance of Scripture would cause men 'to be carried away beyond the world by the sublimity of their conceptions and involve things absurd and superstitious' – 'if a man consult only with reason without the testimony of sense he will be rapt away with mere phantasies' but on the other hand 'when the sense judgeth the moon to be bigger than Saturn or an oar to be broken under water reason rectifies it by certain documents of experience'.[23]

In biology Comenius was influenced by the command to Adam that he should name all creatures and plants and in consequence the 547 separate items in the *Janua* dealing with them consist largely of names. The descriptions, though showing some evidence of keen observation, are based on the assumption that the world of nature is subservient to human purpose. The general approach is similar to that of Aristotle or Pliny with emphasis on habits and breeding and curiosities of information and less moralizing than in the medieval bestiary or the early encyclopaedias with which he was familiar, especially Isidore. In the search for a 'natural' classification of plants there had been little advance since ancient times and there was no fundamental difference between the *Herbal* of Theophrastus in 300 B.C. and that of Gerard in 1600 A.D.[24] Since Comenius held the Scriptural view of the separate creation of all the species he was bound to take structure rather than evolution as the basis for his classification as, indeed, did Linnaeus a century later.

To Comenius the ultimate foundation of the universe was metaphysical, not material. The clock presupposed a maker, the multitude of beasts, a Creator. Like Plato's *Republic*, the universe of Comenius was a manifestation of a single pervading law and therefore knowledge of it must go further than sense perception to the pure form of which it was an approximation or a particular instance. It is clear that Plato's Cave simile was very frequently in Comenius' mind and he thought of knowledge as the entry of light. Thus 'When the internal lamp is not lit, but the torches of strange opinions are carried around the effect must be as if lights were carried round a man shut up in a dark dungeon; the rays, indeed, penetrate the chinks but the full light is unable to enter'.[25] The vision of the universe given by the 'full light' was substantially that given by Plato in the

Timaeus: 'The world has received animals mortal and immortal, and is fulfilled with them, and has become a visible animal containing the visible – the sensible God who is the image of the greatest, best, fairest, most perfect heaven'. It sounds bizarre but in A. N. Whitehead's view it comes nearer than any other book to providing the philosophical setting required by the ideas of modern physical science.[26]

KNOWLEDGE OF SELF

Though Comenius took the universe as his theme and God as the soul of the universe he sometimes wrote as if man himself were its centre. It was man as the image of God, indeed, but man reshaping the universe in the image of his desire and ascribing reality to the fiction. The significance of man was that he embodied the universe and projected himself into it – he was 'a microcosm' or epitome of the universe, since he inwardly comprehends all the elements that are spread far and wide through the Macrocosm or world at large.[27] This view was not uncommon in the seventeenth century and illustrates a tendency to concentrate attention on the human problem and away from the metaphysical preoccupation of the Middle Ages. The thought was that as God had imposed unchangeable laws on the innumerable forms and events of nature so must man develop his ideals into external forms and to do this he must first understand himself. 'As you find man to be,' writes Jacob Boehme, 'just so is eternity'[28] and if this is so, Comenius asks: 'What is the voice from heaven that resounds in the Scriptures but "Know thyself, O man, and know me".'

If, therefore, the proper study of mankind is man it must begin with the study of the body since in this marvellously contrived mechanism the secrets of the universe are revealed. In physiology and anatomy the first half of the century produced some discoveries as important as those in physics but unfortunately Comenius did not get to know them. In the first place they originated in the University of Padua with an attack on the teaching of Galen by Vesalius, and Comenius had little opportunity of learning of them. The most important was the discovery by William Harvey of the circulation of the blood and the action of the heart but his book *De Motu Cordis* was not published until 1628 and it was thirty years before this was widely known.[29] The importance of Harvey's discovery was that it opened up the way to the other physiological systems – respiration, oxygenation and digestion – which would almost certainly have had a great appeal to Comenius because of their exemplification of the principle of order. The discovery of the microscope in 1608 and the thermometer in 1621 opened up the way to more exact observation of the human body but they were not available to Comenius. Consequently he fell back on the old classical system of spleen, gall, humours and vital spirits. Thus in the *Janua* he says, 'The heart beateth without rest and guarantees the vital spirit which it distributes throughout the whole body' while 'a cold is the dripping of a moist humour'. In the *Orbis Pictus* the illustrations show that he retained the old misconceptions though, in places, he gives evidence of detailed knowledge as, for instance, when he names thirty-four bones in the hand and thirty in the foot.

He has no great respect for the physicians who, he says, 'kill their patients with impunity' and he recommends mothers to 'avoid giving medicine to their children except in great need'.[30] He has much positive advice to give about natural therapy in which the great principles are moderation in all things and the cultivation of habit.

Although Comenius was mistaken in his physiology he does establish (or, at least, take over from Aristotle) some truths of general application. His definition of an animal – to be endowed with 'life, perception and motion'[31] or to be self-sufficing through 'life and motion'[32] – leaves the essential human characteristic as the power of thought and this is the theory of Aristotle's *De Anima*. It is from the *De Anima* that Comenius quotes the 'great truth': 'There is nothing in the understanding that was not first in the senses'.[33] He accepts the concept of a 'body-mind' entity in which there is harmony between the physical and mental aspects – 'For just as the great world itself is like an immense piece of clock-work . . . thus it is with man. The body is indeed constructed with marvellous skill. First of all comes the heart, the source of all life and action from which the other members receive motion. The weight, the efficient cause of motion, is the brain, which by the help of nerves, as of ropes, attracts and repels the other wheels or limbs. . . . Man, then, is in himself nothing but a harmony as in the case of a clock or a musical instrument'.[34] The position of Comenius is uneasily somewhere between the dualism of Descartes who separated the soul from the body and even located it in the pineal gland and the pantheism of Spinoza who said: 'Since God is Being absolutely infinite there cannot be any substance other than God and consequently none other can be conceived'.[35] Thus in the *Orbis Pictus* (Ch. XLV) the Soul of man is represented as an indistinct outline of the human form surrounded by a white cloth and described as 'the Life of the Body, only vegetative in plants, withal sensitive in animals, and also rational in man'. In the *Physica* the Soul of man is made to differ from the Soul of an animal only in quality and rationality. In many places Comenius tends toward the conception of the *De Anima* that the soul is really a function of the body and uses such similes as the blank tablet (*tabula rasa*) 'potentially written on'[36] or a seed which possesses 'everything rolled up within itself'.[37] His view seems to be the same as that of Aristotle that the question whether the soul and body are one is meaningless. What he does emphasize is the unlimited potentiality of man.

Comenius believed that sex was a God-given function to be associated with piety rather than pleasure. Thus:

'The Creator could have created the human race in full number as He did the angels but He took pleasure in showing His wisdom in another way. The human race is a divine seed but it continues in the same way as the seeds of other plants and animals. In order that this should be done holily the care for children is placed in parents' hands instead of in God's whose seed they are ordered to seek.'[38]

The 'pleasure' of sex comes from the sense of association with God and in heaven marriage would be 'not widely separated from virginity'.[39] The idea of sex differentiation is taken almost exactly from Bacon:

'Having formed the two sexes that one might do the part of the plant bearing the seed and the other, as it were, cherishing and hatching it . . . this alone and none other is the end of the two sexes. The members whereby the sexes differ are the same in number and form and differ in nothing almost unless it be in regard to exteriors and interiors, to wit the greater heat of the male thrusting the genitals outward but in the female by reason of the weaker heat the said members containing themselves within.'[40]

The idea that pain is a necessary part of sex is shown by the prayer suggested for expectant mothers: 'I do not ask for exemption from the punishment Thou hast laid on our sex'.[41]

Comenius based his optimism concerning the future on the Platonic notion that man will naturally embrace good if it is presented to him clearly enough and will choose evil only through ignorance.[42] Though this might appear what Erasmus called a 'divine folly leading the soul from visible corporeal things to the invisible and divine'[43] for Comenius it gave ground for boundless hope – 'for the mind, neither in heaven nor anywhere outside heaven, can a boundary be set'.[44]

KNOWLEDGE OF PRACTICAL UTILITY

Despite occasional criticisms, Comenius gained from his Herborn teacher, Henry Gutberleth, a high regard for Aristotle. No one at that time could disregard the one who had 'formed the European mind' and had 'like a Colossus bestrode the centuries'.[45] What he rejected was the Scholastic tradition arising from Aristotle. It was the 'turning over of dead papers rather than the living book of the world' and the 'vanities of learning – verbalism, controversy, plagiarism and subtlety – that made it impossible for philosophers to do their proper work. This was 'to remedy the deficiencies of men' but though they 'sat round the tree of nature' and 'gnawed the nuts till their teeth shook' yet 'the kernel lay intact'.[46] Erasmus had wished that 'there could be an end of scholastic subtleties and that Christ could be taught plainly and simply'[47] but Comenius went further and came to believe that the whole body of human knowledge could be made available for use.

The man to whom more than any other he owed this belief was Francis Bacon. He came to know Bacon's work while he was in hiding at Brandýs, for the *Novum Organum* was published in 1620 and the *Advancement of Learning* was translated into Latin in 1623 and he found it 'an admirable work which I look upon as a most bright beam of a new age of philosophers'.[48] When he was almost at the point of despair he read Bacon's words: 'By far the greatest obstacle in the advancement of the sciences, and the undertaking of any new attempt or department, is to be found in men's despair'.[49] It was Bacon who infused new hope that if the false ideals of learning could be cleared away, man could through a study of nature 'find the highest link of the chain which must needs be tied to the foot of Jupiter's chair'.[50] But the first links must be established by careful observation and collection of facts for 'We have observed that nothing has been so injurious to philosophy as this circumstance namely, that familiar objects do not arrest and detain men's contemplation'. Nevertheless the study of familiar objects must always be guided by reference to 'first causes' and Bacon showed his lack of prescience by condemning those who wasted their time 'on probing some solitary matter, as Gilbert's magnet'.[51] On the other hand he recognizes the 'wonderful exertions of Galileo', speaks with enthusiasm of the invention of the compass, gunpowder, silk and the telescope[52] and suggests as topics for research those which Newton took up later – gravity, rotation of heavenly bodies, heat and light, density, liquidity and motion. Bacon's 'true key' to the study of nature is induction – the 'store and collection of particular facts' so that there might be 'a better compilation of natural history'. He realized the limitations of induction since 'simple enumeration' was puerile.[53] Induction and deduction must be combined, for 'notions' abstracted from things would have no solidity but the collecting of facts must have as its aim the defining of notions.[54]

Comenius had already derived from John Henry Alsted at Herborn a passion for the collection of facts into a comprehensive encyclopaedia but he was tied to the traditional framework of classical learning and Scriptural history. The medieval encyclopaedias such as the *Etymologies of Isidore* had been little more than voluminous catalogues of ill-arranged facts trying to encompass the whole of human knowledge. Alsted was already working on a more rational survey when Comenius was his student but he did not publish his work until 1629 (*Scientiarum omnium encyclopaedia*).[55] Fired by this example Comenius projected his own encyclopaedia and regarded it as his '*magnum opus*' to 'replace a whole library of books' until it was for the most part destroyed at Lezno. From the Table of Contents it is clear that the plan was still dominated by Christian theology and prophecy but the central part dealing with 'human activities, crafts and arts and world geography and chronology' must have been more mundane while the intent expressed in the Preface: 'I love my country and my language and my greatest wish is that it should be cultivated and improved as much as possible' indicates the practical purpose.

Also at Herborn and Heidelberg Comenius came under the influence of the writers of Utopias, Thomas Campanella and John Valentine Andreae and there is a close connection between the 'new philosophy' of Bacon and these projections of ideal societies. It is unlikely that Comenius would have known the 'New Atlantis' but the basic conception of all the Utopias of the time was the same – it was a portrayal of the 'good society' where knowledge was at the disposal of man or, as Bacon put it, 'a rich storehouse for the glory of the Creator and the relief of man's estate'. Utopia was not an enchanted island for escapists but a clarion call to follow Andreae's motto: 'It is inglorious to despair'. Campanella's *Civitas Solis* was published in 1623 and Comenius read it with 'incredible delight'. It envisaged a state in which science would be used for man's welfare, where ships would move without sails. Even more remarkable were the allegories of Andreae – the *Peregrini in Patria Errores* of 1618 and the *Reipublicae Christianopolitanae Descriptio* of 1619. In writing the *Labyrinth* Comenius borrowed freely from Campanella and Andreae[56] and he regarded the city of Christianopolis as a suitable ideal for the 're-dedication of minds' since it had as its innermost shrine the 'seat of religion, justice and learning'. The integration of spiritual, practical and intellectual aspects of life seemed to Comenius essential for each of them. His aim was 'to enlighten all men with true wisdom; to order their lives by true government; to unite them with God by true religion'.[57]

Comenius saw the danger that men would interpret useful knowledge as that which contributed to earthly comfort and efficiency. This was the tendency against which he warned the Royal Society. 'Let us assume,' he writes to them, 'that you have conquered the whole domain of Nature. If you rest content with that . . . your work will be a Babylon turned upside down, building not towards heaven but towards earth.'[58] The theme of man's Utopia had already been dealt with by a Czech – Václav Porcius Vodňanský – whose title *The Spiritual City or The Joy of the Soul* expressed the hopes of Comenius better than the Preamble to the Statutes of the Royal Society which was frankly utilitarian.[59]

On the other hand it would be wrong to think that Comenius was not acutely concerned for the 'relief of man's estate'. Though he was a minister of religion his text-books for children give a high priority to science. In the *Janua* thirty-six chapters are given to science as compared with twenty to religion and morals and only six to the liberal arts. The remaining thirty-seven chapters are given to human activities but over half of them are concerned with severely practical crafts from which stimulus for scientific activity arose. He does try to show the relevance of knowledge to every-day life – 'the disciplines of mathematics are as useful as they are subtle' (para. 755). The chapters in the *Orbis Pictus* dealing with crafts, though brief, show a surprising range and accuracy of practical knowledge. There are a number of traditions concerning his manual skills for which evidence is given by Kvačala – for instance that he was apprenticed between leaving Strážnice and going to Přerov either as a blacksmith or as a miller and that at Fulnek he taught his parishioners the art of bee-keeping. His account of printing in the *Great Didactic* makes it hard to believe that he did not frequently use the press at Leszno. His approach to learning is not always philosophical – for instance he opens Chapter XXII of the *Janua* cheerfully, 'Well now let us inspect the bowels' and there is no squeamish avoidance of unpleasant facts concerning violence or false modesty concerning the sexual temptations of youth.[60]

Comenius had a high regard for the value of the dissemination of knowledge as such. Paradise could only be regained on the basis of an understanding of Paradise lost and the 'ways of God to man' must be justified in the humblest and most ordinary affairs of life. Between 1628 and 1632 he wrote an amazing collection of books for almost every situation – a handbook for mothers, a manual for teachers, a series of text-books for children of all ages, a natural philosophy 'exposed to the censure of those that are lovers of learning', a compendium of the Bible for Church members and all the time he was continuing with the encyclopaedia and turning his mind increasingly to an even greater work on pansophy.[61] He wanted to accomplish the aim set forth by Vives – 'all that knowledge which leads to the life of greatest usefulness'.[62]

He believed that the Baconian method of induction was the true 'key to nature' but complained that 'the noble Verulam had not opened the secrets of nature'.[63] What was needed was an intensive and extensive study of all the phenomena with emphasis on verification of the facts. Thus the Universities should 'pay closest attention to the demand: 'Give a proof'. 'Let them teach, if they are well advised of trees, of beasts and of fowl . . . Let them teach the composition of the world and the strength of the elements . . . of the power of ghosts and the thoughts of people'.[64] If encyclopaedic knowledge was beyond the capacity of ordinary people in the seventeenth century how much more in the twentieth but yet there is something in the words of a modern writer: 'The ideal of complete all-round knowledge cannot be realized but it is worth striving for'.[65] He concludes: 'Encyclopaedic education is neither practical nor desirable; pansophic teaching is both'. It is certain that at a very early stage Comenius was searching for a method of organizing facts so that they expressed wisdom and would therefore constitute knowledge of practical utility.[66]

J. A. COMENIUS

NOTES

(a) *Knowledge of the Universe*
1. *Labyrinth* Ch. XI.
2. F. Bacon: *Novum Organum* I.69.
3. Quoted by H. Butterfield: *Origins of Modern Science* p. 100.
4. cf. 1649 Edition of *Janua* and *Diatyposis* (Tr. of J. Collier) p. 91.
5. A. Rupert Hall: *From Galileo to Newton* p. 18.
6. H. Butterfield: *Op. cit.* p. 18.
7. A. Rupert Hall: *Op. cit.* p. 32.
8. R. G. Collingwood: *The Idea of Nature* p. 97.
9. *Janua* XI.22.
10. *Via Lucis* X.8 and XIII.9.
11. *Amphitheatrum Universitatis Rerum*: Preface.
12. *Orbis Pictus* VIII and IX.
13. cf. *Via Lucis* XII.
14. *Panorthosia* VIII.
15. A. A. Krasnovskij: *J. A. Komenský* quoted by Otokar Chlup. (*Archiv pro Badani* XVIII.)
16. *Via Lucis* XIV.7.
17. *Via Lucis* XVI.12.
18. *Physica*: Preface.
19. Rufus Jones: *Spiritual Reformers* p. 138.
20. V. Jelínek: *Analytical Didactic* p. 20.
21. *Great Didactic* XIII.13.
22. Galileo: *Il Saggiatore* (Opere 1800) p. 232 Quoted by H. Butterfield, *Op. Cit.* p. 102.
23. *Physica*: Preface.
24. Lancelot Hogben: *Science for the Citizen* p. 923.
25. *Great Didactic* V.8.
26. R. G. Collingwood: The Idea of Nature p. 79.
Knowledge of Self
27. *Great Didactic* V.5.
28. J. Boehme: *The Threefold Life* VI.47 Quoted by Rufus Jones: *Spiritual Reformers* p. 18.
29. H. Butterfield: *Origins of Modern Science* p. 37-54.
30. *Informatorium* V.
31. *Janua* XIV.
32. *Great Didactic* VI.3.
33. *Analytical Didactic* 53. Aristotle: *De Anima* III.VIII.432a.
34. *Great Didactic* V.15.
35. Spinoza: *Ethics* Prop. 14.
36. *Analytical Didactic* 80. Aristotle: *De Anima* III.IV.430a.
37. *Great Didactic* V.5. Aristotle: *De Anima* II.412.25.
38. *Pampaedia*: VIII.1.
39. *Labyrinth*: L.
40. *Physica* II. cf. F. Bacon: *Novum Organum* II.27.
41. *Informatorium* V.
42. *Analytical Didactic*: 98 cf. Plato: *Protagoras* 357.

43. Erasmus: *Praise of Folly* 120 ff. Quoted by E. F. Rice: *The Renaissance Idea of Wisdom* p. 158. (Tr. H. H. Hudson 1941.)
44. *Great Didactic* V.4.
Knowledge of Practical Utility
45. J. A. K. Thompson: *Ethics of Aristotle* p. 18.
46. *Labyrinth* XI.
47. Rufus Jones: *Spiritual Reformers* p. 3.
48. *Physica*: Preface.
49. *Novum Organum* I.92.
50. *Advancement of Learning*: 1.1.3.
51. *Novum Organum*: I.69.
52. *Novum Organum*: II.39.
53. *Novum Organum*: I.98 and 105.
54. *Novum Organum*: I.14.
55. P. R. Cole: *J. H. Alsted – A Neglected Educator*. Max Lippert: *J. H. Alsted*.
56. Von Criegen: *Comenius als Theolog* Quoted by Lutzow in *Introduction to Labyrinth*.
57. *Pampaedia* I.9.
58. *Via Lucis*: Dedication p. 19.
59. Vodňanský was executed in 1621.
60. *Janua*: 661.
61. *Informatorium*: *Czech Didactic*: *Janua and Vestibulum*: *Physica·Manualnik*.
62. L. Vives: *De Tradendis Disciplinis* I. VI.
63. *Physica*: Preface.
64. *Panorthosia* XXII.
65. W. K. Richmond: *Permanent Values in Education* p. 36.
66. A. Turek: *Comenian System of Education* Sec. III p. 9.

CHAPTER 4

THE CONCEPT OF THE GOOD SOCIETY

COMENIUS believed that universal education could never be achieved without a complete change in the social structure. The 'good man' could not live in a social vacuum any more than a 'good society' could be created without the reformation of its component units of individuals. Therefore the 'relief of man's estate' could only come about through a parallel change of man and society and education was necessary at three levels. First there must be effected a change of attitudes from suspicion to trust and from aggressiveness to co-operation and this would operate invisibly whatever the particular form of external organization. Nevertheless a structure was necessary and Comenius believed that there was no inherent threat to the liberty of the individual in a 'well-ordered' society. But both the invisible society and the well-ordered society would be sterile unless its members were inspired by a perspective beyond their present experience towards a Utopian society. Universal education depended upon all three aspects being developed simultaneously and in harmony with each other.

Comenius focused his social criticism on the fact of human aggressiveness. This reached its peak of horror and futility in the incidence of war with the 'military estate' claiming 'every kind of liberty' and deliberating among themselves 'how to give wings to death'. The inhumanity of man to man constantly forced itself upon his attention – the useless treatment of criminals attested by the prevalence of 'prisons, stakes, gibbets',[1] the torturing of human beings, not for their crimes, but for their heresies, the close imprisonment of men of blameless character like John Augusta.[2] Comenius concludes the sad story of the persecutions of the Unity of Brethren with the cry, 'Why should I produce more examples of their cruelty'[3] though he was aware that the violence was not all on one side but was part of a pattern of life affecting everyone. Even in a school text-book he found it necessary in order to give a true picture to describe the manifestations of human cruelty as the Chapters in the *Janua* on 'The Tormenting of Malefactors' or the 'Besieging of a City' will prove.

Though Comenius believed with Vives that 'all wars are civil wars' he was prepared to accept that in certain circumstances the use of force might be justified. He did on occasion use the argument of some Anabaptists that the sword might be used to 'hasten' the Day of the Lord. It was a dangerous argument apt to recoil on those who used it. Persecuted minorities have always been tempted to resist tyranny and this has been the not unreasonable excuse of rebels and regicides. Men have usually convinced themselves that in extirpating heretics or punishing criminals they were acting as instruments of divine justice. But what excuse could there be for prostitution of law for self-interest or the slow, remorseless pressure of oppression? How came it about that even in the small, intimate group of school or family violence could become, not occasional, but habitual?

The Brethren believed that in the famous Letter of Majesty of 1609 they had a firm legal foundation for the future: 'No decree of any kind shall be issued by us or by our heirs and succeeding kings against the above religious peace' and to make doubly sure they had their representatives in the twenty-four Defenders appointed to defend it. Within twenty years Comenius had fled from the Proscriptive Decrees of Ferdinand II 'inhibiting any persons (except Jews), who would not conform, from residing in Bohemia and Moravia or from owning land therein'. There were many thousands who could not go into exile and they had no escape. Yet there were many thousands more who had suffered oppression from their overlords all their lives for whom there never had been any legal redress – 'Some fill and overfill their houses meanwhile others, equally servants of God, have hardly wherewith to feed and clothe themselves'.[4] Who would write a 'Letter to Heaven' on behalf of the serfs?[5] Comenius was continually appalled at the low motivation of those who should have been leaders of society – the time-serving intrigues of Bohemian nobles – the almost fantastic double-dealing of the negotiators of the Peace of Westphalia[6] – the mercantile rivalries of the two leading Protestant powers, England and Holland, in 1664. Even among scholars and ministers the situation was no better. At the beginning the Church of the Brethren was so intent on holy living that they had no time for learning but under the guidance of Jan Blahoslav they changed somewhat and began to send students abroad. Comenius was one of these and later as Secretary of the Church he supervised the studies of young ordinands. He was not hostile to learning yet he complained of ill effects on those who returned with 'worldly courtesy and eagerness for strifes, drinking bouts and jewellery'.[7] In the religious leaders he found other faults just as harmful because of their wrangling and bigotry through which the most hopeful ecumenical conferences foundered.[8] But of all aspects of human stupidity the one that gave most urgency to his demand for reform was the oppression and neglect of children – the 'sticks, canes and birch-rods of the teachers' and the 'grievous conduct of mothers (especially of the upper classes) who find it irksome to cherish their own children'.[9]

This was the background from which Comenius drew his pessimism so that 'death seemed more desirable than life' and his conclusion: 'O miserable men, such is then the end of your activities, of your ambitions, of your glory, of your arts and your learning'.[10] But it also gave him a strong motivation for reform.

THE INVISIBLE SOCIETY

Since the earliest days of the Christian Church there have been two concepts concerning its nature. The first was of an authoritative and supernatural instrument of salvation as the visible embodiment of Divine grace. The second was of a fellowship of seekers with the minimum of organization as the invisible body of Christ in the world. Since Augustine, the first predominated, though the City of God was not equated with the visible church, but Catholics and Protestants rejected the ideal of an unorganized fellowship as worthless. Both Hus and Calvin rejected the orthodox hierarchy but put in its place an invisible body indeed but consisting of those chosen by God. Nevertheless there were always some who took the view that the church had no power beyond the witness of its members and no authority, except through experience, to discover and refashion truth. One of such men was Peter Chelčický and the key to his position was the complete repudiation of force – 'The temporal order of force and Christ's way of love are far removed from each other'.[11] From this principle he drew the logical conclusions: The first was of conscientious objection to fighting since 'neither the king nor the princes nor the rulers do the fighting themselves but compel their peasants to do it for them. If all refused whom would the rulers find?'[12] It is perhaps ironic that this exponent of pacifism owed his own immunity to the protecting presence of the 'terrible warriors' of Tábor and the successful outcome of a bloody revolution.[13] Chelčický saw further that a Christian social order was inconsistent with fixed class divisions – 'I shall never assent to the doctrine that these two arrogant estates (nobles and clergy) should exempt themselves from hard work and lay the burden on the common folk'.[14] The Christian cannot shelter behind social convention or necessity – 'The executioner who kills is just as much a wrong-doer as the criminal who kills'.[15] The only possible penalty that can be supported by the Christian is recompence for wrong done or penance and forgiveness and if both fail 'then no harm should be done him but let him be sent away thereby preserving our own purity'.[16]

When the Kunvald community was established with a complete repudiation of the secular power of Church or State they still desired some visible link with the historical Church and sought as their leader the Waldensian Bishop Stephen who was not contaminated with secular associations but claimed unbroken Apostolic succession.[17] They refused to take public office or to take part in the process of law. There was a hierarchy of Beginners, Proficients and the Perfect but the highest class consisted of those who embraced voluntary poverty and gave up their possessions for the common good.

However much the early Church of the Brethren may have wished to exemplify the invisible society working like leaven in the lump of human society they were prevented by two facts. One was that visible society refused to leave them alone and the other was that the Brethren themselves made a compromise with society. Comenius was profoundly interested in the history

79

of his Church. He collected the story of their persecutions from 894 A.D. and in 1649 published the eighth book of their history by Jan Lasicki, the Polish historian of the sixteenth century. To it he added an introduction and a summary of the whole. He made notes on the 1633 Edition of the Rule of Discipline and gave a description of the Order and Discipline as an Appendix to the *Exhortation to the Church of England* of 1661. Yet he makes no mention of Chelčický or of the Schism of Lukáš of Prague which occurred in 1494. The radical views held by the Brethren for forty years seem to have been forgotten and Peter Brock suggests – 'The desire to avoid giving prominence to – indeed the impulse to forget altogether – any discussion of ideas long ago discarded but liable to be regarded as subversive by the authorities was undoubtedly one of the motives which dominated the historiography of Blahoslav and Comenius.'[18] Jaroslav Goll even suggests suppression of the facts.[19]

It would be wrong to think of Comenius or his Church as having abandoned the ideals of their origin rather than having modified them as they worked out the theory into practice. The extreme radicalism of Chelčický presupposed the maximum potentiality of human nature and therefore had a strong appeal for Comenius and it gave him a strong link with the post-Reformation sects such as the Mennonites, Quakers, Behmenists and Socinians. In fact Comenius showed no subservience to authority, even when he was living under the protection of a noble as at Fulnek, in his attitude to social problems. His ideal was not a re-distribution of wealth but opportunity so that 'each one who was not idle might raise himself from poverty'.[20] There is no doubt where his sympathies lay – 'The knights spend their time sitting either on the backs of horses hunting or at long tables laden with divers dishes while they drive their serfs to soccage and place them in towers'.[21] He was deeply moved by the cries of the oppressed poor rising to heaven 'while the rich have their barns and larders so full that the mice despoil them.[22]

The invisible society can be thought of in terms of leaven, or salt, or, in modern terms, vitamins as a prophylactic for the body politic. The Unity of Brethren tried to fulfil this function by repudiating the principle of force. Their dilemma was that they could only survive under the protection of the powerful. It was within the domains of a sympathetic noble that they could make their witness most effective and in exile there was no refuge for them except by consent of someone in power. They could not remain invisible and therefore could not survive if their protest against social inequality should bring them under the dreadful charge of subverting the peace. The witness for spiritual equality under God might carry with it economic implications but they were not essential since if rich and poor were living in the will of God there could be neither oppression nor resentment. Comenius notes a 'wondrous thing' in the Paradise of the Heart: 'There were some among these holy men who had an ample supply of riches – silver, gold, crowns and sceptres (for there are such men among God's chosen). Others had scarcely anything beyond a half-naked body. Yet the former said they had nothing and the latter said they had everything'.[23] Thus the primary function of the Church was to seek the will of God and penetrate society with that will.

The concept of people unknown to each other but bound together in a mystical union as the body of Christ on earth was one that sustained Comenius whenever it seemed that the visible Church was failing or might be destroyed. The Kingdom of God came not 'with observation' but within the minds of those who belonged to it and that was the Bequest which a dying church might pass on. In the Paradise of the Heart it was 'worthy of wonder that men who had never seen each other were quite familiar'.[24] Not that this mystical body could remain inert for it was also the Bride of the Lamb of God preparing in secrecy with 'fine linen, clean and white as a holy trousseau'.[25] Often these men of faith have to be hidden from the Baal to whom they will not bow the knee as when Charles Žerotín 'like Obadiah of old, sustained Lanecius and many others in their caves with bread and water'.[26]

There would always remain the Secret Seed and Comenius, sadly surveying the wreckage of his Church, reckoned that in 1620 there were 96 out of 200 ministers still alive and some 7,000 of the faithful in Bohemia and Moravia.[27] Constantly he urged his friends to wait until the storm had passed and meanwhile to maintain their ties. Some degree of group support was essential in order to keep alive the feeling of being a 'family of

F   81

God' and therefore 'great intimacy, openness and holy companionship'.[28]

Intimacy and companionship are only possible with the small group living close enough to each other to cultivate close personal relationships and each might have its local or historical peculiarity without destroying the unity of the Church universal. The Brethren did not regard themselves as a sect and the word which they used of themselves – Jednota Bratrská or Unity of Brethren – indicated a local fellowship belonging to the universal and invisible Church – Církev. That it was small should be no disparagement as Comenius remarks when writing to the Church of England. They were 'a special, peculiar group on nobody's side'[29] not wishing to align themselves under any special leader or name.

Though he makes no mention of them it is easy to believe that Comenius had knowledge of a movement in Holland known as the Collegiants or Rynsburgers. They began in 1619 as a result of the rejection of Arminianism by Dutch Protestants and formed a 'Society' with very much the same aims and principles as those of Chelčický. Similar groups or colleges were formed in a number of Dutch cities. While Comenius was living in Amsterdam these groups were active and Spinoza was a member at Rynsburg for three years (1660-1663).

Certainly Comenius would have known of several attempts to establish societies of Christians cutting across sectarian divisions and devoting themselves to the reformation of the world. There was the proposal of Andreae in his book *Fama Fraternitatis* published in 1614.[30] The outbreak of war put an end to these plans but in 1628 Andreae founded a Christian Union at Nuremberg and this probably had the same aims as the Antilia Society inspired by Samuel Hartlib and which was revived under various names until in 1661 he wrote: 'Of the Antilian Society the smoke is over, but the fire is not altogether extinct. It may be it will flame in due time, though not in Europe'.[31] Then there were the efforts made from time to time to bring Protestants together to work for peace amongst themselves on a more informal basis than official conferences could provide. Thus David Pareus, his 'most learned' teacher at Heidelberg, proposed in his book, the *Irenicum* of 1614, a Synod of all

Evangelicals 'which would cause the strifes to cease'. Again the Thirty Years War interrupted such plans but Comenius was always ready to join a group, large or small, devoted to this purpose. Thus from 1638 onwards there was a kind of pact between John Dury, Samuel Hartlib and himself to 'doe things with mutuall advice' of which Dury says: 'Though our tasks be different we are all three in a knowledge of one another's labours, and can hardly be without one another's assistance'.[32]

In the seventeenth century there was no sharp division between religion, science and the humanities and groups of people, sometimes with official support, formed themselves into academies or societies to cultivate their common interests but also to promote the public good. At first they were mostly philosophical or literary such as the Platonic Academy of Florence whose origin went back to 1470. Comenius mentions two societies concerned with the study of language – the Florentine society, La Crusca, whose emblem was a sieve to sift and purify the Italian language, and the German Fruitful Society (Die Fruchtbringende Gesellschaft) founded in 1617.[33] He himself played an important part in maintaining the purity of the Czech language and he speaks of the zeal of the Brethren 'for the enrichment, purification and development of our beloved, melodious mother-tongue'.[34] He believed that a common language would be the means of keeping alive in the scattered remnants in Bohemia a sense of spiritual unity and therefore he continued to write in Czech 'for all the scattered sheep of Christ' and designated by letters the centres where the faithful were known to be as, for instance, at Fulnek.[35]

Gradually the societies took more interest in science but they still kept in the forefront their social aims. The group, of which Comenius had been a prominent member, began weekly meetings in 1645 and became known as the 'Invisible College'. It was partly necessity but partly a change of emphasis that made them exclude politics and philosophy and, as Robert Boyle said, to 'value no knowledge but as it hath a tendency to use'.[36] The motion to the English Parliament made by J. Hall in 1649 well expresses the relationship between an 'invisible society' and the 'good society'.

'What more seasonable opportunity can we have than that we

see the highest spirits, pregnant with great matters, and in despite of the tumults and troubles which environ them on every side, labouring with somewhat, the greatnesse of which they themselves cannot tell, and with a wonderful deale of courage attempting the discovery of a new world of knowledge.'[37]

THE WELL-ORDERED SOCIETY

One of the lessons of history is that groups of enthusiasts need organization in order to survive but flexibility in order to grow. Comenius felt that the Unity of Brethren had both these essentials. The Schism of 1494 was concerned with making it possible for members to retain their ranks, to continue in public service and to engage in occupations for profit. In consequence they became a well-organized, efficient and prosperous body of some 200,000 members taking a broad view of their civic responsibilities and anxious to unite with other Protestant bodies in Europe. They even began to see themselves as possible leaders of a national revival in education, literature and culture. Yet the Unity accepted a discipline almost as severe as that of the Jesuit Constitutions and Luther was justified in saying of them: 'These Brethren do not surpass us in purity of doctrine but they far excel us in the regular discipline by which they govern their churches', and Seifferth adds: 'The testimonies of Melanchthon, Bucer, Calvin and others all concur in the same judgment'.[38] Comenius in his notes on the Brethren's Rule of Discipline (Ratio Disciplinae) brings forward tradition in his support and after quoting Origen and Chrysostom adds: 'Why give more quotations. There are none of the ancients who do not speak in praise of order. . . . It is plain that any church is less liable to be broken up the more order it has within it although it be weak enough in other points as may be seen in the Greek and Roman Churches'.[39] Comenius was not unaware of the dangers of discipline – its tendency to produce legalism if not Pharisaism, the temptations of power, the setting of the letter of the law above its spirit. He even complains: 'Discord in the Church about everything comes from the ministers . . . understanding must be sought in the common people'.[40] But yet he says: 'It is a matter of astonishment that some persons in our time on account of the abuse of order have come to dislike order itself and wish to have its bonds removed'.[41]

The Brethren's *Ratio Disciplinae* was prepared at a Synod at Žeravice in 1609. Comenius was then a schoolboy at Přerov and there was every reason to believe that with the signing of the Letter of Majesty they could look forward to peaceful expansion. It was not published until 1616 by which time the clouds were gathering with the prospect of the accession of Ferdinand of Styria. It was republished at Leszno in 1633 with extensive notes by Comenius and its provisions reflected closely his ideal of a good community. Essentially it was a means of redirecting human will into constructive channels and thus demonstrating how the 'vast evil' of the world could be overcome.[42] In different terms it was 'everyman's' super-ego by which the weak ego could restrain the *libido*.[43]

The constitution outlined in the *Ratio* was an attempt to create a strong hierarchy without the evils associated with power. It was based on a system of checks on authority 'since it is hazardous to commit absolute power to a single individual or to a few'.[44] The most important check of all lay in the belief that the whole community was under the control and direction of God and so it was theocratic but it was also a mixed constitution which, claimed Comenius, in addressing the Church of England, 'suits a monarchy because it has bishops: an aristocracy because it has a senate: and a democracy because it has a Synod'.[45]

The seventeenth century was an authoritarian age but the Brethren held certain democratic principles. They held that everyone must be under the law of the community and this rule was frequently maintained even against the richest and most powerful members. Careful regulations were laid down concerning the right ordering of all the relationships of daily living with degrees of punishment for infringement from private admonition to rebuke by Elders and finally exclusion from Holy Communion and there were no exemptions. Thus: 'If any irregularity occurs it is reduced to order by timely admonition. All must submit to discipline: the highest and the lowest, the senior and the con-seniors, the ministers and the assistants: all the members, noble and of the commonalty, even the magistrates'.[46] Comenius gives an instance of 'an itching' of the rich patrons of the Church 'to choose preachers after their own tastes' thus:

'I remember one illustrious baron who acknowledged with sorrow his error in this respect. For he had refused to accept the appointed pastor and urged that another be assigned to him whose gift of eloquence he greatly admired: but, finding the man elated with self-confidence, he petitioned for his removal.'[47]

The other principle was that every member bore a responsibility to the community. Thus the education of the young was a concern shared by all and each one 'be he clergyman or politician or physician makes a big mistake if he think that he is on that account exempt from the common task of school reform'.[48]

The function of women is fully recognized:

'In like manner from the females are chosen respectable, prudent and grave matrons to attend to their own sex furnished with like authority as the men. The two sexes are treated exactly alike but separately so that a woman would have to admonish a woman and the matrons would take special care of such things as evil speaking and extravagance in dress.'[49]

The Brethren were firmly against the establishment of a priestly caste with special privileges and status and they emphasized the pastoral responsibility of every member of the Church and the eminence of the Bishop 'is no distinction of honours or of reverence but of labour and care for others'.[50]

Yet in other respects there was an emphasis on authority. The Brethren would not accept the Catholic doctrine that the means of grace through the sacraments did not depend upon the state of perfection of the priest who administered them. A 'true' priest not only held his commission from God, he must also prove his fitness by holy living to give certainty of salvation (*certitudo salutis*) to his flock. The capacity to give absolution for sin implied a God-given faculty for distinguishing good from evil and for seeing beneath the surface of outward behaviour or verbal expression but it also implied a solemn duty to instruct, exhort and discipline without fear or favour. No effort could be too great to ensure that such terrifying power should be in worthy hands and therefore the priest must be under constant surveillance by members of the congregation. The usual word for priest was 'Kněz' corresponding to the New Testament presbyter but the Brethren also spoke of him as 'kazatel' (or minister) and as 'spravce' which means governor and made him equal in status to a Lord of the Manor. He was important because he had the solemn responsibility of 'presenting his people perfect unto God' (Col. 1.28).[51]

The priests of the Brethren elected an Inner Council who then selected the Bishop but any major decision of the Church had to be made by a General Synod consisting of the Bishop and his assistant, the priests, deacons, and acoluths and the lay patrons of churches. The whole organization was based on an identification of status with responsibility and everyone had 'such a classification' that each one knew what place was assigned to him, exactly what authority he should exercise and what obedience he should yield to this or that person. Each congregation was divided into three classes, Beginners, Proficients and the Perfect. Originally the Perfect were those who undertook complete voluntary poverty but in the time of Comenius they had the task of teaching others and acting as Overseers for the welfare, both spiritual and material, of all the people including the priest.

Concerning spiritual welfare the *Ratio* was explicit about the need for supervision – 'It is certain that no order, however skilfully designed, can endure without supervision'.[52] The Civil Elders (elected from the Perfect) had a special responsibility but at least once a year a visitor, appointed by the Bishop, would visit each congregation and after enquiring from the priest concerning the state of the congregation he would question the Civil Elders concerning the priest. Every group in the congregation would meet the visitor separately to account for their way of living. The Lord's Supper was made an occasion for close examination of the conscience of all 'stirred up to spiritual hunger and thirst by the preaching of the Word'. This constant and detailed supervision does not seem to have been resented – 'They regarded it as a preventive of sin to know that there were those watching their life and conversation. All are subject to discipline, from the child to the old man, from the subject to the civil elder, from the acoluth to the bishop'.[53] Young men aspiring to become priests had to satisfy the most careful enquiries concerning their birth, upbringing and knowledge of the Bible but most important of all was the examination of conscience which, says Comenius, 'was very strict and sometimes so affectingly conducted that instances are not wanting of persons having shrunk from the office through alarm of conscience'.[54] A minister of the Unity of Brethren was given high respect and could expect complete support from his congregation but it was always his duty to bear patiently their enquiries about his conduct and to submit to the collective will of the Church as expressed in its Synods or through the decision of the Bishop. Comenius himself showed remarkable capacity for obedience in this respect and on the other hand one of those ordained with him at Žeravice was excluded from preaching because of his failure to conform.

The most careful consideration was given to the material welfare of the congregation. The almoner took charge of the collections for the poor though it was typical of the attitude of the Brethren that there were two other officers to keep a check on him and ensure that meticulous records were kept. Provision was made for orphans, widows, the sick and disabled and 'those in exile for the Gospel'. They found it hard to meet the demand made by Chelčický: 'For the Christian every human being in distress is a neighbour to be helped' for they were fearful of encouraging the lusty beggar or the undeserving. In those days orphanhood was a very real problem and Comenius tried to awaken the consciences of richer members to provide homes for fatherless children. In other matters the Church provided social services such as the settling of disputes without resort to law and even the setting up of a labour exchange. There was an insistence that all work was for the glory of God and for the good of man. There was the same insistence on the 'just price' which so much helped Quakers to establish themselves in business in England and on providing articles of service rather than luxury which elevated industry above money-making.

The well-ordered society is essentially educative and that for two reasons. Its membership fluctuates and this imposes a necessity to educate children and new members but in addition it is striving by its order to attain a spiritual goal and this requires an effort in education by everyone.

The main elements in the religious service were preaching, singing and the reading of the Bible and in each of them there was a didactic purpose. Thus at the conclusion of the noon and afternoon services the elder youths and maidens remained behind and were examined by the preacher with an Elder and Matron assisting him. The Brethren took from the Taborites the tradition of congregational singing long before Luther set the pattern in Germany and they regarded hymns as an important part of religious education. The first *Kancyonál* was published in 1501 and by the time of Comenius there had been ten editions and he himself wrote a number of hymns for the edition of 1669 and some musicologists think he composed the music for some of them. Since copies were scarce they were shared by groups and the congregation sang under the direction of a choirmaster. Esrom Rüdinger says of the Brethren:

'Your churches surpass all others in singing. For where else are songs of praise, of thanksgiving, of prayer and instruction so often heard? Where is there better hymn-singing? The newest edition of the Bohemian hymn-book, with its seven hundred and forty-three hymns, is an evidence of the multitude of your songs. I do not know any who sing more. I will also add – who do it better.'[55]

Insistence on Bible reading was also a tradition which the Brethren took over from the Taborites for even in 1457 the Papal Nuncio Aeneas Sylvius, complained that Italian priests knew less about the New Testament than the women of Tábor and its connection with education is illustrated by the remark of the Jesuit, Balbin, 'Although I cannot accept this knowledge of the Bible by uncultivated people nevertheless there is a warm desire and eagerness for education among them'.[56] The translation of the Bible known as the Kralice version was made, not from the Vulgate but from the original languages, the New Testament being the work of Jan Blahoslav and the Old Testament of a group of scholars. Comenius is well justified in saying of it: 'Few nations hear so pithily, truly and clearly in their own language'[57] and it had an effect upon Bohemian Protestants similar to that of the Geneva Bible in England upon the Puritans.

Since the ability to read the Bible and the Hymnal was so much valued, some form of Primary education existed wherever the patronage of a sympathetic landowner made it possible. Here again the tradition came from the Taborites who according to a fifteenth century writer 'began to accept and to teach in the Czech language little boys and girls'.[58] According to Brock the first Brethren Primary School was at Brandýs in 1482[59] and there is indirect evidence of how widespread the movement became in the rumours spread by Catholics and Utraquists that the proficiency of Brethren peasants and their children was due to Satanic power. After the Schism the Brethren also became interested in grammar education and they opened a number of Latin schools with their own teachers. Hutton gives the names of fifteen such schools of which Přerov was one of the foremost.

Nevertheless the chief means of education was not the school but the family. The *Ratio* lays it down that

'parents should instruct their children and domestics in religion by diligently enquiring at dinner and supper time on Sunday how much each had observed of what had been spoken in Church.'

Both mother and father took part in this regular instruction and it may be assumed that Comenius himself was thus taught by Martin and Anna Komenský. In many cases in the early days family instruction must have been the only one possible since the Brethren were precluded from establishing schools.

What was the relationship of the 'well-ordered society' to the disordered society of the world? This question agitated the minds of the Brethren from the beginning and their thinking gradually moved away from the extreme position of Chelčický that Christians should not participate in worldly institutions though they should conform to them within the limits of conscience and avoid giving offence. Interfering in politics was both a hindrance to the spiritual life and dangerous in itself as

Comenius found when he 'contributed a nail or two' to establishing the throne of Frederick of the Palatinate and decided: 'Let him who will, approach these heights, but not I'.[60] It became obvious that the original ideal of a group of rural communities loosely federated together but owing no allegiance to a civil power was impossible but it was extremely difficult to decide at what point to stop with a clear conscience. Thus, although war was condemned it was justifiable 'to suffer and die against the Turks and not be reckoned as traitors and Anabaptists'.[61] The price which had to be paid for the protection of lords and knights was to present themselves as a party of law and order. Thus it was enjoined upon members who were peasants, artisans and servants that they 'should realize that the world order is ordained by God for their own good: they should know their place and that those in authority are set up for their good and to preserve them from evil. They must be subject to them, not only out of fear, but for conscience' sake. They should refrain from striving after equality'.[62] This point of view might have had some justification on the estates of Žerotín but it was hard to accept when law itself became an instrument of tyranny and in the minds of the Brethren there was always a limit to the duty owed to the civil power. They would never accept the doctrine of the Peace of Augsburg that a prince could determine the religion of his subjects (Cujus Regio, ejus religio) because as Bishop Augusta put it in a letter to Bucer: 'The civil power is insufficient and, indeed, not suited to build Christ's kingdom'.[63] But they had no wish to exchange the tyranny of one sword for another and repudiated also the absolute authority of any Church. This was the historic protest of Hus that Christ Himself was the rock upon which the Church had been founded and not St Peter nor any of his successors.

Since the Brethren were a small minority forming only five per cent of the Protestant population it was difficult for them to make an effective protest against the institution of serfdom which sapped the vitality of the peasants. Seton-Watson dates the evil development of this process from the Diet of 1487 which prevented all movement of peasants from the land on which they were born.[64] It is doubtful whether Comenius realized what a barrier this was to the creation of national consciousness since the exiled nobles feared that the peasantry would gain more freedom if the Hapsburg tyranny were overthrown and the suspicions of the peasants made them less ready to risk their lives in rebellion.[65]

THE UTOPIAN SOCIETY

It was the hope of Comenius that there would be a sudden and dramatic change in the human situation which would immediately solve all the political, social and economic problems of which serfdom was only a symptom. This arose from his belief in the Second Coming of Christ to earth and the reign of God which it would inaugurate. This doctrine of 'Chiliasm is well attested in the Bible even though the terms are often vague and mysterious. Thus the signs which would herald the end of the world as given in the Book of Daniel, the Gospel of St Matthew, the Pauline Epistles and the Revelation of St John can be held to apply to every age. The faithful are always aware of apostasy and evil and they do not have far to look to find an Antichrist. Sometimes the belief brought comfort, as to the Thessalonians in New Testament times. In the second century it caused the Montanists to cease all earthly activity until the 'hour of the Lord'. It always remained the belief of the Catholic Church but it gained new vigour amongst the Protestant sects of the sixteenth century. In some cases it gave a fanatical zeal to 'hasten' the Millenium by killing off the servants of the Evil One. In other cases it gave dynamic energy to men who saw their task as preparing the way of the Lord. Generally this was the effect which Comenius received from his teachers at Herborn and Heidelberg and the immediate task was to heal the unhappy divisions between all men of good will and thus stop the horror of the tearing apart of the mystical body of Christ. Comenius favoured rapprochement with Catholics if only they would repudiate 'the Man of Sin' the Pope, and he had no sense of revulsion even against Moslems whom he found 'clothed in white and great lovers of cleanliness'.[66] There were, indeed, times when Comenius' belief in the Millenium or, at least, his acceptance of prophecies about it, caused him to engage in political intrigue or to raise false hopes in his friends.

This was unfortunate and lays Comenius open to criticism but Chiliasm was not altogether harmful in its effects. If it was a myth it was an energizing one which led him constantly to speculate about and plan for the Utopian society which was to come, and thus it was a 'pattern laid up in heaven', indeed, but with far-reaching earthly implications. At least it forced men to consider what an ideal society on earth would be like rather than losing themselves in dreams of 'Jerusalem the Golden with milk and honey blest'. The creation of an earthly paradise could, of course, make men disregard altogether the bliss of heaven or as Gerard Winstanley, the leader of the Diggers, said: 'When men are gazing up to heaven imagining after a happiness or fearing a hell after they are dead, their eyes are put out that they see not what is their birthright and what is to be done by them while they are here on earth'. To Comenius there was no sharp alternative between preparing for a Millenium and for eternity but there was a sharp alternative between a Welfare State and a theocratic one.

There were times when Comenius felt that the first step towards the Millenium was to remove the enemies who prevented it – the Pope or Ferdinand II or the House of Hapsburg or rapacious landlords but generally he believed that the conflict was with the will of man which inclined to pride and rebellion and not to longing for the kingdom of God. Poverty, inequality and hardship were not so much wrong in themselves as wrong because they struck at the spiritual life of everyone.

Comenius received inspiration for the new Jerusalem from many quarters but principally from John Valentine Andreae. It was Andreae 'who in his golden writings had laid bare the diseases not only of the Church and the state, but also of the schools, and had pointed out the remedies'.[67] He begged Andreae 'not to leave the field of battle before he had trained up successors'[68] and acknowledged that he had obtained from him 'almost the very elements of pansophic thought'. Thus it was Andreae's allegory of a city of God – Christianopolis – that became for him a blue-print of the Utopian society.

Christianopolis was a 'well-ordered' society in that it was governed by the ideals of religion, justice and learning and it was 'as it were one single workshop'. It was an educative society in which the whole community undertook the responsibility of child-care. Over the age of six children were entrusted to 'the most upright preceptors, men as well as women' but this delegation of function was not regarded as absolving the whole community, since all must share in preparing every boy and girl for citizenship. Yet Christianopolis laid stress on the inner life of the spirit by which the 'invisible society' could be maintained. Thus the purpose of leisure was 'to shake off the dust of the earth' and the task of government was to foster creative impulses but to reduce the temptations of possessiveness. Women had an important role in this respect and their 'greatest boast' was of peace in the family nor should they be ashamed of household duties which could be transformed into spiritual service.[69]

Comenius took his inspiration not only from Andreae but also from the Czech writers, Porcius Vodňanský and Nathaniel Vodňanský of Uračova, but his allegory was not a complete rejection of the world. He tried to find a bridge between the Labyrinth which represented the world and the Paradise of the Heart which represented both the inner harmony of the soul and the outer harmony of a reformed society. He did not wish to escape on a kind of magic carpet but rather to plan an educational reconstruction of the world he knew.[70]

NOTES

1. *Via Lucis* III.12.
2. J. E. Hutton: *History of the Moravian Church* p. 105-108.
3. *History of the Bohemian Persecutions* p. 353.
4. *Labyrinth*: XLIV.
5. *Listowé do Nebe* (1618).
6. Bedřich Šindelář: *Comenius und der Westfälische Friedenkongress.* (*Historica* V. 1963.)
7. *History of Lasitius*: Conclusion.
8. The Consensus Sandomirensis of 1570 was one of the few successful agreements. It brought together the Polish Protestants.
9. *Informatorium*. V.
10. *Labyrinth*: XXXVI.
The Invisible Society
11. P. Chelčický: *O Trojím Lidu* p. 48. Quoted by P. Brock: *Op. cit.* p. 46.
12. P. Chelčický: *Replika* p. 393. Quoted by P. Brock: *Op. cit.* p. 61.

13. P. Brock: *Political and Social Doctrines of the Czech Unity of Brethren* p.43.
14. P. Chelčický: *O Trojím Lidu* p. 71. Quoted by P. Brock: *Op. cit.* p. 65.
15. P. Chelčický: *Postilla* p. 181. Quoted by P. Brock: *Op. cit.* p. 55.
16. P. Chelčický: *Síť Víry* p. 21. Quoted by P. Brock: *Op. cit.* p. 53.
17. J. E. Hutton: *History of the Moravian Church* p. 56.
18. P. Brock: *Op. cit.* p. 283.
19. J. Goll: *Quellen und Untersuchungen zur Geschichte der Böhmischen Brüder.* Quoted by P. Brock: *Op. cit.* p. 279.
20. *Labyrinth*: XXXII.
21. *Labyrinth*: XXI.
22. *Listowé do Nebe.*
23. *Labyrinth*: LXVI.
24. *Labyrinth*: XLIV.
25. *Panorthosia*: Tr. Josef Hendrich p. 120.
26. *History of Bohemian Persecutions*: p. 252.
27. *History of Bohemian Persecutions*: p. 374.
28. *Labyrinth*: XLIV.
29. *History of Lasitius*: Conclusion p. 294.
30. F. E. Held: *Christianopolis* p. 39 and 72.
31. G. H. Turnbull: *Hartlib, Dury and Comenius* p. 73.
32. G. H. Turnbull: *Hartlib, Dury and Comenius* p. 362-363.
33. *Methodus*: Ch. XXVIII.
34. *Bequest*: XIX.
35. *Katechysmus pro Mládež Českou Jednoty Bratrské* (1661) Quoted by J. E. Hutton: *Op. cit.* p. 172.
36. R. Boyle: *Works* (Ed. T. Birch 1744) p. 17-20.
37. J. Hall: 'Motion to the Parliament of England concerning the Advancement of Learning' (1649) Quoted by R. F. Young: *Comenius in England* p. 77.

The Well-ordered Society
38. Seifferth: *Church Constitution of Bohemian and Moravian Brethren* p. 13.
39. Seifferth: *Church Constitution of Bohemian and Moravian Brethren* p. 177.
40. *Haggaeus Redivivus*: p. 29.
41. Seifferth: *Op. cit.* p. 177.
42. *Via Lucis*: II.7.
43. The *Ratio Disciplinae* of 1609 was not the first Rule of the Brethren. Gindely gives the earliest as 1496-1500.
44. Seifferth: *Op. cit.* p. 114.
45. *De Bono Unitatis*: 8.
46. Seifferth: *Op. cit.* 169.
47. Seifferth: *Op. cit.* 191.
48. *Great Didactic*: XXXIII.14.
49. Seifferth: *Op. cit.* 179.
50. Seifferth: *Op. cit.* 112.
51. Marianka S. Fousek: *Pastoral Office in the early Unitas Fratrum* (*Slavonic Review* June 1962 p. 444-451).
52. Seifferth: *Op. cit.* 105.
53. Seifferth: *Op. cit.* 169.
54. Seifferth: *Op. cit.* 188.

55. Esrom Rudinger wrote an Appendix to the *Historica Narratio* of 1570 by Camerarius which was the first account of the Brethren.
56. cf. J. E. Hutton: *Op. cit.* p. 154.
57. *Bequest*: XIX.
58. Anna Císařová Kolářová: *Žena v Jednoté Bratrské* p. 170.
59. P. Brock: *Op. cit.* p. 100.
60. *Labyrinth*: XIX.11.
61. Synod of Žeravice 1559.
62. Dekrety: Quoted by P. Brock: *Op. cit.* p. 228.
63. J. T. Müller: *Geschichte der Brüder Gemeinde* p. 119.
64. Seton-Watson: *History of Czechs and Slovaks* p. 85.
65. Bedřich Šindelář: *Op cit.* The war of liberation planned by the peasants of Bohemia and Austria failed because they were hopeless and exhausted and had no leadership.

The Utopian Society
66. *Labyrinth*: XVII.
67. *Great Didactic*: Greeting 10.
68. M. Möhrke: *J. A. Comenius u. J. V. Andreae* p. 21 and 34.
69. F. E. Held: *Christianopolis*.
70. J. B. Čapek: Poutník dvou světů. (*Labyrint* 1941) cf. D. Čapkova and J. Kyrášek: *J.A.K. Zivot a Dilo v Dokumentech* 23.24.

CHAPTER 5

THE CONCEPT OF DIDACTIC PROCESS

INTRODUCTION

THE development of the 'good man', the acquisition of encyclopaedic knowledge, the building up of the 'good society' – these
were high aims only to be achieved, according to Comenius, by
the right deployment of all human resources constituting a
'didactic process'. Comenius describes it in these words:

'We promise a *Great Didactic*, that is to say, the whole art of
teaching all things to all men, and indeed of teaching them
with certainty, so that the result cannot fail to follow; further,
of teaching them pleasantly . . . further, of teaching them
thoroughly . . . in such a manner as to lead to true knowledge,
to gentle morals, and to the deepest piety.'

The starting point of this proposal was a complete rejection
of the aims, content and methods of the existing system and
here Comenius was reflecting seventeenth century disappoint-
ment with the results of the Renaissance and Reformation. Both
of these movements represented a bursting away from the
inhibitions of the Middle Ages and both represented bold bids
for a wider life. The Renaissance was a re-birth of all that was
finest in the heritage of the past to recover the glory of Rome
and Greece. The Reformation was an awakening of the spirit of
the Apostolic Church out of the darkness of medieval superstition. In both cases the intention was to use the past in order
to reconstruct the present, but as the first vigour and enthusiasm
ebbed the new establishment congealed into a form almost as
cramping as the one it replaced. The dead hand of the past prevailed and those who looked for the golden age in front and not

behind were compelled to become critics of a movement which had already become a tradition.

The original aim of Humanism, as expressed by Erasmus, was not dissimilar to that of Comenius. It was 'that the tender spirit may drink in the seeds of piety, that he may love and learn thoroughly the liberal studies, that he may be informed concerning the duties of life, and that from the earliest childhood he may be habituated in courteous manners'.[1] Unfortunately the 'tender spirits' had turned out to be a very small minority who might be an élite but by their education were far removed from the masses and their teachers found themselves engaged on the fruitless task of trying to metamorphose European youths of the seventeenth century into Romans of the Augustan Age. Classical inspiration degenerated into a mad race for Latin eloquence which in the end revolted most of those who took part in it and the spirit of the Ancient world was lost in a senseless worship of forms of expression.

In somewhat the same way the Reformation hardened and lost its impetus. The original aim had not been to exchange one set of theological dogmas for another but to transform life. The letter which John Hus wrote from his prison in Constance 'To the Bohemian Nation' shows how practical and non-theological was his appeal:

'Faithful and Beloved of God, Lords and Ladies, rich and poor, I entreat and exhort you to love God . . . to be kind to the poor and to rule them justly . . . all artisans to follow their craft and take delight in it . . . and students to apply themselves to letters for the sake of God's honour'.

These sentiments continued to be repeated but they lost their sincerity and it was easier to resurrect long-forgotten controversies than to venture into untried ways of individual and communal living. The emphasis came to be on verbal formulation of the truth until the truth itself was strangled in controversy.

The aims of Humanists and Reformers – eloquence and theology – were too narrow to bring about a universal revolution but they might have been less harmful if the content of their educational programmes had been different. The Humanist educators of the sixteenth century might be excused for neglecting undeveloped vernacular literatures but instead of fostering them they proscribed them and affected to believe that all literature must be written in imitation of certain Latin models. Even this would not have been so bad if the emphasis had been on the classical spirit rather than on the style of particular authors. When Johannes Sturm, one of the most prominent Humanist teachers, looked forward to the day when his pupils would speak Latin to perfection he had Cicero in mind and imitation rather than creativity as his ideal. This led inevitably to a concentration on philology and grammar and in the end to a deadening verbalism. Very much the same mistake was made by the Protestant leaders in their programmes of education. They assumed that religion could be inculcated by catechisms of doctrine and that the words of Scripture were not only infallible but also the essential means of pious expression. Thus worship became stereotyped and religion standardized.

Since aims and content of education were so defective it was inevitable that methods should be equally faulty. Here Comenius had personal experience as his painful evidence and maintained that he was one of thousands who 'had miserably lost the sweetest spring-time of life . . . on scholastic trifles'[2] and had undergone the formation 'though not without hardship and anguish'.[3] His condemnation was that teaching method used an excess of violence to produce a minimum of learning and concentrated on the training of the intellect without giving the intellect adequate nourishment.[4] Because the 'art of teaching was in former centuries unknown' the normal child was simply filled with 'windy and parrot-like loquacity' and only the extraordinary child could acquire a sound education in spite of the teaching he received which detained him 'for five, ten or more years over matters that could be mastered in one'.[5] Schoolmasters should be blamed, but even more pitied, because they have been 'for the most part ignorant of their art' and have 'exhausted their strength in laborious efforts, trying in turn first one plan and then another'.

Such complaints had been common in Europe for over a hundred years. At first it was the medieval grammar books such as the *Graecism* of Ebrard (1212) or the *Compendium Grammaticae* of John de Garlande that were condemned summarily by Luther as 'stable-refuse' introduced by the devil.[6] But exactly the same source was suggested for humanist teaching a century later by Lubinus: 'I find myself always led to the conclusion that the entire system must have been introduced by some evil genius, the enemy of the human race',[7] and Comenius adds to this: 'He is only one out of many authorities whom I could quote in my favour'. All the more thoughtful educationalists realized that learning based on a few classical authors was far too narrow. Some, like Erasmus and Melanchthon, urged that nature also should be studied while the great scholars of the sixteenth century, such as Lipsius and Scaliger, explored the full range of classical literature and made some attempt to integrate it with more recent history. It was extremely difficult for anyone at that time to escape from the belief that truth must be sought in the pronouncements of those with authority. Though Comenius quotes with approval the opinion of Campanella and Bacon 'that all Aristotle's doctrines were nothing but a nurserie of disputations' and says that they are 'often farre from the truth',[8] he cannot come to the point of openly questioning the Bible. Concerning the teacher-pupil relationship common at that time there is almost universal condemnation amongst writers on education. Rabelais attacked the whole system in ribald allegory: Montaigne with biting criticism. Roger Ascham suggested that it was often the master who was worthy of beating rather than the pupil while Richard Mulcaster was inclined to blame the Latin tongue when with so much less effort 'the same treasure could be gained in the vernacular'.[9]

The conservatism of teachers has always been an obstacle to educational reform and Comenius realized that he would not only have to shock them with present evils but also enhearten them with future possibilities – to combine the approach of Rousseau and Pestalozzi would be a not unreasonable analogy of what he proposed. The positive task was to reduce the 'mechanical formulas of instruction' to eternal laws of pedagogy and this, as Comenius admitted, was to assume the role of a 'teacher of teachers' and to offer an invention to mankind which 'would deserve to rank with the discovery of America by

Columbus'. He concludes the *Great Didactic*: 'For Christ's sake I beseech you to listen to me . . . the gate is opened to an unfailing method by which the understanding may be developed'.[10]

UNIVERSAL DIDACTIC

The communication of ideas or knowledge is one of the most universal activities of mankind and this, according to Comenius, constitutes the germ of the teaching situation and the art of teaching (which is didactics) is simply the formalizing of this relationship.[11] There can be mass communication where the transmitter is more conscious of the group than of the individuals who compose it, as with a preacher or politician, or there can be individual communication where the group is sufficiently small for the speaker to be more conscious of individuals than of the group or where he is concerned with one person alone. Both methods had been formalized into educational practice. The first gave rise to the lecture system which was inevitable in the Middle Ages because of the scarcity of books and it tended to become the reading of a book which the students copied down. In many cases there would be some commentary and as the supply of books increased the lecture became more concerned with summarizing books and comparing authorities. The tendency towards commentary was increased by the invention of printing since the student was able to confirm for himself what the author said. Thus the dissemination of the Bible greatly increased the value attached to expository preaching which Comenius regarded as the most important teaching instrument of the Church.[12] The second type of communication was commonly used in schools where teaching is usually depicted as taking place in a crowded room with pupils sitting or standing without much regard for order but waiting their turn to recite their lesson to the master and probably also waiting their turn for the ferrule. At its best there was genuine communication as may be illustrated from the description of Roger Ascham: 'First let him (the teacher) teach the child cheerfully and plainly the cause and matter of the letter; then let him construe it into English so oft as the child may easily carry away the understanding of it'.[13] This kind of individual instruction was, as Dr Johnson said, 'the best ever given for the study of language'.[14] It is possible that Comenius enjoyed such teaching under Lanecký and it is certain that he attempted it himself both at Leszno and Elbing. In 1626 he made out a plan of studies for the guidance of the tutor of the children of his protector George Sadovský of Sloupno.[15] In 1637 he wrote a book for the instruction of the sons of his protector, Raphael Leszczyński,[16] and he frequently took private pupils during his years at Leszno.

The problem of combining the advantages of personal tuition with the saving of labour of mass communication had engaged the attention of Humanist teachers even in the fifteenth century and their solution was to devote the morning to public lecturing and the rest of the day to private tuition.[17] Under the direction of Alexander Hegius the school of the Brethren of the Common Life at Deventer became a centre of intellectual activity and the number of its pupils increased to about two thousand. It was divided into eight classes and the lectures took the form of readings from Latin poets and historians while the pupils learnt grammar and prose composition, and gave orations based on the model of Cicero.[18] The man who did most to provide a model of large group education was Johannes Sturm (1507-1589) though it was only for the small minority who could profit by a long training in classical literature. When Sturm was appointed to the Rectorship of the school at Strasburg in 1538 he enunciated in a 'Book on the Right Method of Founding Schools for Literary Education' the principles which he derived from his experience as a pupil at the School of the Brethren of the Common Life at Liége. He was extremely successful with a school of about 1,000 pupils, drawn from a wide area, which he guided for some forty years and by his influence he largely determined the ideal of the German Gymnasium. The school was divided into nine or ten classes based on age and fitness with annual promotions and prizes for industry and success. To facilitate organization each class was divided into groups of ten pupils each under the control of a chosen pupil called a Decurion for the efficient carrying out of such exercises as declamation, disputation and play-acting. The whole course was graded to cover grammar and the Catechism and a selection of classical poets, dramatists and historians, though the emphasis was on Cicero.[19] The teaching was very formal with lectures of the type common in Universities and there was a University course superimposed upon the school course.

One of those who came under the influence of Sturm was John Calvin and the College, which he established at Geneva in 1559 under the leadership of Theodore de Beza, had much the same organization as the Strasburg Gymnasium[20] and a similar success. There was less emphasis on Cicero and more on the use of the vernacular and the Calvinist model was more influential in France, Holland and Scotland because it was more closely integrated with the religious purposes of the community. John Knox's words illustrate this: 'Here exists the most perfect school of Christ which has been since the days of the Apostles on earth; nowhere did I find that morals and faith have been improved more sincerely than here'.[21]

These schools presupposed very large classes where their success depended upon having a teacher of the calibre of Hegius, Sturm or Beza and pupils who had already a grounding in language usage but without these conditions they quickly became formal and mechanical. It was for this reason that Philip Melanchthon (1497-1560) set up a private school in his own house at Wittenburg limiting the number of pupils so that direct personal instruction was possible. This situation was ideal but impracticable and therefore Melanchthon set himself the task of organizing schools so that the evils of superficiality might be avoided and in doing so he well earned the title of 'Preceptor of Germany'. He laid stress on the importance of the first class in which the pupils should remain until they had mastered the elements of Latin grammar and to assist in this process he wrote a number of text-books to lay a solid foundation for later work in oratory and composition.

The development of higher education in Protestant lands offered a challenge to the Catholic Church which was successfully taken up by the Society of Jesus. The Jesuits spent much time in considering the best forms of contemporary education and were much influenced by Sturm before they produced their own Rule of Studies (*Ratio Studiorum*) in 1599. They produced two answers to the problem of the large class apart from the methods they took over from Strasburg. The first was to refine discipline both for teacher and pupil. For the teacher the curriculum was laid down with meticulous care while the pupil was made to feel the constant and inexorable pressure of discipline. The second was to refine the lecture itself into a highly polished analysis of a passage of literature which was to be studied. This 'prelection' required the most careful preparation which could hardly fail to have its effect on the attention given by the pupils. Their success was unquestionable and justified the tribute of Bacon. 'As for paedagogy, it were the shortest way to refer to the Jesuits who, in point of usefulness, have herein excelled'.[22]

The reaction against haphazard, individual teaching and in favour of organized, class teaching was vocal in the time of Comenius. John Brinsley carried it to the logical conclusion by saying, 'If all can heare alike it is the same labour to teach one as a thousand'.[23] Comenius was well acquainted with the famous school of Goldberg established by Trotzendorf in 1531 where the problem of personal contact was met by delegating authority to the pupils themselves. He was well aware of the need for the teacher to be a person of outstanding personality so that he could attract his pupils 'by a certain majesty and authority', as Ludovic Vives expressed it, and supported by 'under-masters'.[24]

Nevertheless the evils still remained so that 'only those gifted with parts beyond the ordinary could obtain a sound education' despite 'the morning glow of the newly-rising age in which God had inspired some sturdy men in Germany'[25] and Comenius wanted a universal method for normal children. For this purpose the most sturdy (and as it turned out the most surly) seemed to be Wolfgang Ratke (1571-1635) whose Memorial to the Frankfurt Imperial Diet appeared in 1612 while Comenius was at Herborn. In it Ratke offered to revolutionize teaching method so that learning became quick, pleasant and thorough. The essence of the Ratke method was to use the vernacular as the medium of instruction so that, for instance, the pupil learnt Latin by committing to memory a passage from the comedies of Terence, first in his own tongue, and then, by listening attentively to the same passage in Latin, learnt it in that language as well. A school of five hundred children, with a printing establishment attached to provide necessary text-books, was used to put the plan to the test but Ratke failed to keep the confidence of the authorities. One of the Professors who had at first supported him, Christopher Helwig, came to the conclusion that Ratke was 'prodigal in promising things which were not in his power to perform'[26] but a modern writer, K. Seiler, has come to the opposite conclusion that he was 'an original thinker who derived his techniques from a study of human nature and the requirements of the curriculum'.[27] What attracted Comenius so much was that Ratke seemed to open up the possibility of making Latin a *lingua franca* for everyone because his plan simply seemed to require a transposition from the vernacular in which the child could already think with facility into a new language. The aim of a universal didactic was to do for the unity of mankind what the Roman Church had done for the unity of the Church so that all people should have a second language of communication.[28]

Comenius was of the opinion that both the Renaissance and the Reformation lacked universal appeal. Sir Thomas More's phrase, 'an order of the learned' implied a narrow and aristocratic approach with little to offer to the common people, except on condition that the individual rose out of his class to receive a training for a higher rank. It is true that Luther advocated popular education and an easier method of instruction which Comenius described as 'indeed a noble counsel' but goes on, 'It is evident that nothing has been done, since in the smaller villages and hamlets no schools have been founded'.[29] As for the 'easier method' Melanchthon's corrective was very necessary for Luther's carelessness of grammatical accuracy. As Comenius saw the problem it was to provide the masses with a flexible tool of communication which would also unlock for them the treasures of past and present literature without attempting the impossible task of restoring Ciceronian Latin – 'that nymph on whom such unbounded admiration is generally wasted'.[30] Thus a universal method would apply equally to the teaching of any language and the claims of Latin should be examined from a strictly utilitarian point of view.

The reform of language teaching occupied the mind of

Comenius from the beginning of his career[31] and he found the 'main bone of contention to be whether Latin should be taught by precept or not'[32] by which he means by grammar or by direct method. It is interesting to note that the Humanists believed that grammar could be freed from the 'subtleties and confusion' of Donatus and Priscian and their imitators so that, according to Matteo Palmieri, 'youth would come to speak and write Latin with a fluency and correctness which it was impossible that our fathers could ever attain'.[33] That was in the fifteenth century and it became the aim of all the leading Humanists. Thus Erasmus wanted Latin to be a living tongue learnt through conversation and the reading of easy texts with grammatical rules reduced to a minimum but in the hands of a less skilful teacher this 'natural' method led to superficiality and militated against advanced study. This was the view of Melanchthon who regarded ignorance of grammar as not simply harmful to the individual but even 'pernicious to the state'.[34] Not, of course, that Melanchthon wanted to go back to Priscian and Donatus. In fact, the method which he used in his school at Wittenberg was, according to Woodward, 'identical with the so-called natural method of teaching a foreign language in our own day.'[35] It was after all, the method by which Comenius himself had learnt Latin tolerably well in the space of two years through the textbook of Johannes Sturm. Various attempts were made to simplify, without destroying, grammar. In 1620 Ezekiel Vogel published a book called *Ephemerides* containing a series of short sentences from the Bible and classical writers so arranged that a short passage could be learnt each day but the sentences were not graded and contained many expressions not used in everyday life. A better collection was that of Casper Seidel and in 1634 a Professor of Rhetoric at Leipzig, Corvinus, announced a universal grammar based on the logical, but mistaken, principle that there must be certain rules common to all languages.

Against these advocates of simplified and 'natural' grammar Comenius notes the arguments of 'direct method'. Thus Eilhard Lubinus (1565-1621), Professor at Rostock, maintained that grammar was 'a needless torment and a represser of talent' and that if children could be brought together at an early age into a 'Coenobium' where only Latin was spoken they would pick it up as they did their mother tongue without the slightest difficulty. A variation of this idea was suggested by Caesilius Frey (1580-1631) who, though a German, was Professor at Paris. It was that children should be put into a school at the age of two where the masters would speak to them in Latin, Greek and French and thus growing up in a tri-lingual society they would master all three. In partial support of such a plan Comenius mentions the case of Montaigne who could speak Latin perfectly at the age of six and he was strongly drawn to the idea of a school 'where Latium would be transferred from the Tiber to the River Bodrog'[36] (where the school of Saros Patak was situated). When his friend, Samuel Hartlib, came to write *A true and readie Way to learn the Latin Tongue* in 1654 it was to Eilhard Lubinus that he turned for support.

Nevertheless, on strictly practical grounds, Comenius rejected the 'direct method' because it could not possibly be applied to a 'dead' language for universal use. In addition he was not convinced that drudgery could ever be completely banished from learning; rather he believed, with Herbart, that the teacher's function was to make it tolerable. Since, however, universal education could not wait for the day when there would be an abundance of good teachers a device must be invented to meet the exigency of the situation. This device was the text-book. 'It is evident,' he says, 'that the success of my scheme depends entirely upon a suitable supply of encyclopaedic text-books' and since 'this task transcends the strength of one man or one lifetime' it should be entrusted to a body of learned men.[37] His hope was that eventually a series of books would be produced covering the whole range of education from birth to maturity which would standardize the process of instruction and make it possible for children to work under the direction of subordinates or even on their own. This was 'the one factor which by its absence or presence could render the whole organization of a school of no avail or aid it in the highest degree'.

Soon after he arrived in Leszno a book was brought to his notice by a Polish friend named J. J. Jonston. It was the *Janua Linguarum* written at Salamanca by three Irish Jesuits – William and John Bathe and Stephen White – first published in 1611 but followed by several later editions of which the one of 1624 was that which came into his hands. Comenius said that he had already had in mind a similar method but nevertheless he 'leaped for joy' to find this confirmation. The basic principle was to use the vernacular as a means of learning a limited range of words, but adequate for normal communication, with their Latin equivalents. Comenius still believed that such a book must be supplemented by a grammar and a lexicon and he acknowledged his debt to a book called *Consultationes* written by a Catholic convert, Kaspar Schoppe (1576-1649) and published in 1636 to go with a Latin-Italian version of Bathe's *Janua* of 1628.[38] It was an attempt to escape from meaningless rules to a philosophical basis for grammar. There was in the seventeenth century a dearth of simple dictionaries and here Comenius wanted to follow the advice of Ludovic Vives: 'Let the master take from a dictionary, perfect and flawless in all its parts, whatever words are needed for daily use, so that he may collect those suitable expressions which the boys will want to use'.[39] His aim was something less cumbersome than the scholarly lexicons of Robert Etienne or Joseph Scaliger but more orderly and contemporary than the *Thesaurus of Polish, Latin and Greek* by the Polish Jesuit, G. Cnapius, which was not selective enough for his purpose.[40]

This project of supplying standardized teaching aids for universal use became for Comenius a self-imposed mission. Had he lived in the twentieth century it is probable that he would have turned to television for his purpose.

NATURAL DIDACTIC

Nevertheless a universal didactic must be based on nature and at this point Comenius gained inspiration from one who had little to say specifically about education. That 'bright beacon of the new age', Francis Bacon, found pedagogy deficient because it was 'so weakly inquired into'[41] but it was his analysis of scientific method that seemed to Comenius so pregnant with possibility – 'I have as vast contemplative ends as I have moderate civil ends', Bacon had said, 'for I have taken all knowledge to be my province; and if I could purge it of two sorts of powers – the verbosities of the Schoolmen and the blind experiments of unmethodical experimenters – alchemists, astrologers, etc. – I hope I could bring in industrious observations and profitable inventions – the best state of that province'.[42] This hope made Comenius envisage something more ambitious than any of his predecessors had achieved. Where they had looked to tradition or experience Comenius turned to nature and the radical difference between books of discipline such as Calvin's *Law of the Geneva Academy* or the Jesuit *Ratio Studiorum* and the *Great Didactic* is clearly shown by the wording of the title-page: 'Its fundamental principles are set forth from the essential nature of the matter, its truth is proved by examples taken from the several mechanical arts'.

The immediate impulse came from a chance visit which Comenius made to the library of Zilvar of Silberstein at Vlčice while he was in hiding at Třemešná in 1627. There he came across a book by Elias Bodinus which put forward a principle which he immediately adopted – the principle that all things in nature are in some sense parallel to each other. The motto of the book made an instant appeal to him – 'Method, Order and Form make all things easy' and it seemed to him that he had found the Open Sesame to scientific pedagogy[43] Two lines of investigation became possible – the first to discover the didactic process through the parallel process of natural development and the second to come to an understanding of 'ideas' through an examination of the 'things' with which they were parallel. Comenius fully endorsed the Aristotelian doctrine of realism – 'there is nothing in the understanding except through the senses'[44] – but he went further to the concept of nature as the most accessible reflection of the wisdom of God. Comenius was deeply impressed by the work of Bodinus and there is evidence that he met him later on in life.[45]

The work of Wolfgang Ratke also influenced Comenius considerably even though it came to him at second hand. The main ideas occur in the *Didactic* of Christopher Helwig, the Professor of Giessen and also in the Education Section of Alsted's *Encyclopaedia*, published in 1630, and they bear some resemblance to the *Great Didactic*:

1. Everything must follow the order of nature.

2. Not more than one thing at a time.
3. Everything repeated many times.
4. Everything first in the mother tongue and from it into foreign languages.
5. Everything without compulsion.
6. Nothing to be memorized unless it is understood.
7. Uniformity in all things, i.e. methods, rules, text-books.
8. First the thing itself, then its function (e.g. in language first vocabulary then grammar.)
9. Everything by experience and step-by-step experiment.
10. All young people, without exception, must go to school.

The most significant aspect of the work of Ratke is its application to popular education in the establishment at Kothen where the emphasis was on the 'German school'. Yet he demonstrated how easy it is for false deductions to be made on the analogy of nature by his insistence on the receptive aspects of learning. Comenius knew from experience how inadequate was the 'Pythagorean silence' which Ratke recommended for the pupil[46] and his own counsel was clear: 'If the pupil is to be merely silent, you will not succeed in making him attentive, much less proficient, though you tear yourself to tatters . . . man is not a block of wood from which you can carve a statue . . . he is a living image, shaping, misshaping, and reshaping itself. Even we adults know from experience that nothing is more difficult than to give a teacher undivided attention; much less is it for children whose interests tend to wander'.[47]

As a minister of the Unity of Brethren Comenius was unlikely to err on the side of informality in the class-room any more than in the church and he endorsed the Minute of an old Synod which said: 'It has been observed that some Brethren, with a view to appearing gentlemanly, have got into habits of facetiousness. This must be amended. The Apostle forbids jesting to all Christians; much more should it be shunned by teachers'.[48] The image of a teacher according to Comenius was of one 'aloof on a raised platform' pouring out 'streams of knowledge as from a spring', and taking the 'greatest care never to speak unless all the pupils are listening' but yet 'teaching with gusto', using 'live-bait to avoid weariness' and even, if necessary, imitating a 'captain of recruits'.[49] Whatever theories Comenius deduced from nature were always put to the test of his own experience as a practising teacher and in this sense he could agree with Ludovic Vives: 'Theory is easy but has no result other than gratification. Practice is difficult but is of immense utility'.[50]

The attempt to make the nature of the child the basis of pedagogy inevitably raised problems of interpretation depending upon the point of view of the observer. There were times when Comenius stared the opinion of his age that the teacher's function was to check idleness in the young 'lest through sloth they be led to evil or contract a tendency to indolence'. Yet he was capable of showing an almost Froebelian attitude towards play as nature's own didactic device, highly serious and of deep significance and in this he owed little to any of his predecessors. Many times he insisted on the 'pleasure principle' in education and here he was following the lead of the most enlightened of the Humanists. It is unlikely that he knew of Vittorino's House of Joy at Mantua but his own school at Saros Patak was intended as a not dissimilar 'garden of delight'. Very frequently Comenius echoes the thought of Erasmus: 'Follow nature, therefore, in this, and so far as is possible take from the work of the school all that implies toilsomeness and strive to give to learning the quality of freedom and enjoyment'. It was not easy for him to escape from suspicion of the pleasure principle, since freedom was generally reckoned as a necessary concession to human weakness not without grave dangers. Thus Quintilian was afraid lest 'children should begin to hate work before they begin to love it'. Vives advised: 'Pupils must not be pressed or driven too much to study, but they must be allowed some respite . . . but still in such a way that they do not glide into mean pleasures'.[52] None realized better than the Jesuits the importance of making concessions to human nature but always so long as they were supervised 'in order to preserve decorum' since the scholars, if left to themselves, 'would fill the whole place with their yells and uproar, their tussling, laughter and jostling'.[53] Comenius had the same fears and often expressed them but still he could say: 'We must comply with nature and permit students, whatever their level of maturity, to do that in which they find pleasure at the time' . . .in this way we shall not struggle against nature but rather act as midwives at her travail'.[54] Yet there is hesitation: 'The teacher should mostly be present at children's games, not as an overseer whose presence makes them tremble, but taking part unobstrusively'.[55] In so far as play was a release of tension Comenius saw its value as a means of conserving energy for higher things but at times he realized another aspect in that it laid the basis for concept formation.

The objections which could be made to spontaneous play did not apply to the 'play-way' under teacher control and here Comenius had before him the brilliant example of the Jesuits who had shown how well enthusiasm for learning could be developed through group emulation. The competition between groups of equal ability in answering questions and correcting mistakes, in conducting discussions arising from school-work, and in organizing dramatic performances created healthy rivalry both between individual 'adversaries' and between large groups especially as the contests often took place in the presence of the public. The good voice control and use of gesture which brought declamation and reading aloud to perfection also built up self-confidence while the giving of responsibility to class readers was not only good for discipline but helped to bridge the gap between teacher and taught.

Ever since Plato's objection that guardians of the state should 'no more act a mean part than do a mean thing' there had been reserve about the dramatic method in teaching. If it was realistic, Vives feared the evil effects upon spectators[56] and most classical drama was in any case unsuitable for children. The Puritan objection was to the bad associations of the theatre and to the thought of boys taking women's parts especially if, as Bacon said, it made them 'ready to be looked at'. Comenius had to meet these objections at Leszno and Saros Patak but his school plays were unlikely to cause moral offence since they were based on the curriculum and could, indeed, hardly be considered drama at all. Instead of Terence and Plautus he wrote 'scenic representations of the facts of the natural world' arising from his text-books, the *Janua* and *Atrium*. Laurie finds it hard to accept that they were popular but, at least, they employed a very large cast, provided a form of revision, and demonstrated to the public the pupils' mastery of Latin. That a legitimate reason for the dramatic method was 'to change school drudgery into a play and enjoyment' few of his contemporaries could accept[57] but Comenius held that even such unpromising subjects as the working of the fulcrum or a table of family relationships could be put into dialogue form. He cites the authority of Plato, Cicero and Augustine for the didactic value of the conversational approach because it is so natural[58] and uses it in his textbooks 'since nothing is more likely to inspire confidence'. Comenius came to feel that any subject could be dramatized though historical subjects were more appropriate but yet 'in the same way as we have divided the *Gate of Language* into eight theatrical plays so will it be possible to translate everything else, pansophy itself, into theatrical scenes for direct demonstration and performance in schools and classes'.[59]

Comenius certainly thought of drama as being characteristic of life and not simply as a form of entertainment and he believed that the teacher should build on the foundations of spontaneous reaction. Thus he says:

'Do not boys derive pleasure from pretending to ride on horseback by using a long stick as a steed; from building houses, joining the army, engaging in mock battle, setting up tribunals and imitating the organization of the state? Others attempt preaching, conduct funerals, etc. Such instances indicate the tendency of individual talents and it becomes apparent that we should not leave them to themselves but keep them wisely instructed. Does he want to ride a horse? Show him a bridle, a saddle and stirrups, etc'.[60]

Motion is more than a release of energy and Comenius recognized its symbolic significance in the expression of ideas since 'human nature delights in activity, especially unhampered movement, whereby it can create things and transform them at will'.[61] The programme of the Pansophic School shows an acute appreciation of the need for activity with half-an-hour for free play after every hour of instruction and even the instruction to be thought of not as labour but as 'amusement with books'.[62]

The thought of making text-books amusing did not occur to

many teachers in the time of Comenius and even Melanchthon's excellent *Grammar* of 1525 devoted thirty-three pages to gender. The purpose of Melanchthon was 'that boys be rightly instructed in Grammar for the sake of Christ's Church'[63] whereas Comenius was more concerned with the 'actual perception of things'. He himself taught, if tradition is true, in the open air with the book of nature open before him but since this is not always possible the next best thing is for representations to be used. He cites the authority of Plautus and Horace for the view that the visual experience is more vivid and lasting than the oral and gives as an example: 'He who has once seen a rhinoceros, even in a picture, can retain the event in his memory more than if it had been described to him six hundred times'.[64] Beyond description of things lies interpretation and for this the teacher must use symbols. As in the Bible, 'the abstruse and invisible must be presented in forms obvious and visible' and the functions of the judge are best represented by the 'blind-fold maiden with scales and sword'.[65] The teacher must bring into his service every means at his disposal – pictures, parables, diagrams and even gestures – so that those 'dumb teachers', books, may be supplemented.[66] Yet even books can be made less 'dumb' if pictorial stimulus is added to verbal. Comenius acknowledges his indebtedness in this matter to Lubinus who discusses it in his Preface to the New Testament of 1617 (which Comenius calls the *Didactic*). He describes it as 'quite a rational method' but 'as the excellent man gave only advice it remains mere advice'.[67] Lubinus, for his part, says that he had often 'counselled and persuaded Booksellers and Artists in the Low-Countreys' to make a picture-book but he blames their 'coveteousness and greedinesse' that nothing was done.[68] Comenius was familiar with the techniques of printing and was doubtless aware of the devices of wood-cuts and copper-plate engravings but, though he frequently advocates their use it was not until 1658 that the *Orbis Pictus* at last appeared. The connection between the didactic purpose of the teacher and the natural inclination of the child is shown by the following passage: 'Such a book will accustom the little ones to the idea that pleasure is to be derived from books'.[69] Yet there are limitations – 'What if the painter made a mistake? What if he tried to deceive?'[70] Though pictures do 'entice witty children'[71] perception is most reliable when all the senses are involved.

NOTES

Introduction
1. W. H. Woodward: *Erasmus concerning Education* p. 73.
2. *Great Didactic* XI.13.
3. *Labyrinth* X.3.
4. *Great Didactic* XI.9.
5. *Great Didactic* Greeting 8.
6. Keatinge: *Introduction to Great Didactic* p. 107.
7. *Great Didactic* XI.12.
8. *Physica*: Preface.
9. R. Mulcaster: *Positions* (Ed. R. Quick) 309.
10. *Great Didactic* XXXIII.19.
Universal Didactic
11. *Via Lucis* I.4 cf. Great Didactic: Greeting 1.
12. *The Art of Preaching* (*Umění Kazatelské*) 1651.
13. R. Ascham: *The Schoolmaster* (1571). Bk. 1 (Ed. W. A. Wright p. 183).
14. P. Monroe: *History of Education* p. 385.
15. John Stadius.
16. *Faber Fortunae* (1637) Published Amsterdam 1657.
17. W. H. Woodward: *Education in the Renaissance* p. 35.
18. W. H. Woodward: *Education in the Renaissance* p. 84-86.
19. P. Monroe: *History of Education* p. 391-392.
20. cf. *Leges Academiae Genevensis* (1559).
21. E. Stickelberger: *Calvin* p. 142.
22. F. Bacon: *Advancement of Learning* Bk. 1. III.3.
23. J. Brinsley: *Ludus Literarius* (1612). Quoted by J. W. Adamson p. 24.
24. L. Vives: *De Tradendis Disciplinis* III. Ch. III.
25. *Great Didactic*: Greeting 8-9.
26. Krause: *Wolfgang Ratichius* (1872) Quoted by J. W. Adamson: *Pioneers of Education* p. 36.
27. K. Seiler: *Das Paedagogische System W. Ratkes* (1931) Quoted by H. Weimer: *History of Education* p. 76.
28. cf. Von Raumer: *Geschichte der Paedagogik*.
29. *Great Didactic* XI.4-5.
30. *Great Didactic* XXIX.3.
31. cf. *Grammaticae Facilioris Praecepta* (1616, not extant).
32. *Methodus* VIII.
33. Matteo Palmieri: *Della Vita Civile* 27. Quoted by W. H. Woodward *Education during the Renaissance* p. 68.
34. *Methodus* VIII.
35. W. H. Woodward: *Education during the Renaissance* p. 220.
36. *Delineatio Scholae Pansophicae*: Add. Deliberation.
37. *Great Didactic* XXXIII.9.
38. *Consultationes de Scholarum et Studiorum Ratione* (Padua). *Methodus* VIII.

39. L. Vives: *De Tradendis Disciplinis* Bk. III. Ch. VI.
40. *Great Didactic* XIX.54. XXII.25.

Natural Didactic

41. F. Bacon: *Advancement of Learning* Bk. II. Ch. XVII.
42. F. Bacon: To his Father (1592) Quoted by P. Monroe: *Op. cit.* p. 470.
43. cf. later contact with Bodinus in 1642 (G. H. Turnbull: *Hartlib, Dury and Comenius* p. 366).
44. *Analytical Didactic* 53 from Aristotle: De Anima III.VIII.432.
45. K. Schaller finds the origin of Realist Pedagogy in Bodinus cf *Die Paedagogik des J. A. Comenius*, Pt.III.
46. *Analytical Didactic*: 24 cf. Methodus Ch.VIII.
47. *Analytical Didactic*: 24.
48. Seifferth: *Church Constitution of Bohemian Brethren* p. 187.
49. Quotations from *Great Didactic* XIX. *Analytical Didactic* 149 and *Pampaedia* VII.
50. *Great Didactic* XXI.1.
51. Erasmus: Quoted by McCallister: *Growth of Freedom in Education* 126.
52. Vives: *De Tradendis Disciplinis* III.IV.
53. T. G. Hughes: *Loyola and the Educational System of the Jesuits* p. 256.
54. *Analytical Didactic* 112.
55. *Methodus*: XIX.
56. L. Vives: *De Causis Corruptarum Artium* IV.4.
57. *Latinitatis Schola Triclassis* para. 89-94. (ODO. III. XV.)
58. *Great Didactic* XIX.34.
59. *Pampaedia* VII.29. Problem XIX.
60. *Pampaedia* VII.16 Problem VI.
61. *Great Didactic* XXII.11.
62. *Delineatio Scholae Pansophicae* cf *Informatorium* Ch. XII.
63. Melanchthon: Preface to *Grammar* Quoted by Keatinge: *Great Didactic* p. 107-8.
64. *Great Didactic* XX.9.
65. *Analytical Didactic* 90.
66. *Great Didactic* XXXII.16.
67. *Methodus*: VIII.14.
68. E. Lubinus: *True and Readie Way to learn the Latine Tongue* (Published by Samuel Hartlib 1654) p. 23 and 34-5. cf. E. Bodinus: *Didactic* also mentions visual methods.
69. *Great Didactic* XVIII.26-27.
70. *Analytical Didactic* 54.
71. *Orbis Pictus*: Preface.

PART II

ASPECTS OF UNIVERSAL EDUCATION

CHAPTER 6

WISDOM

IN his intellectual and spiritual pilgrimage Comenius became aware of the partial nature of the concepts of wisdom normally held. The Stoic definition that it is knowledge of all things human and divine (*Sapientia est rerum humanarum divinarumque scientia*) left unresolved the relation between man and society, between intellect and goodness, between the actual and the potential. The concept of the Good Man made little sense without the Good Society and Encyclopaedic Knowledge presupposed a universal and natural didactic process by which it could be acquired. Above all Comenius was disturbed by the thought that wisdom might be a rare possession of the few because this seemed at once to betray its universal character. The 'pearl of great price' must not be beyond the reach of the multitude yet it must elude the grasp of any particular point of view – even the theological in the seventeenth century or the scientific in the twentieth.

Comenius persisted throughout most of his life in thinking that he could make this break-through in the history of human thought in such a way that all human knowledge could be given coherence, that all aspects of life could be integrated and that all men could share in it – 'all things, in all ways, to all men'. Whereas men had been, in Bacon's words, 'like ants who heap up their store' or 'like spiders who spin out their webs' wisdom would make them 'like the bees who extract matter from the flowers but work and fashion it by their own efforts'.[1] With the right formula men could be initiated into a new dimension of consciousness and education could become this process.

Such a project smacks of the grandiose, if not the ridiculous, and it is not surprising that Comenius has been attacked for chasing shadows of his own imagination. He never quite knew what he meant by the word which he adopted as central to his philosophy – Pansophia – but the prefix 'pan' helped him to put every isolated and particular problem into a universal setting. Division of labour, specialization of knowledge, differentiation of function are so easy and, apparently efficient, that it requires a great effort to realize the wholeness of reality but this was the aim that Comenius took as his life-task. He could not have continued with it if he had not met with support and encouragement from a wide circle of friends as may be seen by the letter which Tassius, a Professor at Hamburg, sent to Hartlib: 'The enthusiasm for pansophia glows in every corner of Europe; had Comenius furnished nothing more than the great crop of incentives which he has scattered in the minds of all, he might be held to have done enough'.[2] Comenius himself says that 'the opinions of the learned were for the most part kindly beyond expectation'.[3] Criticism came from various sources – his co-religionist, Jerome Broniewski, was concerned that he was 'mixing divine things with human' whereas Descartes accused him of 'applying Scripture to an end for which it was not intended',[4] and while Vossius, an outstanding authority on Roman literature, felt that he was 'lacking in antiquity learning'[5] Philip Müller doubted whether he was practical enough.

Modern criticism has tended to concentrate on the pedagogy of Comenius and depreciate his pansophy. Keatinge expresses some regret that the 'inspired schoolmaster' attempted 'the welding of a philosophical system' which was beyond his powers.[6] Jelínek says: 'His practical and realistic notions about teaching became so vitiated by pansophy that they were transformed into a rigid system that deformed the author's ideas like a bed of Procrustes'.[7] Halliday comments: 'When he leaves Didactics for Metaphysics he tends to fall into confusion'.[8] However, it is quite impossible to separate the practical schoolmaster from the theorizing metaphysician. He himself refused to make any distinction and he must stand or fall by the unity of his theory. Laurie put this point of view even in 1887 – 'It was in Pansophism that his real life-work lay, his scholastic undertakings being strictly subordinate to the great task'.[9] Now that a large body of the pansophic works of Comenius is available it is possible to think again since, in Jelínek's words, we can know 'the furniture of his mind'[10] and discover, as Halliday suggests, that his peda-

gogy 'is not quite so usual as has long been thought'.[11] Jean
Piaget places pansophy 'midway between scholasticism and
mechanicalism'[12] but Jan Patočka rightly emphasizes the
dynamic character and links it with Neo-Platonism.[13]

THE INITIATION OF WISDOM

The quest for pansophy was the story of his life and Comenius
believed that he was in fact blazing a trail for mankind. It would
seem that the idea was born in him out of the tragedy of his
childhood because he speaks of being touched with this desire
when he lost both his parents and suffered from the neglect of
his guardians so that he 'could but pity others especially in my
own nation'.[14] He did not use the word pansophy until it was
suggested to him by a book with that title by Peter Lauremberg
(1585-1639), Professor at Rostock, in 1663. He found the book
too Aristotelian and containing 'nothing appertaining to divine
wisdom' but nevertheless he began to hope that he could 'square'
the title with his own work. Klaus Schaller shows that it was a
word used during the Middle Ages and Renaissance and there is
an instance of a writer, Franciscus Patricius, using the prefix
'pan' in much the same way as Comenius came to do later.[15] But
the idea of pansophy had been in his mind for a long time, either
in the *Theatrum* which he began at the age of twenty or perhaps
more clearly in the *Physica* of 1633.[16] Certainly many of the
concepts which he came to develop later may be found in the
first four chapters of the *Great Didactic* which he wrote in
Czech in the same year. The Lord of Leszno, Raphael Leszczyński, became very interested in the wider plans but, unfortunately,
died of apoplexy in 1636 and Comenius began to consider carefully whether he could not go beyond the description of things externally (as he had done in the *Janua Linguarum* which had just
been published in 1633) to a comprehension of 'what each thing
was in its essence'. His purpose in this was not metaphysical but
practical. It was because he had perceived the confusion of
language 'so long as words, not things (the husks of words, I say,
not the kernels of meanings) be in our mouths'.[17] This idea was
in other men's minds at this time[18] but to Comenius it became a
passion to which he wanted to devote his life – 'How badly,'

he says, 'have I imitated that merchant seeking for good pearls, who, when he had found a pearl of great price, went away and sold all that he had and bought it. Would that I, having once struck the pansophic vein, had followed it up and neglected all else'. His enthusiasm was to some extent held in check by his appointment as Bishop of his Church with special responsibilities for ministers in training in addition to his work as supervisor of the school at Leszno. Consequently he made slow progress with the *Janua Rerum* (Gate of Reality) until he came into correspondence, through two of his students at Cambridge University, with a man who was to have a deep influence upon him, Samuel Hartlib. He sent Hartlib a brief outline of pansophy which, to his complete surprise, Hartlib had printed at Oxford under the title *Prelude to the Pansophical Ideas of Comenius* and distributed 294 copies to a wide variety of people asking for their opinion.[19] A second edition followed under the title *Essay of Pansophy* (*Prodromus Pansophicae*) but it was still only an outline whereas Comenius had, by this time (1636) written a fuller account, which, however, was not published although, according to his own account, he had worked on it since 1631.[20] He did, in fact, send it to Hartlib and some copies were distributed but even then it was only a fore-view (*Praeludia*) since Comenius believed that a full working out of the theory of pansophy required a team effort. One of the difficulties in analysing the pansophic theories of Comenius is that he frequently wrote outlines trying to indicate his purpose and hoping that others would take up the work or that he would attain perfection.[21] His hope was that a college (such as the 'illustrious Bacon desired') might be established and he was very much heartened by the support of a Synod of his Church in 1639 to a Description which he wrote for its approval ('*Dilucidatio*) and which Hartlib also published for him. Hartlib tried to make contact with him but he was 'tied to his place by the character of his office'[22] until, after a tempest-tossed journey from Danzig, he finally arrived in London on September 21, 1641.[23] He only stayed in England for nine months but it was a momentous experience. It freed him from the parochial view almost inevitable in a member of a poverty-stricken community of exiles and it introduced him to a wide circle of friends brimming over with exciting ideas. His letters back to Leszno show his amazement at conditions in London – the crowded churches, the well stocked book-stalls, the eager debates on reform. He was entertained to dinner (and even given clothes for the occasion) by the Dean of Westminster and given an official welcome in a sermon to Parliament by John Gauden in which he was coupled with John Dury as 'not unknowne for the fame of his works'. The whole atmosphere was conducive to optimism and on October 20th the Long Parliament 'communicated their plans for assigning some College with its revenues as a Pansophic College. There was even named for this purpose the Savoy, Winchester and Chelsea College'.[24] The influence of Bacon was evident in the University of Oxford which, according to Christopher Hill, became 'for a short time a leading centre of scientific activity until it sank again into torpor'.[25] The indefatigable Hartlib had just brought out a *Description of the Famous Kingdome of Macaria* and then published the two tractates of Comenius (*Prodromus* and *Dilucidatio*) under the title A *Reformation of Schooles*[26] but, more important, he introduced him to a circle of visionaries. There was Theodore Haak, a refugee from the Palatinate whose 'longing to do good and to see unity and peace replace the hatred and chaos' made him an eager member of Hartlib's Macaria Society for 'propagating religion and endeavouring the reformation of the whole world'.[27] Of a different character was the shy John Pell whose book, the *Idea Mathescos* of 1638, endeavoured to do for mathematics what Comenius hoped to do for all knowledge. This man and Joachim Hübner were recommended by Hartlib as collaborators for Comenius and Hübner was particularly suitable since he had done research for Hartlib in the Bodeleian Library at Oxford since 1637.[28] There were a considerable number of men linked together by enthusiasm for pansophy and ready to exert their influence in Parliament or University on its behalf such as Robert Boyle, who was to take an active part in the Royal Society later on, Cheney Colepeper, a gentleman of whom Comenius had a very high opinion,[29] and John Sadler, who wrote a book on education.[30] But the man with whom Comenius had the closest connection next to Hartlib himself was John Dury who came to England with him and was the third member of the pact in which Comenius was given responsibility for 'the waies of schooling and pansophical learning'.[31]

The winter of 1641-42 was unfortunately filled with rumours of war but Comenius worked as if eternal peace were imminent. He drew up an impressive list of books to be written 'for reforming the studies of the young' including a 'Handbook for Parents', an 'Elementary Reading Book', an 'Encyclopaedia of Sense Experience' an 'Epitome of the Bible', and a 'Book of Pansophy'. He continued to work on outlines of pansophy as a guide for the future and to emphasize particularly the universal scope, including even the Indians of America in his schemes. The *Via Lucis* or *Way of Light* gave a plan for universal books, universal schools, a universal language and a universal college while the *Diatyposis Pansophiae* or *Pattern of Knowledge* was a sketch of the seven Temples of Wisdom.

As it became clear that Civil War was inevitable, several possibilities opened to Comenius. There were some French scholars and scientists who held that Paris and not London was the proper place for an international college and Cardinal Richelieu was willing for Comenius to guide its establishment along pansophic lines. Comenius had great admiration for the civilization of France and the prospect of collaboration cutting across barriers of religion and nationality made a strong appeal to him. But Richelieu was at the point of death. The tradition that Comenius was asked to become President of Harvard College is based on the evidence of Cotton Mather writing in 1820 and on the fact that John Winthrop, who wanted Harvard to be a centre for the new 'experimental philosophy' met him in Europe[32] and to this Comenius himself was drawn by his concern for the Indians whom he saw as 'white unto harvest'[33] and by the thought that New England might be a kind of laboratory for social experiments.[34] It was his ill fortune to find patrons in Sweden who wanted school text books but regarded pansophism as impracticable, if not dangerous.

Comenius left England on June 21, 1642, though he 'never forgot that beautiful dream of Jeremiah concerning the wonderful church and the restoration of the world' and promised his friends that he would not be diverted from the pansophic project or 'delay by reading authors, but proceed to search into the very mines of real things'.[35] The six years spent at Elbing in the service of Ludovic de Geer and Axel Oxenstiern, the Swedish Chancellor, proved a stern test for Comenius personally and for pansophy generally. His aim was not to write text-books but to transform them and for this purpose he set himself an impossible ideal. He wished that he had 'either greater powers or fewer desires' but found that 'with every step forward a further insight was granted which made it impossible not to strive after what was better or deeper.[36] He had always maintained that pansophy required collaboration but he found himself working with men who, however willing, were only amanuenses.[37] When he did find people who might have helped him more positively, such as George Vechner or Cyprian Kinner, personal difficulties arose.[38] He was constantly distracted by other problems – financial stringency, the illness of his wife, sectarian quarrels and the tortuous proceedings at the Peace Conferences at Münster and Osnabrück.[39] That, in such circumstances, he should have attempted singlehanded to commit to paper his pansophic schemes as a whole is matter for astonishment. He did not, as Keatinge thought, 'fling them to the dust-heap' while he wrote 'text-books for little boys'[40] although it is difficult to date his work exactly because he frequently made fresh attempts and changed his titles. According to Professor G. H. Turnbull one version of the *Janua Rerum* was written in 1642, probably while Comenius was in England, and published after his death in 1681. In addition Professor Turnbull found amongst Samuel Hartlib's papers (now in Sheffield University Library) two manuscripts which were published at Prague in 1951. The first part, which Comenius calls *Praecognita*, consists of an Introduction and three Books concerning the necessity, possibility and the ease of Christian pansophy. The second is dated 1643 and is entitled the *Gateway of Things (Janua Rerum)*. It was probably planned as part of the *pansophia* of which Comenius himself says that, up to the time of his going to England, he did 'nothing greatly therein'.[41]

However, by 1644 Comenius was engaged upon that great collection of works that together make up the *Consultation* with an intensity that made him plead that he was only 'a man, not an angel; flesh not iron'.[42] He often worked on different parts simultaneously and constantly revised until almost the hour of his death. The manuscripts discovered in 1935 show the following parts of the *Consultation*:

1. *Panegersia*: Universal Awakening. He was still working on this in 1654.[43]
2. *Panaugia*: Universal Dawning.
3. *Pansophia*: *Universal Wisdom* (Seven volumes).
4. *Pampaedia*: Universal Education.
5. *Panglottia*: Universal Language.
6. *Panorthosia*: Universal Reform.
7. *Pannuthesia*: Universal Admonition.

In addition there are three closely associated works:

1. *Lexicon Reale Pansophicum* – An alphabetical list of definitions of pansophic concepts.
2. *Spicilegium Didacticum* which was published in 1680 by Nigrinus.
3. *Sapientiae primae Usus Triertium Catholicum* – the Three Universal Forms of Wisdom published in 1681.

There can be no doubt that the most loyal friends of Comenius were at times somewhat anxious about his progress. John Dury, for instance, in 1646 hints that pansophy has 'hitherto been only to make people gaze, and raise expectations'.[44] Colepeper in the same year, says of Comenius: 'He calls loud for attention, and hath (methinks) too many soundings or '*prodromuses*' before he enters the stage'.[45] The difficulties increased when Comenius finally settled in Amsterdam and realized that he was racing with death for the completion of his work and the following extract from a letter of Peter Figulus, his son-in-law, tells its own sad story: 'The greatest labour is to keep him upon one resolution, and to persuade him that he hath alreadie brought it to such a perfection as can be imagined, or required from him. . . . When one thing is built he ever still over-turns it again and buildeth a new'. The reason was partly physical. Figulus reports that he was 'withering and decaying' and so crippled with sciatica that he 'went crooked' and yet determined to give himself 'whole for the Pansophicall worke'.[46]

Klaus Schaller suggests that Comenius often had Plato's simile of the Cave in his mind and his view of the 'initiation of wisdom' may therefore have some resemblance to Plato's:

'the faculty by which man learns is like an eye which cannot be turned from darkness to light unless the whole body is turned; in the same way the mind as a whole must be turned away from the world of change until it can bear to look straight at reality, and at the brightest of realities which is what we call the Good'.[47]

Education is the initiation of men into the light of God and Comenius was willing to make that his day and night pre-occupation for forty years. He was not unaware of the dangers of 'importing an imaginary harmony which it will not find in the facts'.[48] He wrestled with metaphysical concepts, not to achieve learned subtlety but so that pansophy might be 'easy to read and apprehended by simple people'.

THE DYNAMICS OF WISDOM

The concept of pansophy as a principle of democracy, 'not in an unknown language but unto all mankind so that even the meanest might understand'[49] presupposed a power greater than had hitherto been discovered. Firstly, the men of learning must turn away from the idols that made their knowledge 'not answerable to the proposed end; seldom attaining to any substantial uses of life but rather ending in opinionative brawling'.[50] Secondly, education must begin on the right lines from earliest infancy so that the young child is introduced to the essential categories of reality, only, adjusted to his understanding. Metaphysics is only impossible for those 'to whom God has denied understanding' and this is 'a rare phenomenon'.[51] Thirdly, all men everywhere must be convinced that escape from the evils of the world is not only desirable but possible. It is not 'the Cafres and similar tribes' but the majority of Christians who need an awakening from the state of living 'like beasts of burden, in deep ignorance of God, of themselves and of all things'.[52] The conviction of sin which theologians took as the first step necessary for personal salvation Comenius took as the preliminary for universal salvation from the 'perpetual confusion of human affairs', the preoccupation with 'vain and frivolous things' and the 'vexations of learning'.[53] But the hungry sheep must not be left unfed and therefore the Book of Pansophy must be presented in the 'popular style'[54] and not 'so beset with thorns' that even such a Prince as Gustavus Adolphus banished 'the study of metaphysics out of his kingdom'.[55]

One of those to whom Hartlib sent the Prelude to Pansophy replied that it was 'very ingenious in detecting the defects of Learning' but that it remained 'for the physician who hath found out the cause of the disease to go through with the cure'.[56] Apart from the general diagnosis that 'the chief cause of this vast evil is to be found in the Prince of darkness himself, Satan',[57] Comenius found two factors in the sickness of mankind. The first concerned the content of education which omitted the subjects of most importance. Even those who were to be leaders – divines, politicians and physicians – skip over the studies of Metaphysics, Mathematics and Natural Philosophy'.[58] Yet in the Gateway of Things he argues that metaphysics is the easiest of all subjects because it has only a few general principles which are so obvious as to be beyond contradiction and from these can be deduced all the sciences of the mind. As for mathematics and natural philosophy Comenius was often wrong in his opinions but he was not wrong-headed. Though he believed in 'unmoveable principles of natural truth' he knew that human understanding of them changes continually and the accepted opinions of one age may be 'quite confounded by the optic glasse of Galileo'[59] and 'discreet and understanding men' must thank Tycho Brahe for removing 'useless stuff' out of astronomy.[60] New hypotheses must be tested not simply against observation and experiment but also against the total picture of knowledge. The second factor in any diagnosis of the human dilemma concerned the will. Comenius realized that perfection was not possible on earth[61] but yet 'the most perfect restoration of human nature to the likeness of God' would be 'if no man were bidden to desire anything against his will'.[62] This is a linking of Rousseau's dictum concerning freedom as desiring only what is possible and Kant's limiting of desire to what is consistent with law. The emancipation of the will from the 'scraping together of money, the vapour of reputation, or the gratification of the body'[63] is only possible if the will of man is actively engaged in the struggle in the soul between the 'contraries of light and darkness' on the right side.[64] Only then can there be that 'inward accord' instead of the 'slippery business of external agreement'.[65]

The *Pansophia* is an attempt to answer these two problems of knowledge and will, by discussing the spiritual structure of the universe as it concerns man. The Possible World (*Mundus Possibilis*) consists of the ideas which correspond to objective reality. The human mind comes to them by intuition or introspection and all that is needed is readiness to wait for inspiration. This concept of the Inner Light or the Seed within was common to many groups in the seventeenth century who believed that 'the Light of Truth which enlighteneth every man' was 'not far to seek but was within the mind'.[66]

Comenius believed that the Possible World of ideas led inevitably to knowledge of God since the Inner Light was 'that of God' and therefore, as he said before, 'since by its own innate notions the mind measures all things, it is able to get knowledge of God Himself, its own Archetype, better than from any other source, gathering that God is such as the mind itself is, or, at any rate, such as its hidden aspirations long to become'.[67] For Comenius there is no need for the kind of arguments for the existence of God that Leibniz put forward to Spinoza since, as Spinoza put it, 'God is Being absolutely infinite, therefore there cannot be any substance excepting God and consequently none other can be conceived'.[68] Thus the thoughts that come spontaneously into the mind lead to God as the Archetype of them all.

From a realization of the world of God the mind, working freely, comes next to a world of spiritual Beings (*Mundus Angelicus*) who realize (or thwart) the will of God by expressing the ideas of the possible world. Psycho-analysis would describe this as the projection of hopes and fears or the displacement of unwanted or unacknowledged desires, and according to this guardian angels are personalized mother figures and avenging angels are projections of the 'stern father'.[69] But such a rationalization does not dispose of the thought in the mind and for Comenius the possible world was a thought system not an objective reality in any material sense.

The fourth, the World of Nature (*Mundus Materialis*) is just as much a creation of the mind as the world of spiritual Beings but at the same time it is not an abstract Platonic world. Comenius firmly believed in the reality of material things through the observation of which man could realize the Possible World of ideas and though he may not have had much conception of the tedious processes of scientific method, as Keatinge says,[70] he was drawing attention to something as important – imaginative introspection. It is this alone which makes observation and experiment insightful, and there is no fundamental difference between the physical sciences and the mental sciences. As Wundt, an ardent exponent of objective methods said: 'All Psychology begins with introspection, but there are two auxiliary methods – experimentation and history'. In all the worlds arising from the ideas innate in the mind man is, as it were, 'a spectator in the amphitheatre of God'[71] since 'the corporeal world is the visible theatre of God, mobile on all sides, constructed with an amazing mechanical skill . . . revealed for the enjoyment of Himself and all His creatures'.[72] Experience of it is necessary before man can begin the upward movement to his starting point which Comenius insists is that of being the image of God – 'not the corruption which has laid hold of men but the condition to which he must be recalled'.[73] Pansophy does not require high intelligence so much as a Socratic 'torpedo touch' which will stimulate the will. When the truth can be clearly shown to man he will immediately grasp it and follow paths which are already laid for the eye of faith but not for the eye of Cartesian doubt. As Schaller says: 'Method for Comenius is not the creation of a path but the following of one already there'.[74] Will is the key, but not so much in terms of resolution as of effort of attention to an idea, similar to the concept of William James. The dynamics of pansophia might be summed up in the words of the mystic, Meister Eckhart: 'God with His own nature, His essence, is in the soul, and yet He is not the soul (i.e. He is infinitely more than the soul). The soul sends back a divine reflection to God, so that they are both the same light. The Word or expression of God becomes God'.[75] In one sense Comenius sees man as humble and acquiescent[76] but in another sense, fired with ambition to climb Jacob's ladder up to heaven.

The second half of *Pansophia* is an attempt to indicate the steps of the ladder. 'Man has seen the theatres in which eternal wisdom plays its games' (Ludos) – the Mind of Man himself, the activities of Spiritual Beings, and the world of Nature – but now the initiative lies with men to imitate God in all their economic, industrial and cultural activities.[77] Comenius sees no danger that human ambition will become vaulting – 'Pansophy teaches us that there is nothing in heaven or earth, in the air or water or anywhere else, that was not destined for human use, either directly or indirectly'[78] provided, of course, that everything serves its 'rightful purpose'. Material things must be used 'according to their nature' but, under that condition, men act as creatively as God in making a new world which is only artificial in the sense that it goes beyond the original nature of things. Art is 'knowledge of how to treat things rightly according to their nature'[79] and Comenius gives special attention to the utilization of light and fire and to the promotion of health of the body.[80] The point at which the use of nature becomes the exploitation of nature is when it becomes an end in itself so that labour is prostituted, wealth is wasted, and the 'godless children of Cain' imprison themselves 'in the cage of this world'.[81] There is no sharp division between science and art or between industry and culture since 'by art we understand whatever is compassed by human industry in thought, word or deed'.[82] His interpretation of utility is closer to that of John Ruskin than Herbert Spencer, since all human activities have in them the possibility of creative skill and, without that possibility, labour is degrading. Comenius believed that the world of art and craft (*mundus artificialis*) should free men from drudgery to the point where all can live 'in decent comfort' but those who want to go further than this 'deviate from God's will'.[83]

The social activities of man are regarded by Comenius as a higher step on Jacob's ladder and this is the subject of the Sixth Book of *Pansophia*. In the Introduction he maintains that social relationships have a moral basis in the identity and equality of all men as images of the divine nature. Social relationships which arise from the motivation of hunger are not moral because they are concerned with the appropriation for use by the individual of that which is other than himself. The Moral World (*Mundus Moralis*) elevates social life above the level of dominance, or even of contract, because it imports into it other elements of value, responsibility and intention. This transcendence can be seen most clearly in the family[84] where sexual love (*Eros*) and compatibility (*Philia*) have their place but are redeemed by the fact that husband and wife are united by the value which they put upon their marriage, by the mutual sacrifices which they make for each other, and by their intention of off-spring. Comenius has no place for the egalitarian family in which there is no authority and no obedience but he believed that these opposites are relieved from tension when they partake in a universal situation. A modern writer, Carl Brunner, puts the argument thus: 'I, as father, as well as the mother and child, know irrevocably that this fact of relationship is permanent and that we three persons are bound to each other . . . in an unparalleled and indissoluble union'.[85] This does not mean that Comenius rejected divorce where marriage has become 'a cruel captivity' where he asks: 'Can they not be untied and set free from one another'.[86] The family, like industry, is not an end in itself but a means by which man can rise above lust, egotism and expediency and it contains within the social institution, a divine order of creation. Other forms of social organization exist at the contractual or compulsory level but they only become moral as individuals intend to realize through them the universal community.

Thus Comenius comes to the Spiritual World (*Mundus Spiritualis*) in which this universal community is freed from dependence upon finite groups even though its life is transient and episodic until at last the Eternal World (*Mundus Aeternus*) brings about 'the simplest and most perfect and therefore the most blessed state'.[87] The dynamics of wisdom, as Comenius sees it, is a cyclic movement from the possible world of thought, through all the manifold forms of the expression of thought to a re-creation of nature, community and contemplation back to God, the source of all.

THE PARALLELISM OF WISDOM

Normally an immeasurable gulf separates human reality from human utopia. The 'pattern laid up in heaven' is too far removed from the compromise possible and consequently idealism breeds inertia. It was the passionate conviction of Comenius that this need not happen and that man could become an active agent in the creation of the New Jerusalem. Pansophia must include man as the conscious agent and steward of God. The mystery remains, however, that the world of experience is so full of disharmony as to suggest some limitation in either the power or the intention of God. Therefore the hypothesis that God even exists has to be made in the face of contrary evidence but, for those who can accept it, there is the great advantage that increase of knowledge and experience, which might correct or overthrow other hypotheses, only serves to give it clearer meaning and ampler range.

With the hypothesis of God parallelism becomes feasible even in the face of contrary evidence because it stimulates further search for evidence of correspondence between one thing and another. Since all comes from God all must express the mind of God and the task of pansophy is to co-ordinate all the separate items of knowledge. It is like the co-ordination made by an army advancing on a wide front and making petty gains in one sector after another until the final break-through. It is precisely here that Comenius has so much to say as a corrective to narrow specialization.[88] The isolation of one aspect of reality from another may be necessary for the sake of analysis but it should always be followed by integration. Thus in psychology the early experimentalists – Weber, Fechner and Wundt – tried to measure sensation as a specific physiological phenomenon and made some valuable discoveries but it then became necessary to bring together the separate factors and re-establish the wholeness of perception. Whether colours, sounds, shapes, etc., are imputed by the mind to the external world or whether the external world provides signals that set off mental activity is a problem that must in the end be subordinate to the harmony which there is between the perceiving subject and the active order of things.[89] Similarly whether sensation, intuition and reason are separate faculties or not must be subordinate to the successive differentiation of sensation by which concept formation is achieved.[90] When Comenius says: 'Show the reason clear truth: it will necessarily understand it' he is not speaking of reasoning power or the logical faculty but of the total response of the mind in the sense used by Henri Bergson: 'By intuition I mean instinct that has become self-conscious and capable of reflecting upon its object and enlarging it indefinitely'.[91] This indefinite enlarging of knowledge is necessary because, according to Comenius, God has 'concealed His works as with a curtain' and man discovers them as he develops 'the desire for the good and the useful'. It means the search for similarities and the constant subordination of particular things to wholes – 'Pansophy by wholesome counsel takes all things in general into its consideration, that it may evidently and most clearly appear, how lesser things are, and come to be, subordinate to the greater'.[92]

In the Via Lucis Comenius speaks of the 'Books of God's eternal nature' of which pansophy is 'nothing less than a transcript duly arranged' and the Books of Via Lucis are almost the same as the Worlds of Pansophia. The innate notions of the mind, the revelations of God, and the things of nature are each microcosms of the others and each of them corrects and supplements the others. Hence knowledge is both a structure and an organism. As a structure it is compared with the Temple of Ezekiel with architectural plan, elevation and model and seven courts leading from the threshold to the Holy of Holies and the Fountain of Living Water.[93] But as an organism it is described as 'a perpetual mover or a tree rising from its roots' and not simply 'a chain neatly framed with links' or 'a pile of wood tied together'.[94] Compared to a clock it is 'so interconnected that not even the smallest part is superfluous' but as music it is not only 'the sweet consonance of divers tones' but also 'the perfect agreement of opposites'.[95]

In the Lexicon (Lexicon Reale Pansophicum) he gives a definition of pansophy which agrees with the more detailed description in the Gateway of Things (Janua Rerum) and the Diatyposis or Plan. Pansophy is a 'universal science' because it is based on truths so clear to common sense that they can hardly be contradicted. It is an attempt to find the few simple classes,

structures and laws to which every single thing must be connected. Each thing has an essence which puts it into a general
class, a mode of being which is the general idea which makes it
operate as it does, and a purpose or principle of being which
determines its possibilities. Knowledge is concerned with things
(real being), ideas (mental being) and words (verbal being).
Things can be divided into three general classes – substance,
accident and defect. Substance is what the thing is wholly in
itself (e.g. a man). Accident is what owes its existence to something else (e.g. health). Defect is something which takes away
from another thing its essence (e.g. sickness). Although knowledge comes from within the mind it has to express itself in
words and it has to derive its stimulus from things and
Comenius seems at times to suggest that the essence of things
is a material entity since 'the Hermetical Physicians have by
Chymistry extracted qualities out of natural bodies and have
extracted the very essence'[96] but generally his point of view is
that 'everything is made in accordance with its idea by which it
is able to be what it is'.[97]

It was a firm belief of Comenius that pansophy could be
adapted to any level of complexity provided certain rules were
adhered to. Thus statements should always be 'plain and per-
spicuous without any exceptions, limitations or distinctions and
the conclusions (axioms) should 'flow of their own accord'. Extreme cases should be avoided in favour of what is normal or in
'the middle course'.[98] Amongst the examples given by Comenius
of how this procedure can be worked out in practice the topic
of the Sun may be taken as typical:

The SUN
Definition: The greatest star in heaven destined by nature for
enlightening the earth through its circuit.
Idea: It is constituted of (1) a very great mass of shining light
made up into one body, (2) of very lively virtue flowing through
its beams, (3) of motion perpetually circular.
Note: If anything here might seem doubtful, as that which is
here spoken of the motion of the sun being attributed by others
to the earth, this controversy cannot be decided. Let this in the
meantime be decided as certain – that there is need of circular

motion whether it be in the sun or in the earth.

Axioms: 1. The sun is the chief fountain of light.
2. The essence of the sun is light.
3. The light of the sun flows out by beams.
4. The light of the sun issues out every way.
5. Therefore the body of the sun is round.
6. The sun ministers light and heat.
7. The sun puts vigour into things.
8. The sun lights one half of the world while the other is in darkness.
9. By how much the sun is vertical the more it shines.
10. The return of the sun to the same vertical position makes the year.

A distinction must be made between the validity of fact (which in this case is missing) and validity of method for which Comenius gives certain conditions:

1. 'The truth and certainty of science depend more on the witness of the senses than on anything else.'[99]
2. The deduction of axioms must be made 'with exquisite care for the main strength of truth lies in them'.[100]
3. Truth must not conflict with intuition for 'knowledge is obtainable by the guidance of the common ideas innate in every mind.'[101]
4. Truth must be consistent with reason which 'measures all things better than any other source, gathering that God is such as the mind of God is.'[102]
5. Truth must 'be approved by the general suffrage of mankind . . . interwoven with significant and brilliant judgments.'[103]

Comenius had affinities with all the scientific methods of his day which were challenging the scholastic tradition. Thus he accepted the need for 'an inductive history in which all things are collected' which is hardly anywhere possessed 'except in astronomy'.[104] Yet he criticizes induction as being 'of no great advantage towards our design because it is intended for the discovery of the secrets of nature but we drive at the whole universality of things'.[105] Though himself no mathematician he was strongly drawn to the mathematical method because of its certainty. It prevented people from 'rushing into contrarities' and gave a 'solid demonstration by which assent is wrested'.[106] He was not the only one at that time to apply the methods of Euclid to philosophy and he found the new mathematical inventions (of which he mentions Napier's Logarithms as one) opening up 'fair and great hopes'.[107] In many ways his approach to knowledge was empirical despite his confidence in universal principles. Thus he speaks of 'the continuous struggle between the forms of Nature and Matter . . . between Law and Custom . . . and the experiments by which the hidden powers of things are tracked out and the instances in which they have been disappointed of success'.[108] Yet his criticism of the Royal Society indicates his suspicions of a materialistic philosophy.

However, the method to which Comenius attached special importance is what he calls 'syncrisis' since it is based on his fundamental idea that the world is constructed in a series of strata each one of which expresses in a special way the same ideas. The word was not unknown in England since John Smith, the Cambridge Platonist, speaks of it in 1657 as 'a comparison of contrary things'. But Comenius places very strong emphasis on it in many of his works[109] and deals with it specifically in a book which has not been preserved ('*Wisdom made visible Two and Three Times*'). Nevertheless until recently this subject has received little attention. Although the term is not used in the *Great Didactic* syncrisis forms the basis of the argument there. At first it might appear that the *Great Didactic* is simply using examples from nature as analogies but, in fact, syncrisis is used as an instrument for applying general principles from the world of nature and of mechanical arts to the problems of education. An example of syncritical method will illustrate this:

Chapter XVI. Sixth Principle

Principle: Nature, in its formative processes, begins with the universal and ends with the particular.

Example: The process of incubation from egg to bird is from an integrated pattern (the foetus) to a differentiated one.

Imitation: (a) The artist outlines his subject as a whole before he puts in the detail.

(b) The sculptor starts with a block of stone and comes to individual parts in turn.

(c) The gardener takes a single shoot for transplanting and from this the new plant develops in detail.

Deviation: In teaching it is wrong to teach subordinate parts before a general idea is given.

Rectification: Teach each subject or topic first in simplest outline and then add the details.

The syncritical method assumes a comparison between every form of nature or of human activity 'since all things partake one of another' and therefore each can be compared with its own principle, with its environmental setting, with its parts, and with its species.[111] Therefore, also, 'no one knows a thing perfectly if he knows only that one thing, even though he knows it analytically and synthetically; he comes to understand it perfectly only when he understands how and why it resembles other things'.

Comenius complains of the ill effects upon education when the principle of syncrisis is ignored: 'I remember well that, when we began to learn dialectic, rhetoric and metaphysics, we were, at the very beginning, overburdened with long-winded rules and knotty questions . . . so that we, poor wretches, were so confused that we scarcely understood what it was all about'.[112] On the other hand it is basic to creative thinking. Isaac Newton apperceived the comparison between the elliptical orbit of the moon and the fall of an apple because he believed that the same laws must govern both,[113] and modern psychologists now emphasize the significance of analogical thinking in intelligence but particularly in creative ability.[114]

In the *Gateway of Things* Comenius takes the syncritical method further by bringing it into line with intuition. Not only is there some correlation between every external thing in nature but the innate notions of the human mind are also harmonious with nature. Thus, in trying to make sense of the jig-saw which is the universe we already have a pre-view, as it were, of the complete picture. Contrarities are simply a challenge to the mind to bring about an agreement inherent though not yet apparent. Optimism is justified because the mind is always potentially able to go through the recesses of the labyrinth of nature.[115]

Comenius had sanguine hopes concerning the benefits of pansophy. He thought it would solve the problem of prejudice 'when things themselves have been reduced to harmony.'[116] He believed that it would make universal education possible, 'not so much to make men learned as to make them wise'.[117] He said quite plainly, 'We want all men to become pansophists' because then they could achieve 'perfection if they so desire it',[118] and these words contrast forcibly with what Rousseau said: 'Everything is good as it comes from the hand of the author of nature; but everything degenerates in the hands of man'.

NOTES

1. F. Bacon: Nov. Organum I.95.
2. Letter from Adolf Tassius to Hartlib quoted by R. F. Young: Comenius in England. p. 37 (ODO. p. 454).
3. Continuatio: 48.
4. Continuatio: 48 cf. Kvačala: Analecta Comeniana p. 159-160.
5. Quoted in a letter from Rulice to Hartlib (G. H. Turnbull: Hartlib, Dury and Comenius, p. 343).
6. M. Keatinge: Introduction to Great Didactic p. 52.
7. V. Jelínek: Analytical Didactic p. 20.
8. J. C. Halliday: The Pampaedia of J.A.C. p. 66.
9. S. S. Laurie: J.A.C. p. 38
10. Jelínek: Op. cit. p. 226.
11. J. C. Halliday: Op. cit.
12. J. Piaget: Introduction to Selections. p. 14.
13. J. Patočka: Philosophical Basis for Comenian Pedagogy (Pedagogica 1957 (2) p. 145).
The Initiation of Wisdom
14. Prodromus: 78.
15. K. Schaller: Pan p. 14. F. Patricius: Nova Philosophia (in Four Parts – Panaugia – Panarchia – Pampsychia – Pancosmia) cf. W. Begemann: Monatsheften der Comenius Gesellschaft (1896) 210-221.
16. J. V. Novák: Monatsheften (1895) 243. G. Beiswanger: Comenius als Pansoph (1904) J. Hendrich: J.A.C. (1924).
17. Continuatio: 44.
18. cf. Letter from J. H. Bisterfeld to Hartlib (1638) Quoted by R. F. Young: Op. cit. p. 32.
19. G. H. Turnbull: Op. cit. p. 343.

J. A. COMENIUS

20. G. H. Turnbull: *Two Pansophical Works* p. 23 cf. J. Ludvíkovsky: *Acta Comeniana* (1957.2) p. 173.
21. Letter from P. Figulus – Kvačala: *Korres.* II.97.
22. *Continuatio*: 50.
23. cf. Letter from Comenius to Leszno – Patera: *Korres* 38-41.
24. Introduction to Part II of *ODO* cf. R. F. Young: *Op. cit.* 54. cf. G. H. Turnbull: *Hartlib, Dury and Comenius* p. 361.
25. Christopher Hill: *Century of Revolution* p. 180.
26. G. H. Turnbull: *Op. cit.* p. 90. cf. Kvačala says the '*Reformation of Schooles*' is a translation of the *Prodromus* and the *Dilucidatio*. (Comenius (Appendix No. XLII)).
27. Pamela Barnett: *Theodore Haak* p. 35-37.
28. Letter from Hübner to Hartlib – Kvacala: *Korres.* 32-42 cf. R. F. Young *Op. Cit.*, p. 38 and 47.
29. Letter from Comenius to Hartlib – Kvačala: *Korres.* 1.191 cf. R. F. Young: *Op. cit.* p. 43. For Robert Boyle see J. B. Capek: *Archiv* XXI.
30. G. H. Turnbull: *Op. cit.* p. 431.
31. G. H. Turnbull: *Op. cit.* p. 362.
32. Cotton Mather: *Marginalia* (1820) cf. A. Matthews: *Comenius and Harvard College* (Publications of Colonial Society of Mass. XXI.146).
33. cf. letter from Comenius to Hartlib – Patera: *Korres.* CXI cf. R. F. Young *Comenius and the Indians of New England* (1929).
34. Christopher Hill: *Op. cit.* p. 84.
35. *Continuatio*: 57.
36. Letter from P. Figulus (1646).
37. From Leszno came P. Figulus, Daniel Petreus, Paul Cyrillus and David Nigrinus cf. Patera: *Korres.* 64. cf. Heyberger: *Op. cit.* p. 70.
38. G. H. Turnbull: *Op. cit.* p. 382-413.
39. cf. Kvačala: *Korres.* 102. Patera: *Korres*: 71-72.
40. Keatinge: *Op. cit.* 51.
41. J. Ludvíkovsky: in *Acta Comeniana* (1957-2) 113-151. G. H. Turnbull: *Two Pansophical Works* p. 19-24 and 147-150.
42. October 1645.
43. Kvačala: *Korres.* 191.
44. Letter from Dury to Hartlib August 1646 (Turnbull: *Op. cit.* 363).
45. Letter from Colepeper to Hartlib Jan. 1646 (Turnbull *Op. cit.* 371).
46. Letter from Figulus to Hartlib July 1658 (Turnbull: *Op. cit.* 380).
47. K. Schaller: *Pan* p. 21 et seq. cf. *Republic* VII. 518.c.
48. *Via Lucis* XVI.11.
(b) *The Dynamics of Wisdom*
49. *Dilucidatio*.
50. *Prodromus* 7.
51. *Great Didactic* XVIII.2 cf. Bovet: J.A.C. p. 29.
52. *Via Lucis* II.3.
53. *Prodromus* 28. 46.
54. *Prodromus*: 41.
55. *Prodromus*: 12.
56. Letter from Hainhofer to Hartlib (Turnbull: *Op. cit.* 343).
57. *Via Lucis* IX.1.
58. *Prodromus*: 33.
59. *Prodromus*: 26.
60. *Diatyposis*: *Orthographia* 15.

61. *De Bono Unitatis.*
62. *Via Lucis*: Dedication 12.
63. *Via Lucis*: II.4.
64. *Via Lucis*: IX.1.
65. *Prodromus* 28-46.
66. Peter Balling: *The Light on the Candlestick* (Rufus Jones: *Spiritual Reformers* p. 128-9).
67. *Via Lucis* I.11.
68. Spinoza: *Ethics* Prop. 14.
69. cf. J. C. Flugel: *Psycho-analytical Study of the Family* (1921).
70. Keatinge: *Op. cit.* 45.
71. *Prodromus* 48.
72. *Pansophia* Bk. IV.1.
73. *Great Didactic*: V.1.
74. K. Schaller: *Pan.* 61.
75. Pfeiffer: *Meister Eckhart* (1857) p. 181. Quoted by R. Jones: *Mystical Religion* p. 231.
76. cf. Truchlivý (*The Afflicted*).
77. *Pansophia* Bk. V. Intro.
78. *Pampaedia* II.20.
79. *Lexicon Reale.*
80. *Pansophia* Bk. V. (Ch. III and VII).
81. *Pampaedia* III.27.
82. cf. Heidelberg Thesis: 'Artis Fundamenta in Natura quaerenda' cf. P. Bovet: *J.A.C.* p. 4 cf. *Prodromus* 60.
83. *Great Didactic* XXIV.18.
84. *Pansophia* Bk. V. Ch. IV-V.
85. Karl Brunner: *The Divine Imperative* p. 346.
86. *Labyrinth* VIII.
87. *Pansophia* Bk. VIII Intro. 1.
(c) *The Parallelism of Wisdom*
88. J. D. Bernal: *Acta Comeniana* (1959.2) p. 67.
89. J. Piaget: *Introduction to Selections* p. 15.
90. V. Příhoda: 'The Psychology of Comenius' – *Acta Comeniana* (1958.1)
91. Quoted by Bertrand Russell: *Hist. of Western Philosophy* p. 821.
92. *Diatyposis* 16.
93. G. H. Turnbull: 'Pansophiae Diatyposis' – *Acta Comeniana* (1957.2).
94. *Prodromus* 39.
95. *Prodromus* 65-66.
96. *Prodromus* 46.
97. *Prodromus* 69.
98. *Diatyposis* 45.
99. *Great Didactic* XX.8.
100. *Diatyposis* 55.
101. G. H. Turnbull: *Acta Comeniana* (1957.2) p. 121.
102. *Via Lucis* I.11.
103. *Via Lucis* XVI.9.
104. *Via Lucis* XVI.14.
105. *Prodromus* 57.
106. *Prodromus* 27.74 *Diatyposis* 42.
107. *Diatyposis* 42 (Napier published his work on Logarithms in 1614).
108. *Via Lucis* XVI.12.

J. A. COMENIUS

109. cf. *Pansophia* Bk. 111. E. *Scholasticis Labyrinthis* (ODO. IV 63-76), *Triertium Catholicum* and *Ventilabrium Sapientiae*.
110. *Prodromus* 64.
111. *Panaugia*.
112. *Great Didactic* XVII.38.
113. A. Koestler: *The Act of Creation* (1964).
114. C. Burt: *Brit. Journal of Educ. Psych* (1962) p. 292.
115. cf. J. Kyrášek: *Syncritical Method of J.A.C.* (1964).
116. *Panorthosia* VIII.
117. *Via Lucis* XVI.10.
118. *Pampaedia* I.15.

CHAPTER 7

LANGUAGE

THE objective of pansophical wisdom was 'that the entire Youth of both sexes' should become learned 'in all things necessary quickly, pleasantly and thoroughly'. This aim required an efficient instrument in language and Comenius was well aware that this was the heart of his problem. The need for speed seemed to determine the choice of language because 'to attempt to teach a foreign language before the mother-tongue has been learned is as irrational as to teach a boy to ride before he can walk'.[1] If knowledge of a foreign language is required in order to have access to learning it must be taught in as natural a way as possible through first-hand experience because 'it is as impossible to talk sensibly about matters with which we are not acquainted as it is for a virgin to bring forth a child'.[2] But it may be that 'thoroughness' of learning requires the devising of a language in which there shall be perfect parallelism between word and thing so that ambiguity is impossible, and this would be 'the most beautiful instrument for illustrating the wisdom of God'.[3]

The rise of vernacular languages in seventeenth century Europe was partly due to the new sense of national cohesion in some countries and partly to the revolt against scholasticism and verbal learning. In fact the conservative forces prevented any radical change in education and the grammar schools continued in the old tradition but Comenius reflected in his suggestions a considerable body of opinion. Most of the Humanist teachers despised vernacular language and tried to prohibit it in conversation but in England and the Low Countries the advantage of using the vernacular as a basis for Latin was generally recognized.[4] Ludovic Vives took a stronger line and spoke of the teacher as a 'Prefect of the Treasury of his mother-tongue'. The two arguments may be illustrated from the work of Richard Mulcaster and Hezikiah Woodward. Mulcaster, writing in 1582, maintained that to teach Latin without a foundation of the vernacular was 'hardly any good, the groundwork being so rotten'.[5] Woodward, nearly sixty years later in 1641, gave another reason for making the mother tongue 'the foundation of all'. Instead of Latin he concentrated on sense-experience – 'the child goes on with ease and delight when the understanding and the tongue are drawn along parallel lines, one not a jot before the other'.[6] In France the Jansenists went further than making the vernacular the initial means of approach to Latin by their belief that it could become an independent source of culture. The Little Schools of Port Royal had, indeed, a short life (1646-1660) owing to the opposition of the Jesuits but their teachers continued to put forward the view that the vernacular could be rescued from barbarity and given sufficient clarity to serve the purposes of learning as well as social intercourse. Coustel, writing in 1687 after the death of Comenius, said: 'Considering the point of perfection which our language has reached, it surely deserves that we should cultivate it a little. It would be shameful for children to be barbarians in their own country'.[7] The possibilities of German national unity were foreseen by Wolfgang Ratke and he proposed that all German children should have an education in their own language up to University level: 'Now the right practice and course of nature is that the dear youth should first learn to read, write and speak their inherited mother-tongue'.[8] Ratke failed but his ideas were taken up by Duke Ernest the Pious (1601-1675) in the state of Gotha until it became a byword that his peasants were better educated than noblemen elsewhere. The programme put forward by Andreas Reyher in 1642 showed the potentialities of national education based on sense-experience.[9]

Comenius reflected, and indeed pioneered, all these aspects of the use of the vernacular. From the beginning of his career he was fired with the desire to make the Czech language a vehicle for universal knowledge and for expressing the most profound truths in a form that common people could understand and yet in a style as elegant as the classics. The *Theatre of the Universe of Things* which he began at Herborn had a Preface in Czech and at the same time he started on a *Treasury of the Bohemian*

Language. Thus the 'complete picture of the universe' was accompanied by a collection of words, idioms and proverbs and continued until both were involved in the fire of Leszno. Especially during the period of hiding (1621-1628) Comenius used the Czech language in his bid to sustain the faith of his Church. He wrote to comfort distracted women,[10] translated the Psalms into classical metres, and put forward the arguments of faith to all the 'Afflicted'. A. Skarka fixes a date between 1623 and 1626 for the composition of a work on Czech poetry in which he tried to prove 'the exceptional aptitude of the language for poetry' in comparison with the Germanic and Romance languages.[11] Comenius followed Hus and Blahoslav in regarding language as a means of ideological revolution or, at least, of survival. The ruthlessness with which the Hapsburgs endeavoured to stamp it out for nearly two centuries afterwards shows their appreciation of its potentiality but for Comenius it was a potent instrument of faith. He solemnly charged his countrymen 'to purify, cultivate and ennoble' their native language.[12] He recognized that language is more than a manipulative device of social communication in that it has emotional functions by which the individual expresses his sense of belongingness and that it plays an important part in giving a sense of historical continuity through the emotive associations of words and phrases. Consequently, when he found himself in exile he appointed himself a guardian of the language and thus gained the everlasting gratitude of his countrymen. He made collections of Czech proverbs and antiquities[13] but his chief contribution to the hoped-for national revival was through his educational books. *The Brief Proposal for the Renewal of Schools in the Czech Kingdom* had a solid basis in the Didactic works which he hoped would establish a Bohemian Paradise.

Pansophy grew out of concern for the language and culture of a small national group but of a group that had established a unique literary tradition since the Hussite movement broke away from the Latin influence of the Middle Ages.[14] In turning from Czech to Latin as his medium Comenius was not rejecting his native language but accepting the situation that he could not communicate with mankind as a whole in any other way. His belief was that a vernacular could, and should, be made adequate for every purpose and if it were 'obscure, or insufficient to express necessary ideas' the fault would be 'not of the language but of those who use it'.[15] Comenius quotes with approval a Dutch mathematician and inspector of dams, Simon Stevin, who died in 1633, who said that technical terms could always be constructed out of native words without having resource to Latin or Greek but, on the other hand, he strongly disagreed with his old master, John Henry Alsted, who argued that only those 'destined for manual labour' should devote their time to the vernacular. For all children the only justification for learning Latin must be strictly utilitarian as it is expressed by Ludovic Vives: 'Since language is the instrument of human society and the treasure house of learning, it is essential to the welfare of men that there should be one single language which all people should use'.[16] Comenius looked forward to that 'most delightful' prophecy of Claudian that thanks to the genius of Rome 'the guest might be at home in whatever region he travels'.[17] He therefore admits that 'if another language cannot be found, Latin should be assigned to this purpose' so that all people would be bi-lingual, with a language of the home and neighbourhood and a *lingua franca* for travel and communication. However, his speculations began 'to take a higher flight' in recommending an entirely new language.[18] He gives a number of reasons for rejecting Latin despite the very strong arguments in favour of it. Latin is not known to uncivilized people at all and this would place them at a disadvantage especially as it has so many irregularities and anomalies. It is poor in composite words for which it has to borrow from the Greek. However, the chief defect of Latin is that there is no parallelism between things and words although in this it has 'as little felicity as other languages'. One point which Comenius does not mention is that he, as a Czech, did not have the advantage of Descartes or Hobbes of a mother-tongue already a major European language. He could hardly have foreseen that, even for the learned, Latin would soon lose its supremacy for international use and that, in fact, he himself would be one of the last Europeans to use it.

Nevertheless it was in England, whose language was eventually to gain world-wide currency, that the idea of an artificial international language was given most attention. Amongst the

Hartlib group were a number of men who saw the possibility of a language based on mathematical symbols. John Pell wrote his *Idea of Mathematics* soon after 1630 and there was some correspondence with Marin Mersenne, the French mathematician, on the advantage of an artificial language as a system of numerical signs as opposed to a 'natural language'.[19] Joachim Hübner acted as go-between in the negotiations for Comenius to go to France and he had 'much speech with Mersenne on pansophic matters'. Rene Descartes was another Frenchman who corresponded with the Hartlib group and who shared with Mersenne the ideal of bringing mathematical exactness into the language of philosophy. Thus Hartlib, writing in 1634, speaks of 'the excellency of Descartes' being especially in mathematics and that he has a 'new algebra by plus and minus to discover truths by falsehoods'[20] while Comenius records his four-hour interview with him at Leyden in October 1642 in which Descartes 'expounded the mysteries of his philosophy'. They parted 'in friendly fashion'.[21] However, for about forty years, England became the centre of the endeavour to find an artificial language. Comenius was very impressed with the popularity of shorthand 'even among country folk' by which a 'large number of men and youths copied out sermons . . . using symbols to signify whole words'.[22] In 1641 John Wilkins published a work entitled 'Mercury or the Secret Messenger' in which he discussed the possibilities of a secret language for commercial use and Comenius, writing at the same time, speaks of a 'Mercury, or messenger, who must make his way among all nations alike' but demands that it should be 'affable and easy to all'.[23] In 1653 Thomas Urquhart of Cromarty published an *Introduction to the Universal Language* in which he put forward the possibility that each letter could be made to correspond with a well-defined characteristic so that any particular thing could be designated by its properties. Four years later, in 1657, George Dalgarno wrote a book entitled *Universal Character and a new Rational Language* and sent a copy to Samuel Hartlib. A copy must also have been sent to Comenius in Amsterdam, for in January 1658 he wrote to Hartlib that 'Dalgarno's inventions' could be considered wonderful ('if they last').[24] The book was published in 1661 under the title *The Art of Signs (Ars Signorum)*. Dalgarno firmly believed that human ingenuity could overcome all the anomalies and confusions that bedevil natural languages – 'by cutting off all redundancy, rectifying all anomalies, taking away all ambiguity . . . contracting the primitives (primary words) to a few number, and even those to be of a rational institution'. He shared with Comenius the dream of bringing philosophy itself under control, 'not only to remedy the confusion of language, but also to cure even philosophy of the disease of Sophisms, etc.'. Essentially the system proposed was to make a classification of 'notions' each represented by a consonant and then to subdivide into sub-groups by vowels and consonants alternately. The following specimen of the new language will illustrate the structure: '*Dam semu Sava samesa Nam tyn Nom*=In the beginning God created the heaven and the earth'.[25]

Just before this, in November 1660, the informal 'Invisible College' which had been meeting at Oxford and London since 1645 organized itself on a permanent basis and began to hold weekly meetings at Gresham College. From the beginning the members had been interested in a universal language and a Committee recommended to the King, in 1664, that Dalgarno's new language might 'facilitate communication between people of different languages, advance all parts of Real and Useful knowledge, civilize barbarous nations, and propagate the Gospel'.[26] It is clear that they regarded a universal language as coming within the aims of their constitution: 'To improve the knowledge of naturall things, and all useful Arts, Manufactures, Mechanic practices, Engynes and Inventions by experiment . . . but 'not meddling with Divinity, Metaphysicks, Morals, Politics, Grammar, Rhetorick or Logicks'.[27]

Some members of the Royal Society wanted to improve on Dalgarno's system and probably at the instigation of Seth Ward, Bishop of Salisbury, John Wilkins wrote his *Essay towards a Real Character and Philosophical Language* which was published in 1668.

Comenius was not able to read Wilkins' book but his correspondence shows that he followed the preparatory work of the author with keen interest.[28] He must have had it in his mind when he sent the *Via Lucis* to London dedicated to the 'Torch Bearers of the Enlightened Age, Members of the Royal Society, now bringing real philosophy to a happy birth'. It was a pity that Wilkins did not realize the great contribution which English could have made to a universal language through its lack of inflexion but nevertheless his system was an ingenious one. He proposed that every thing and every notion should be assigned a distinct mark or symbol with provision for indicating inflexion. Thus each thing would have a 'real character' not simply a word to signify it. He judged that about 2,000 symbols would be enough to express the really essential classes but he made no provision for any expansion of the system to include new knowledge.

THE PHILOSOPHY OF LANGUAGE

Comenius was deeply concerned with the search for a universal language because he realized how much his pansophic dreams depended on it. But his approach to the problem was both wider and deeper than that of the Royal Society. Their point of view had changed somewhat since the days of the Hartlib group. Hartlib himself was dead (1662) and even the strictly utilitarian aim of their constitution soon gave way to a dilettante approach far removed from industrial arts and crafts.[29] Comenius gives a hint of this in the Dedicatory Letter of the *Via Lucis* and it would seem that in return for royal patronage (or at least acquiescence) the Society dropped off those elements of the pansophic scheme concerned with education, politics and religion. J. D. Bernal has suggested that Comenius did not realize 'the power and persuasiveness of the individualism which was characteristic of nascent capitalism'.[30] Robert Boyle, indeed, was a kindred spirit whose 'charity was so extensive that it reached unto everything called man'[31] but for others a narrower aim sufficed to discover a means by which written communication amongst scholars might be facilitated.

For Comenius language reform was only a means to a universal end. It was 'Ariadne's thread to lead mankind out of the labyrinth' as he wrote to the Amsterdam printer, Montanus.[32] It was the means by which the 'morning glow of the new age', almost snuffed out by war, might be restored. A language so plain that it could act as intermediary between individuals and peoples seemed to Comenius the essential instrument by which the Angel of Peace could bring concord[33] while the expansion of trade to unknown lands beyond the seas would only be justified if the barbarous people could be converted through a word of truth they could readily understand.

Consequently Comenius insisted that the new language must be simple – 'ten times easier than Latin . . . and a hundred times more perfect' and he rejected any suggestion of a 'language for the learned different from that for ordinary and common use'.[34] Nevertheless he demanded that language should have a philosophical basis such as was not given by the schemes of Dalgarno or Wilkins. This lack of a philosophical foundation was criticized by Leibniz later on and he was influenced in this by Comenius and it may be that they were both following a will-o-the-wisp in this matter. But, at least, they realized that language is more than a system of signs and this position is held by modern linguistic scholars. Thus Louis Hjelmslev says that a sign-system is 'only concerned with the external functions of language . . . but not with its proper internal functions' and adds, 'Linguistic theory is led by an inner necessity to recognize, not merely the linguistic system in its schema and in its usage . . . but also all man's sphere of knowledge and human society behind language'.[35] Speech, according to Malinowski, is 'never detached from the situation in which it is uttered',[36] and for that reason any attempt to revive a dead language, such as Latin, for common use is bound to fail. The American linguist, B. L. Whorf, points out how profoundly our outlook on life is determined by the linguistic framework of our environment and our deepest attitudes are conditioned by the particular form of language we use 'even while we think ourselves most free'.[37] The definition which Comenius gives of a 'perfect language' shows some awareness of the deeper problem. In the Panglottia Comenius thus defines his idea of the perfect language, though he agrees that only amongst the angels could speech be really perfect: 'It is firstly, an extension of the world in its totality, secondly, an equal richness of the mind whose concepts it communicates to others, and thirdly, a regularity, like musical harmony, by which it establishes between things and concepts and between concepts and words a context in which it is possible to conceive things as they are and to express them as they are conceived'.[38]

Comenius wanted something more than a computer for translating words into signs with no bond between them and therefore he saw the vernacular as the primary tool of language which he begged 'the learned men of all nations to cherish and develop'.[39] If this were done each national language would have enough words to express all things and ideas, the words would be unambiguous, and the grammar clear and adequate.[40]

Throughout his life Comenius gave his attention to the problems of language but certain works have special significance. Towards the close of 1648, and after six years of work, he produced the *New Method of Languages* (*Linguarum Methodus Novissima*) usually known as the *Methodus*. Although it was chiefly concerned with Latin the author claimed on the title-page that it could be adapted 'with great profit, to other languages' and in the Preface he defined his field of reference as covering the origin, nature and development of language in general before he could deal with the question of method. In fact, he gave nearly two-thirds of the book to such philosophical bases and discussed more than forty great Renaissance scholars whose works he had utilized. There have been three Czech translations – one by Fr J. Zoubek in 1874, one by J. Šmaha in 1892 and the most recent in 1964 with an Introduction on the Philosophical Significance by Dr Jirina Popelová. Dr Popelová speaks of the *Methodus* as a junction of the main lines of Comenius' thinking and certainly it forecasts many of the ideas which he came to develop in the *Consultation*. Of the seven Books of the *Consultation* the one which deals specifically with language is the Fifth Part called the *Panglottia* (Universal Language) to which there is attached a First Attempt at a new Harmonic Language (the *Tentamen*). Professor Hendrich believes that it was the last of the seven Parts to be completed and dates it between 1665 and 1666. He was, therefore, working under the influence of the English language reformers, though he did not attempt, like Dalgarno and Wilkins, to devise a complete system but rather to give a new orientation to the whole problem. The third work which must be considered to have special significance for a philosophy of language is the *Lexicon of Things* (*Lexicon Reale*) which was found with the *Consultatio* in 1935 and was probably written between 1662 and 1665 as indicated in Comenius' letter to Montanus of December 1661. It was put together, after the death of the author, from a number of detached sheets and the Preface explains that it belongs to the first two volumes of the Pansophia.

Consideration of the philosophy of language raises two fundamental questions – the origin of language which is an historical and comparative study and the meaning of language which is metaphysical. As to the first Comenius was a very fair linguist with competence in German and Polish and a good knowledge of the classical languages but he lived before the day of comparative linguistics and accepted the Biblical account of the development of language. According to Genesis, language began with the naming of animals in the Garden of Eden and presumably with an extension of the naming process to all other parts of the external world. Accordingly there was a single original language which was brought to diversity (and confusion) as a punishment for the pride of the Tower of Babel. This multiplicity of tongues was further complicated by the passage of time and by the mixing of tribes and nations but nevertheless they all had something in common which a Pentecostal miracle could bring again into consciousness. Comenius believed that it was possible to prove the identity of the four European language groups – Greek, Romance, Germanic and Slavonic – and their common link with Hebrew as the primary language.[41] Apart from the linguistic evidence there were strong cultural arguments in the origin of Christianity and the links with Islam through Arabic and, in addition, the short verbal roots of Hebrew made it well suited for the development of new words and the long and careful preservation of its grammar by the rabbis seemed to have preserved it from the corruption of time. For Comenius there was a further philosophical reason in that the monosyllabic roots of Hebrew seemed to him to support the idea that once they had reflected the true nature of things. Though he did not claim that Hebrew was a 'natural language' it seemed to offer the best indication of such an ideal.[42]

Even Comenius recognized the difficulties of this monogenetic theory of language. He gives Hungarian as an example of a

European language which he says must be 'cognate with the languages of Asia, whence it came',[43] but he gives no explanation for these Asian languages although he was well aware of the antiquity of Chinese which did not even have an alphabet. He follows Bacon in assuming that there must be a parallelism between Chinese characters and the things they represented and speaks of them as 'mental characters which express not letters and words, but things and notions'.[44] His knowledge of Chinese probably came from his meeting with Jacob Golius, an Arabic scholar of Leyden, who in turn had profited from the experience of Jesuit missionaries from China.[45] He knew also of the work of the Jesuit, Athanasius Kircher, who in 1663 produced a new system of writing based on oriental languages.[46] However, the greatest difficulty was that the discoverers in America and the Far East were bringing back news of many peoples who seemed to have no connection with the Genesis story and who had developed languages that Comenius could only describe as 'barbarous' but who were yet 'part of the human race'.[47] However impressive the range of Indo-European languages might be there were too many exceptions to support a monogenetic theory, but, at least, Comenius showed his awareness of the need for a comparative study of languages as a basis for a universal language rather than a purely arbitrary system of signs. He favoured an empirical approach to the problem by combining the best features of a number of languages such as the short roots of Hebrew or German, the 'soft pronunciation of Latin, or the 'economy' of inflexion of English.[48] There were few people in the seventeenth century who could have contemplated jettisoning the whole apparatus of inflexion but Comenius did recognize the need for very much simplication. Thus he says: 'The Italians, in removing irregularities, may seem to have corrupted Latin: but they have at any rate achieved this result, that Arabs, Turks, Tartars and other barbarians are not indisposed to learn their language though it still suffers under a load of anomalies'.[49] In fact: 'Among existing languages there is hardly one so unhappy that it has no elegance which is proper to it . . . consequently one could not go wrong in selecting from one or other something superior to the others'.[50] It is, therefore, clear that Comenius took the view that language is like an organism rooted in evolution or a tissue of interlacing elements which cannot be separated from each other. From this fact he derived certain principles for devising a universal language. Thus he says: 'It is necessary to observe above everything that the roots must be monosyllabic. We must distribute the first and simple roots among the syllables'.[51] Then he was impressed by the onomatopoeic quality of roots in many languages and he thought this parallelism between sound and thing could be extended to particular letters. Thus if K could be taken to signify gross size and U immobility then KU might stand for the earth and from such simple bases a new language could 'grow completely from its roots without taking in anything else' and at the same time each word would also act as a definition.[52] If every element in a word could have some significance 'from the smallest to the greatest then the number of roots would be small (Comenius suggests 200 to 300) and they would be easy to understand because of their 'natural' sound yet capable of easy formation into compounds. At first, Comenius shared the opinion of most people in his time that roots should be substantives and this was in line with his insistence that every 'thing' must have a name, and that the number of things, distinguished by form from each other, must tally with that of words; no more and no less'.[53] However, in the *Tentamen* he changes his ground somewhat by admitting that substantives could be given the impress of the temporal thus allowing for flexibility within the framework of things. It may be that he was alive to what Malinowski calls 'the sliding of roots and meanings from one grammatical category to another'. Comenius also found it hard to escape from the conviction that grammar and syntax were basically determined by logic and that all would be well if the anomalies and irregularities could be removed and he could hardly have accepted the stricture of Professor Brunot concerning Latin grammar books: 'Incomprehensible abstractions, pretentious yet for the most part empty definitions, false rules, indigestible lists of forms – one has only to turn over the pages of any textbook to find variegated specimens of these sins against reason and truth'.[54] Comenius did, indeed, devote many wasted hours to the task of reducing grammar to logical rules but he renounced this in his scheme for a universal language because he wanted its regularity to be a reflection of the harmony of the universe itself and in particular of the human mind – it should be 'a language which corresponds by the quality of its structure to the structure of the concepts of the mind and which serves in consequence as an exact vehicle for conveying mental notions from one mind to another'.[55]

The fundamental philosophical question which Comenius faced was concerned with the meaning of meaning. Language, which should be an instrument for the transmission of ideas, seemed often to be an iron curtain so that 'men commonly do not speak but babble: that is, they transmit, not as from mind to mind things or the sense of things, but words not understood or ill understood'.[56] Until the problem of meaning could be solved Comenius saw no hope of using that peculiarly human faculty of speech as 'a perfectly open way for teaching all necessary things to all men'.[57] Nor could any progress be made if scholars used words without any clear concept of their meaning which would be instantly recognized by others so that there was no confusion between them. It seemed to Comenius inconceivable that speech, the invention of rational man, should be completely arbitrary and irrational and therefore it must be presumed that the original perfection had somehow become corrupted but that reform was feasible.

For this corruption Comenius is inclined to blame the affectations of the learned more than the simplicity of the common folk. Thus rhetorical ornament, which satisfies man's desire 'not only for truth but also for beauty', is dangerous when it leads to a change of the 'notions'.[58] Words that 'have become blurred' form a barrier between the mind and reality, but the chief evil is 'the astounding confusion of homonyms, synonyms and paronyms' and 'the shifting meaning of idiomatic expressions'.[59] Comenius feels that well-educated people are specially prone to use words which are divorced from 'the inner constitution of the things' so that 'when in conversation they name God, Angel, Man, Satan, Law, Sin, Virtue, Vice and the like, yea in speaking of that which hath body such as Light, darkness, wine, water, wind and the like . . . they know not the essence of what they name'.[60] This blurring of meaning is the most obvious evil of language but Comenius complains also of the 'enormous number of exceptions' in grammar which he thinks could easily be cured by rational examination, leading to a complete nomenclature of things, a complete consent as to meaning and a complete system of grammatical rules.

A number of objections can be made to such facile optimism. Firstly Comenius greatly over-estimated the accuracy of observation through the senses but especially visual observation. Thus he contrasts hearsay evidence with eye-witness which Plautus says is ten times better and concludes: 'He who has carefully observed a real elephant knows for a certainty what sort of creature it is, and no one can deceive him'.[61] Secondly he over-estimated the rationality of man. Even such a thing as inflexion is much less systematic than it appears and the impression of system comes from the way in which we learn. E. P. Morris says on this point: 'A glance at the facts of Latin morphology furnishes convincing evidence that irregularity and absence of system are not merely occasional, but are the fundamental characteristics of Latin form-building'.[62] Thirdly he over-estimated the importance of the 'word' as opposed to the 'sentence'. As a translator Comenius did not make this mistake and the *Didactica Magna* is not a literal rendering of the Czech *Didakitka* nor was he unaware of the 'loading' effect of context on meaning. But this would seem to invalidate the argument that each word should correspond with a thing 'in such a way that it is impossible to attribute it to another thing'.[63] In this he is at variance with modern linguistic theory that language is 'always and everywhere a system of arbitrary symbols'.[64]

The idea that language in its pure state has an exact relationship of word and thing was not invented by Comenius nor was the possibility of constructing a perfectly logical language. The first goes back to the *Cratylus* of Plato while the second was a common dream of seventeenth century philosophers from Bacon to Descartes.[65] Nor need his plans for language reform be dismissed as a wild-goose chase for there is a subtle bond between word and thing which is due not to onomatopeia but to association. Throughout the ages men have ascribed occult powers to particular words so that they have become sacred or obscene. A rose by any other name would take some time to smell as sweet or as Yeats puts it: 'All sounds evoke indefinable and yet precise emotions . . . or, as I prefer to think, call down among us certain disembodied powers whose footsteps over our hearts we call emotions'.[66] But this extreme flexibility by which every lover makes his own language and every mother communicates with her child may only be feasible with the native speech which has become part of the mind itself. Ogden and Richards have shown how inadequate is a definition of language simply as a system of conventional signs because words only have 'meaning' when they form an act of reference to the user and listener alike; otherwise they are nothing but reverberations in the air.[67] However, a great deal of communication has to be beyond the level of a 'family language' and it was for this purpose that Comenius asked for a constructed speech as an 'algebra of thought' which would be free from the ambiguities of any existing language and yet would make use of the best features of all. That he recognized the dimensions of the problem is indicated by the following words: 'A perfect language, if one might hope to realize it, can only be hoped for from Pansophy (Universal Knowledge) and Pampaedia (Universal Education).

The first requirement meant that where there was no natural connection between word and thing an artificial one must be made which would eventually become natural by association. Thus Comenius suggests that the letter 'l' might be expressive of a soft thing, while 'm' might indicate haziness. Vowels could symbolize certain concepts such as 'a' for separation, 'e' for defect, 'i' for diminution, 'o' for excess, and 'u' for increase.[68] Thus there could be built up a nomenclature for each field of knowledge (as has, in fact, been done in chemistry) and this has good possibilities but within a narrow range of meaning. But such a system would not give the total essence of a thing, only its essence in one particular respect, and beyond that no system could cover all the characteristics of any one thing in every situation.

As for the second requirement Comenius attached very much importance to a 'complete and universal lexicon fixing the significance of all the sounds of human speech . . . and a complete description of things'.[69] He composed this *Lexicon of Things* by putting down words as they occurred to him and then defining them as occasion demanded in such a way as to show their 'essence'. Throughout his life Comenius was trying to define abstract concepts and, as Ogden and Richards say, 'there is no harm and much service in this linguistic machinery'.[70] The charge that it simply results in circumlocution would apply equally to any modern dictionary of psychology or a Thesaurus of words and phrases[71] and the difficulties of linguistic interpretation are faced by A. J. Ayer in his Preface to the Second Edition of *Language, Truth and Logic* (1946). At least Comenius was aware that he was trying to define a 'thing' and not the word which symbolizes it, the noumenal meaning of the 'thing in itself' and not the phenomenal meaning of its observed qualities.

THE MECHANISM OF LANGUAGE

For Comenius language was not fundamentally a philosophical question but an educational one – at least it was only philosophical in so far as it depended upon the proposition that nature is the creator of forms, which, being reflected in the human mind, make the ordering of the educative process automatic. Human nature is part of the Common nature and therefore the key to the development of a universal language must be sought in the spontaneous development of language in the infant.

Thus it is clear that speech begins with vocal symbols and not with writing and furthermore that these symbols at first convey feeling rather than information or communication of thought. Comenius places much emphasis on this first 'babbling' stage by which rapport is established because it provides the basis for the whole structure of rhetoric with gestures, rhythm and alliteration.[72] It was because the vernacular had so many homely associations with the situations of infancy that it must be the medium for arousing emotion in the adult which must be accepted as a proper and legitimate function of religion. That, according to Comenius, ordinands for the Brethren's ministry could seldom go through the service without tears[73] was evidence of the strength of their infant experience where 'the home was as a church with prayers, singing and reading every morning'. Thus language is not simply a means of need reduction, as some psychologists seem to assume, but also a recognition of cues by suitable responses.

Nevertheless Comenius says that, as soon as the child's tongue becomes more supple, baby talk should be left behind and he passes on to the 'naming' stage.[74] He is quite clear on the interdependence of sense experience and language learning: 'Words should not be learnt apart from objects . . . but objects cannot be apprehended without words'.[75] When Comenius says that the starting point of language is in metaphysics it is not abstractions that he is thinking of, but rather general concepts such as 'something, nothing, where, when, like, unlike, etc.'.[76] Thus 'children see, hear, taste, and touch, but are ignorant of the exact object of their sensations . . . they commence, therefore, by learning the general concepts'.[77] Their perception might be described as syncritistic because it goes from the whole to the part. It could be said that the fundamental factor in the first stages of perception is not so much the association of one thing with another as the dissociation of parts of an obscure total situation and that this is achieved by naming. The first major concepts are, in fact, metaphysical fields – spatial, causal and temporal – and 'the mother-tongue is intimately concerned with the gradual unfolding of the objective world' through all the subjects that will later become the school curriculum. Comenius mentions particularly the need that thought should be internalized action and that the word gains meaning when it is acted out while the experience is heightened by association with the word. There is, indeed, a quite surprising similarity between the account of language development in Chapter XVIII of the *Great Didactic* and in the *School of Infancy* and the results of Piaget's experiments with children.[78] Many examples of this could be given – 'speech is a special kind of action' – 'I maintain that a baby immediately in its first or second year is able to understand what a wrinkled and an unwrinkled forehead means' – 'the child should not do anything that cannot be named'. At the same time the child needs to learn to listen as well as to speak and Comenius speaks much of the need for 'prescriptions' which should be brief, clear and certain and for continual verbal contact between mother and child which modern research confirms to be so necessary.[79]

Comenius viewed school education as simply an extension of home education but both are closely concerned with language development. The Activity School would have little point without the accompaniment of speech. The dice games he suggests for little children are for sounds and words.[80] The *Orbis Pictus* and Bible stories should be given to children by the age of six so that they can localize words and before they start in the Vernacular school they should be 'gathered in circles' around 'honest women' in a kind of Reception Class.[81]

As for the Vernacular School, as Comenius envisaged it in the *Great Didactic and the Pampaedia*, it may be thought of as a mirror of nature on the one side and of society on the other and, although he wants it to be a 'garden of delight', its purpose is very serious. 'We must not think that children are not able to take things seriously *but* in their own way'.[82] Children will be the successors of those who now build church and state and they can become conscious of this through literacy.[83] Klaus Schaller says of the mother-speech in school: 'It is not simply to be understood for the presumed realistic tendency but also for the first possibility of human organization and the ordering of men in the presence and service of God'.[84] It is clear that oral language is the aim and object of the Vernacular school since speech is 'the painted picture of the world'[85] and the school should create an atmosphere of 'oracy'.[86] At the same time Comenius firmly held that the school must be supported by a society where literacy is highly prized and in the seventeenth century this meant a society, where, in the words of Charles I of England, 'People are governed by the pulpit more than the sword'.[87] Comenius believed that a 'climate of literacy' was essential for national democracy or world government and that it would be a waste of time to return children from school into a 'stubbornly uncultural society'.[88] He believed also that language was itself a means of refining thought processes through metaphors and idiomatic phrases especially in the intimate conversation of friends and he himself was an ardent collector of such figures of speech in his own language. He was also keenly aware of the cultural value of linguistic study and may be counted one of the greatest Czech linguists.[89]

The acquisition of other languages beyond the vernacular

could, in the opinion of Comenius, only be justified on grounds of utility and should not take up time which could be better spent on more realistic knowledge.[90] The best way would be 'to send children at the age of ten or twelve to the country concerned' where they should be taught from text-books parallel to those with which they were already familiar.[91] The chief need, however, was for an international language which would go beyond the *lingua franca* of the market-place to the 'communication of the inner imaginations'.[92] Although in the end Comenius rejected Latin for this purpose he always maintained that the difficulties were exaggerated by bad teaching and that it could, with proper teaching, become a 'mediator' between languages. Indeed, if every nation took the same Latin text as the basis for its school books it could become a guide for the cultivation of each vernacular with the great advantage of preserving the common framework of European civilization. He agrees that 'a complete and detailed knowledge' of Latin is unnecessary but that it could become an alternative medium of thinking if colleges could be established where it was used for the 'commonest tasks of life'.[93] Thus the Pansophic school might be a 'Latin community' of which the ultimate purpose would be to make the scholars genuinely bi-lingual and this did not seem an impossible ideal.

However, bilingualism, though desirable for communication, is not an end in itself. Language has a higher function in universal education in the development of personality.

NOTES

1. *Great Didactic* XXIX.4.
2. *Great Didactic* XXX.5.
3. *Via Lucis* XIX.17.
4. W. H. Woodward: *Education in the Age of the Renaissance* p. 157.
5. R. Mulcaster: *Positions* 1.
6. Hezekiah Woodward: *The Child's Portion* (1640) cf. *A Light to Grammar and a Gate to Science* (1641).
7. Coustel: *Rules for the Education of Children.* Quoted by H. C. Barnard: *The Little Schools of Port Royal* p. 119.
8. Wolfgang Ratke: *Memorial* (1612).

9. Andreas Reyher: *School Method* . . . showing how the Children of this Principality . . . can and shall be plainly and successfully taught (1642).
10. cf. *The Name of the Lord is a High Tower* (1622).
11. Jan Patočka: *Present State of Comenian Studies* (Historia 1959) p. 199.
12. *Bequest*: XIX.
13. Jan Jakubek: J.A.C. (1928).
14. Josef Hrabák: *Acta Comeniana* (1959.2) p. 11-23.
15. *Great Didactic* XXIX.14.
16. *Great Didactic* XXIX.1. 12 L. Vives: *De Tradendis Disciplinis*. III.
17. *Via Lucis* XIX.7.
18. *Via Lucis* XIX.9.
19. Mersenne: *Questiones ad Genesim*.
20. G. H. Turnbull: *Hartlib, Dury and Comenius*. p. 167 from Hartlib's *Ephemerides* for 1635.
21. *Continuatio* 59.
22. Patera: *Korres*. XXXII Quoted by R. F. Young: *Comenius in England* 65.
23. *Via Lucis* XIX.8. cf. V. T. Miškovská: *Communio Viatorum* 1959.IV.
24. G. H. Turnbull: *Op. cit.* p. 106. 378.
25. George Dalgarno: *Ars Signorum, vulgo Character universalis et Lingua Philosophica* (1661) Appendix.
26. Quoted by F. Bodmer: *The Loom of Language* p. 445.
27. Hoole: Draft Preamble to Statutes of Royal Society (1663).
28. V. T. Miškovská: *Philosophy* (London July 1962) p. 238.
The Philosophy of Language
29. Christopher Hill: *Century of Revolution* p. 238.
30. J. D. Bernal: *Acta Comeniana* (1959.2) p. 75.
31. Robert Boyle: *Works* I.20 cf. J. B. Čapek: *Archiv pro Badani* XXI. 1962.
32. Patera: *Korres*. 1892. CCX.
33. cf. *Angel of Peace* (1667).
34. *Via Lucis* XIX.8.
35. Louis Hjelmslev: *Prolegomena to Theory of Language* (1953) p. 7.
36. Quoted by Simeon Potter: *Language in the Modern World* p. 137.
37. B. L. Whorf: *Metalinguistics* (1952) p. 5.
38. *Panglottia*: III.6.
39. *Methodus*: XXVIII.
40. *Methodus*: V.
41. *Methodus*: III.
42. *Methodus*: IV.
43. *Methodus*: III.
44. *Methodus*: III cf. F. Bacon: *De Dignitate et Augmentis Scientarium* VI.1.3.
45. V. T. Miškovská: *Communio Viatorum* (1959, IV) p. 340.
46. A. Kircher: *Polygraphia Nova et Universalis* (1663) cf. Kvačala: *Korres*: (1898.1) CCLXVII p. 318.
47. *Pampaedia* II.10.
48. *Panglottia* VII.3.
49. *Via Lucis*: XIX.10.
50. *Panglottia* VII.2.
51. *Panglottia Tentamen* II.
52. *Panglottia* VIII.

LANGUAGE

53. *Panglottia* VIII.
54. Brunot: *L'Enseignement de la Langue* p. 3 Quoted by Ogden and Richards: *Meaning of Meaning* p. 232.
55. *Panglottia* VI.15.
56. *Continuatio* 44.
57. *Via Lucis* XVI.8.
58. *Methodus* XVI.
59. *Methodus* V.46. *Analytical Didactic*: 108.
60. *Continuatio* 44.
61. *Analytical Didactic* 54.
62. E. P. Morris: *Principles and Methods of Latin Syntax*. Quoted by F. Bodmer op. cit. p. 317.
63. *Panglottia*: *Tentamen* 3.
64. Simeon Potter: *Language in the Modern World* p. 52.
65. cf. F. Bacon: *Novum Organum* Bk. I.56-61.
66. Quoted by Ogden and Richards: *Op. cit.* p. 45.
67. Ogden and Richards: *Op. cit.* p. 205.
68. *Panglottia* cf. V. T. Miškovská: *Philosophy* (London 1962) p. 240.
69. *Panglottia* III.8.
70. Ogden and Richards: *Op. cit.* p. 109.
71. cf. Drever's *Dictionary of Psychology*. Roget's *Thesaurus*.
The Mechanism of Language
72. *Informatorium* VIII.
73. Seifferth: *Church Constitution of Brethren* p. 189.
74. *Informatorium* VIII.
75. *Great Didactic* XXII.4.
76. *Great Didactic* XXVIII.2.
77. *Great Didactic* XXVIII.2.
78. cf. Jean Piaget: *Language and Thought of the Child* p. 132-145 and *Construction of Reality in the Child*.
79. cf. John Bowlby: *Maternal Care and Mental Health* 1952.
80. *Pampaedia* IX citing Saavedra.
81. *Pampaedia* IX cf. Plato: *Republic* II. 377.
82. *Pampaedia* X.
83. *Pampaedia* X.
84. Klaus Schaller: *Die Pädagogik des J.A.C.* cf. H. Geissler: *Comenius und die Sprache*: Conclusion.
85. *Panglottia* III.3.
86. A Wilkinson: *Spoken English* (1965)
87. C. Hill: *Op. cit.* p. 77.
88. Simeon Potter: *Op. cit.* p. 187.
89. V. Skalička: *Acta Comeniana* (1959-2).
90. *Great Didactic* XXII.10.
91. *Great Didactic* XXIX.19.
92. *Pampaedia* XI.16.
93. *Methodus* XIX.

CHAPTER 8

REFORM

THE outstanding characteristic of Comenius was insuperable optimism concerning human affairs. The blacker he painted the picture of the present the brighter became his vision of the future and his confidence, though at times naïve, was based on the conviction that human corruption was only superficial. Essentially man was the image of God and all that was necessary was a return to the place from which he had lost his way.[1] Reform could be immediate; there need not be any waiting for the slow grinding of the mills of God; nor was it sensible to tinker with a system that could be radically altered; nor could the saints look for a safe retreat in heaven where all tears would be wiped away. But it was necessary for all men to 'hear the whisper of the gentle breeze, bidding them go forward to the mouth of Elijah's cave and hold colloquy with God about the restoration of the ruins'.[2] That troubles had so greatly increased was no reason for abandoning attempts – 'Far from it! While the disease continues, measures for cure must continue. We must redouble our labours and vary our processes'.[3]

Throughout his life Comenius was engaged in varying the processes of reform. In 1618 the newly-inducted minister of Fulnek voiced the deep complaints of the poor in his 'Letter to Heaven' and when he was a refugee, only existing through the protection of nobles, he did not hesitate to make the most astringent criticisms of those 'invested with authority'. He was undoubtedly on the left wing of his church and his social criticism in the *Labyrinth* was influenced by such works as Václav Porcius Vodňanský's *Spiritual City* of 1610.[4] He gives a hint of his own part in the events leading up to the crowning in Prague of Frederick of the Palatinate thus: 'Now I, thinking it well to act for the common welfare ... contributed a nail or two to strengthen the new throne' but he found politics too dangerous and sadly concludes that 'town halls, law-courts and chanceries were as much workshops of injustice as of justice'.[5]

As the limitless implacability of Ferdinand became obvious Comenius turned for relief to the prophecies of the young girl, Christine Poniatowska, and the Silesian tanner, Christopher Kotter, and, buoyed up by the victories of Gustavus Adolphus, he made plans feverishly for a model Bohemian state. When these proved abortive, he stretched his imagination to the wider world. His brief stay in England opened his eyes to immense possibilities and it was in this mood that he wrote the *Via Lucis*, outlining a new social order. Even the long wrestling with text-books at Elbing did not subdue his ardour for reform and he began on those parts of the *Consultation* which dealt with it. Part I (Universal Awakening) and Part 2 (Universal Dawning) were published as a Folio Trial-Print in 1657 and about six years later as an Octavo Edition. Part 6 (Universal Reform) was prob-ably finished about 1655 and ten chapters were included in the 1657 Edition of Parts 1 and 2.[6] A Czech translation of the whole work was made by Josef Hendrich and published at Prague in 1950.

During the four years at Saros Patak (1650-1654) Comenius was mainly concerned with educational reform but he was drawn to politics through the prophecies of Nicholas Drabík. He came to think that the House of Hapsburg had committed so many crimes against humanity that it had incurred divine judgment and all that remained was to find the instrument of the Lord to carry it out. Thus in the Tractate entitled *The Happiness of a State (Gentis Felicitas)*, after discussing the essen-tials of good government, he urged the Prince of Transylvania, George Rákóczi, to organize a Protestant alliance for the over-throw of the Hapsburgs. Events seemed to favour an alliance between Rákóczi and the new King of Sweden, Charles Gus-tavus, and, when the Swedes invaded Poland, Comenius wrote a Panegyric on their king which aroused the anger of the Poles. Thus the burning of Leszno on April 29, 1657, had some justi-fication in the political activities of Comenius. He narrowly escaped with his life and eventually found a refuge in Amster-dam. It was a fitting place for him to pick up the threads again and make a last effort to persuade the world that universal reform was possible.

Supported by the vitality of the Dutch atmosphere Comenius continued to use prophecy as a means of political intervention, and in this he was encouraged by his patron, Laurence de Geer, to publish a collection of prophecies over many years, the *Light out of Darkness* (*Lux in Tenebris* 1657). Comenius proceeded to distribute copies of this book to whoever he thought might be inspired by them to join an alliance against the Hapsburgs. Thus of the twelve he sent to Hartlib he asked that three be delivered to Cromwell. Drabík continued to make prophecies which Comenius continued to believe and from time to time these were published and distributed but with less success than the appeals for financial help for the exiled Brethren. In 1660 Comenius wrote an *Exhortation to the Church of England* (*De Bono Unitatis*) which he dedicated to King Charles II on his restoration to the throne and in which he outlined the constitution of the Brethren's Church and showed some appreciation of the Anglican system. His last attempt at political or religious propaganda was in 1667 when he addressed himself to the English and Dutch delegates to the Conference of Breda urging them to compose their differences in a spirit of Christian amity. This book, the *Angel of Peace* (*Angelus Pacis*), tried to show how ridiculous it was for Protestant nations to fight for commercial advantage or for nationalist pride.

The contrast between pacifist theory and political intrigue, between submission to the will of God and restless searching for support from prophecy, between universalism and partisanship, illustrates the inescapable dilemma of those who would reform human affairs.

REVOLUTIONARY REFORM

The starting point for reform must always be the recognition of abuse but the problem of reform is how to deal with the powers that support abuse. At what point and under what circumstances must force be used to curb power wrongly used and thus become revolutionary? Comenius had no doubt of the corruptions of power in the affairs of men. 'Look at government,' he explains, 'for six thousand years men have been taking counsel on the best form of government yet there have been wars and disputes . . . almost to the extinction of the human race'.[8] Rulers are more often 'defenders of disorder than of order'.[9] And he wonders why the people 'entrust law and justice to men who lack the members necessary for the purpose'. Yet he shrinks back from rebellion, because it may lead to even greater evils and 'it is better to trust to a chosen few than to be the prey of all'. Comenius is deeply suspicious of the exercise of power or even of the science of state-craft which began with 'Nimrod's dominion over other men' and continued with 'Machiavellian skill in controlling them'.[10] His conclusion is that 'neither one nor the other form of government is in itself bad' and 'the main political theories on which the present rulers of the world support themselves are treacherous quagmires'.[11]

The first reaction, therefore, to oppression is not revolutionary reform but patient acquiescence. Faced with corrupt government and unjust laws the Christian could do nothing but resign himself and at the conclusion of his account of the Bohemian Persecutions Comenius can only say, 'The good Protestants, understanding that the laws were not serviceable to them and that nothing remained in which they might appeal . . . did this one thing – solicit God with sighs and groans to be the revenger of such malice. Otherwise there was no helper'.[12] Did this mean that the Christian should reject politics altogether? At times Comenius favours this. 'It is indifferent to true Christians who sit on the throne; indeed if one of the godly sits on it (and experience proves this) many flatterers and hypocrites come . . . the Christian lets all such matters fall as they will'.[13] Submission to the temporal power was Christian doctrine since St Paul and the attitude of the Brethren was to avoid giving offence, by conforming to human institutions when they found them 'not hurtful or contrary to the Word of God'. Faced with a choice of evils between submission to oppression and awakening the violence of revenge Comenius was inclined to the same attitude as Luther, when confronted with the Peasant uprising of 1525. Serfdom was wrong but violence might be worse. At another level the same argument was in the mind of Žerotín concerning the Hapsburgs. The Czech Kingdom had a long history of autonomy going back to the Premysl dynasty even though the 'Great Moravian Empire' was perhaps never more than an illogical and loosely knit structure.[14] It had a tradition of independence going further back than the Hapsburgs claim to be its hereditary rulers and Žerotín argued that the rule of law would outlast the tyranny of Ferdinand II.

Nevertheless there was some danger that unlimited submission would take away the will to resist[15] and there must come a point at which it was right to look for 'another Žižka' to assist God in removing the 'cruel bloody sword'.[16] Comenius had no difficulty in identifying his Protestant heroes with the Old Testament saviours raised to be scourges of the enemies of God though, of course, the 'just war' must be limited to 'moderate chastisement' of the incorrigible. It was an interim measure using war as an instrument of peace and clearing the way for just rule and only justified in fulfilment of divine purpose.

Comenius completely accepted the necessity for obedience to lawful authority. He believed that every man should be 'trained for his own special vocation so that those who have high position should learn how to rule, and those who have subordinate position should learn how to obey'.[17] Thus he entreats the common people to submit to 'the mystery of reasonable obedience' since 'a constant gradation is necessary in all things',[18] and it is 'in the interests of things themselves to be administered by wise men'. Thus government (a 'mystery which cannot be explained to boys') is guidance according to law until the day when each can be 'his own law within himself'.[19] Thus in the labyrinth it was not the division of society into estates that was wrong but that they were 'broken through in many places'.[20]

The search for a 'natural law' as a theoretical basis for obedience pre-occupied seventeenth century thinkers. According to Hobbes it was a necessary condition for peaceful existence for which 'covenants without the sword have no strength to secure a man at all'.[21] The 'original compact' by which men secured some liberties by surrendering others was a subject for discussion from Althusius to Locke but Comenius emphasizes the common good more than rights of property as when he says: 'Every man will understand that the welfare of each individual (including his own) depends upon the general welfare of all; but this general welfare cannot be kept undamaged or unshaken, unless every man safeguards himself in his own proper station, neither lowering it nor thrusting it in advance of others'.[22] Comenius has doubts about that 'milder method' of government by which 'a definite number of men, after certain covenants have been entered upon, agree upon some common good and unite their resources, their counsels and their plans' because 'human intelligence is often clouded'.[23] As for the law governing nations Comenius was influenced by the thought of Grotius that 'there is a common law among nations, which is valid alike in peace and war'.[24] The 'universal law' which according to Comenius must 'be established to serve the whole of the human race'[25] has exactly the same foundation as that of Grotius 'proceeding as it does from the essential traits implanted in man' which can nevertheless 'rightly be attributed to God, because of His having willed that such traits exist in us'.[26] Comenius did not work out a theory of government since he held that 'neither one form nor the other is in itself bad'[27] but he recognized the dichotomy between power and freedom so that 'man longs for power under the sway of which other things may be brought' but yet 'there is inborn in human nature a love of liberty which can by no means be driven out'.[28]

Thus there are two basic problems of government – first how to select the best men to govern and second how to curb their power from abuse. Comenius recognized that there must be authority at different levels, each one autonomous in certain respects, but with a 'constant gradation'. So each family, each community, each province, each state and finally the whole world must have its tribunal. At the top of the hierarchy there should be 'custodians', outstanding among their fellows, chosen to 'keep watch as from a high tower' whose function it is 'to preserve peace and quiet'.[29] Whereas according to Hobbes the people should 'confer all their power and strength upon one man' so that they may 'reduce all their wills unto one will' Comenius envisages a more negative role for his custodians of 'preventing a slipping back into the old disorder' and preventing 'aberrations from creeping in'.[30] An outline of the functions of these rulers (the Dicastery of Peace) is given in Chapter XVII of the Panorthosia (Universal Reform) as follows:

1. To stop corruption and abuse of power at every lower level so that 'judges are such as the peace requires'.

2. To act as court of appeal, or like the Danish Ombudsman, so that 'nobody may be left without refuge, defence and protection'.

3. To survey social evils which cause trouble to human society so that 'tranquillity may be preserved without prisons, swords, nooses, gallows, etc.' Here Comenius suggests collecting cases.

4. To prevent inter-group tension. Here Comenius gives the example of a nation 'so hard-pressed by reason of its numbers that the native soil is not enough for all'.

5. To teach people 'not to lower their human dignity by starting hatred and litigation over material things'.

Comenius makes certain provisions for preventing the abuse of power by the custodians though he is willing that their office should be 'perpetual' since their jurisdiction is based on a kind of common law and not on personal absolutism. Comenius has no place for absolutism in government. There must be a number of custodians (here he cites Matthew XXIII, 8-10) with decentralization in every kingdom. Then there must be other tribunals for religion and education which are independent of the dicastery of peace. Thus Church and State must be separated and neither must be an instrument of the other as happened with opposite emphases in the Lutheran and Calvinist churches. Comenius would not agree to the principle of the Peace of Augsburg that religion must be determined by political decree but yet he was against a priestly class with exclusive rights. Both judge and priest were human agents under God but to these Comenius added a third – the man of learning – and these represented the 'estates' from which the 'Senate of the world' should be formed and this triumvirate of power should operate in each kingdom. Despite all he still has a haunting fear of absolutism, however benevolent and whether monarchic or papal, and whether of priest or squire. Thus peace will come to pass 'if every one of the rulers is content with that portion of government which has fallen to his lot . . . let him not go beyond this or disturb the rule of others in their own sphere'. Comenius gives this solemn warning: 'If any man seek to rule over all things, he is seeking Babylon, bringing confusion into the world again'.[31] At the more local level he was clear that 'the clergy must have no part in secular government'[32] but on the other hand 'such a polity (as that of the Brethren) will lose nothing of Church liberty however much it submits to the politics of the world . . . it comports itself with every well-constituted state and never disturbs it'.[33] The combination of Church and State under a king seemed to Comenius not incompatible with the independence of both and of the Church of England he says, 'Verily, thou art, indeed, in this age, a city set upon a hill'.[34]

Ultimately power must be backed by force. Thus Comenius accepts, 'if any man is determined to be obdurate in the extreme, the judges must seek and find means of subduing this indomitable malice'.[35] If priests failed in their responsibility they must be checked – 'Kings and princes and others in high places, why do you not by the power of the sword (if pastors by the power of the keys cannot) restrain Christian people from outrages? Why do you not by coercive power bring the pastors into order?'[36] Freedom must be within an ordered framework with 'some to govern and go before and others to follow and obey'.[37] Comenius would agree with Milton that 'liberty hath a sharp and double edge, fit only to be handled by just and virtuous men' and therefore there must be effective power to control it with 'one judge in every town as there is one horologue'.[38] But on the other hand there must be effective safeguards against abuse. Above all no one must be exempt from the rule of law, and therefore there must be a system of checks and in this respect the constitution of the Brethren had certain similarities to the American constitution. The Senior Bishop and the youngest acolyte were both under rule and what Comenius wanted from the secular power in return for obedience was non-interference in church affairs. All ceremonies and forms of worship should 'stand awhile without the bolster of penal statutes (not yet are we sure that even in heaven we shall all be of one size or posture)'.[39] There is always the chance that rulers will forget that their primary duty is not to rule but to secure peace and only if the 'men of politics hold it unworthy of their honour to give cause for dissension' can the common man 'live in safety against the unlawful attacks of kings'.[40]

The power at the disposal of the church was essentially

different from the secular power. It was not to impose uniformity nor offer opportunity for dissent or schism and although Comenius hated sects that made a 'sad and derogatory exhibition of themselves',[41] he had no admiration for the uniformity in which the 'Roman Catholics are known to be steadfast'.[42] Church discipline was for the good of the individual not for imposing standards and directed more against those 'in whom something of the insolence of Antichrist remains under cover of spiritual power' than against the weak or wayward. The Church of the Brethren was familiar with a system of mutual surveillance which they did not find incompatible with freedom because it was preventive rather than coercive, relying on 'wise and holy guidance rather than force'.[43]

RADICAL REFORM

Revolutionary reform was necessary to deal with the problem of power but it was only an expedient, and radical reform of human nature itself was necessary if permanent change was to be achieved. Comenius saw that the perfect republic required the education of the followers as well as of the philosopher kings and obedience must be more than passive acquiescence, The universal awakening though addressed primarily to scholars, rulers and ministers was only possible on the assumption that all men, not an élite, had, buried in their nature, a desire for the sublime,[44] and though the first response must come from Europeans the prize would not be won until the peoples of Asia, Africa and America were drawn in.[45] Comenius therefore puts the question: 'Since the earth, by its nature, is one whole why should not mankind be able to establish a moral universe'.[46]

The education that Comenius had in mind was not bookish – 'not for the sake of learning . . . but for the sake of exercise, in order to obtain the goal of all activities, which is rest and happiness'.[47] Within that definition there could be 'no readier remedy than this, namely, that the lower orders should not be ignorant of what it is to be learned'[48] but yet Comenius makes clear 'not that mechanics, rustics and women should devote themselves heart and soul to books but that not one of such persons should be left out in regard to those matters which are necessary for all men'.[49] The 'one thing necessary' is 'that man should know himself, should master himself, and employ his faculties usefully'.[50] Politics can only 'facilitate his amicable relations with others' but universal philosophy should enable him to 'exercise his legitimate dominion over all creation' and the scholar leaders must be the universal 'watchmen' for this purpose and not become immured within ivory towers.

Comenius discusses three aspects in which there must be radical reform, through education, of the inner attitudes of mankind. In the first place they must be transformed from an egocentric to a socialized point of view. Comenius rejected the idea of individual salvation as a withdrawal into beatific union with infinity. The Christian must of necessity take a world view; he must have an intense realization of the present needs of all men; nor can he be insulated from the world. Men are so bound together that 'if any one of them, even the smallest, is affected it is immediately felt by them all, and one sick limb easily affects another . . . He, then, who would seriously not wish well to the whole of the human race, injures the whole human race'.[51] Thus radical social change must be brought about by the perceptive social action of individuals in concrete situations not by doctrinaire slogans. The English Quakers produced such a man in John Bellers (1654-1725) whose 'colleges of industry' for organizing the poor into a fellowship of usefulness, and whose proposals for 'an Annual Congress of Europe' for settling disputes, showed the kind of initiative possible from unlearned men. The cultivation of good neighbourliness is the duty of the true Christian, 'if he but sees what can benefit a fellow-man, he does not hesitate, does not delay, spares no trouble, does not extol the service he has rendered – whether he meets with gratitude or ingratitude he continues serving quietly and gaily'.[52]

The second aspect of radical reform is concerned with the displacement of cupidity by contentment. Cupidity is, in Comenius' view, the prime cause of human disunity to escape from which is 'the royal road, hitherto unexplored, of light and peace'.[53] Although he did not equate the Millenium with a redistribution of wealth unless it should be accompanied by a change of heart there can be no doubt but that his sympathies lay with 'the poor of all ranks who came forth with a supplication in which they complained of the great inequality in the world'.[54] In recent years there has been considerable attention to the connection between Comenius and the English Puritan Radicals known as Levellers and Diggers.[55] The common ground between these two groups lay in the fact that both claimed the law of nature as their justification as, indeed, did almost all seventeenth century philosophers. The difference was in interpretation and here the Levellers emphasized individual rights, including property rights, as opposed to hereditary privileges while the Diggers took the law of nature as meaning communal rights to the means of subsistence, of which land was the most important. The outstanding writer among the Diggers was Gerard Winstanley whose *Law of Freedom* was published in 1652 addressed to Oliver Cromwell and in it he expressed the voice of proletarian utopianism that 'the earth is free for every son and daughter of mankind to live free upon'. Although Comenius could not have read the *Law of Freedom* he frequently put the same point of view. Thus he says, 'It is no wonder that the Son of God purposely desired to have no property'[56] He believed that 'the great abundance with which God has endowed the house of His world'[57] is quite sufficient for all men 'to learn the art of being rich; that is to say all men should have enough, not to be in want and therefore not to covet the goods of others, nor to disturb the peace by their coveteousness'.[58]

As befitted a divine, Comenius takes a jaundiced view of luxury and trade – 'What,' he asks, 'have precious stones, pearls, silken materials and similar Asiatic gewgaws brought us but luxury, pride and effeminacy.'[59] The eager, bustling commercialism of England and Holland filled him with foreboding as he says, 'We have, indeed, grown richer in possessions but also in the worst possible vices'.[60] Comenius was never against progress but he saw grave dangers in materialism and wondered 'if all that was useless, unnecessary and sinful were taken away, the larger part of men's trade would sink to the ground'.[61] What profit would a gold-rush bring if 'a hundred thousand gold pieces would not be more than several ducats in the days of our forefathers'.[62] Human inventions were 'immeasurable gifts of God' but they must be controlled so that 'men were not slaves of circumstances but circumstances serve them'.

Selfishness and cupidity between them could wreck the prospects of any ideal republic but Comenius found still another aspect of radical reform. It was that men should actively seek roads to agreement and practise tolerance. Throughout his life Comenius was appalled by the intolerance of Christians which even a life-time effort by his friend, John Dury, could not penetrate. Poor Dury was turned out of the Church as a heretic in 1677 and the only fruit which he reaped by all his toils was 'to see the miserable condition of Christianity'.[63] Comenius was singularly free from intolerance. With individual Catholics he had no quarrel and he rejoiced whenever he found Lutherans and Calvinists living in harmony.[64] He was always afraid of being 'mixed up with divisions and debates'.[65] When he went to Ecumenical Conferences (as at Thorn) he found men discussing without serious intention to agree because there was no trust between them and here he found the procedure of his own Church a remarkable contrast. In the Senate of the Brethren the members spoke in order of seniority until finally the President weighed up the arguments and gave his conclusion which was then entered up in the records by the Secretary. This was, in fact, Comenius' own duty for some years and he says of the whole procedure: 'The effect of this rational method is that all can see the mind of the whole church, can speak of matters as with one voice, and can act with unanimity'.[66] It was, as the Quakers found in England, the active determination to come to unanimity which prevented divisions of opinion. But the rules for business meetings given in the *Panorthosia* are only possible for men who trust each other – decisions never to be enforced upon a minority, matters in dispute to be held in abeyance, conclusions to be avoided which bring more difficulty or absurdity than their negative. Very wise is the advice, 'the beginning of reform must be made by halting and by an almost general silence so that agreement may arise' or 'let what can neither be upheld as evident truth nor refuted as evident falsehood be left undecided until God and time unveil it'.

His whole approach to dogma is somewhat pragmatic and he seems at times to accept the view of William James that an idea is 'true' if it is profitable in practice since 'errors are less dangerous if we keep a middle position'. It is even better to tolerate error than 'to cut to pieces everything in exaggerated zeal'. Right or wrong, persecution is 'below human dignity' and only makes 'the decline of humanity obvious'. But there is an additional reason for compromise in that 'a third solution, previously unnoticed, may be lighted upon' and contradictory opinions 'often leave the truth unimpaired lying between them'. Comenius seems often to be saying that the simple confrontation of opposite points of view if expressed with sincerity is in itself a good – since 'all opinions have some truth in them' they should all be reduced to a 'golden mean'. No truth is worth pressing to the point of 'disdainful distaste' and 'if something cannot be conciliated theoretically it should be attempted in practice . . . and the object of contention should be changed into works'. Comenius lived in a contentious age from which men were already beginning to turn with scepticism where he would counsel infinite patience in hope of the 'uncovering of many a mystery'.[67]

The same caring for conciliation rather than convincement that was necessary in religion applied in politics. This is the message of Comenius in the *Panegersia* and he diagnosed only too accurately the futility of international peace bodies based on power blocs. All the machinery of peace making would grind to a halt if mutual trust were lacking.[68] Were the delegates of Münster and Osnabrück or of Breda the realists or would it have been better if, in Comenius' words, the Angel of Peace had called a halt and taken the 'safest way to peace which is the remission of suffered wrongs'.[69] Comenius argued, not without justification, that the arts of peace should be cultivated as eagerly as hitherto the arts of war.

The family is an institution that radical reform cannot ignore for it can be either the enemy or the foundation of utopia. A man can be hampered in his civic duties by family ties; he may sublimate his cupidity by making provision for his dependents; he may fortify his ego-centricity within the fortress of the home. Because of these temptations Plato wanted to abolish the family from his republic altogether. The argument for a celibate priesthood was that a man could be more free for the service of God if unencumbered by wife and children. Campanella found the family incompatible with the ideal City of the Sun since love for the state could only be effective if self-love were taken away. On the other hand there were philosophers like the Frenchman, Jean Bodin, who regarded the family as the keystone of the state though most agreed with Aristotle that, although the family was prior in time, the state was prior 'by nature'. Thus Sir Thomas More regarded the family as the basic political and economic unit but redeemed it from selfishness by a communistic system. Andreae recognized the psychological function of the family but projected many of the domestic duties on to the community and particularly the care of children into the charge of 'upright preceptors'.

Comenius as a family man was not unaware of the tendency of a wife to bring in 'eagerness for private comfort'[70] but also not unaware of her restraining influence upon 'frequenting taverns or being absent from the home at night'.[71] On balance he found his solution in the theory of parallelism according to which 'any human society is a living body harmonically built up . . . be it one man or one family or one community or one region or the whole world'.[72] The harmony of each unit depended upon it being a microcosm of the whole so that every family was also a tribunal, a church, a state in itself. There was therefore no basic unit since each had the characteristics of the others and even the individual had within himself the pattern of the good family with 'temple and altar' in his own heart.[73] The outline for the conduct of private life which Comenius devised for one of his students showed the same scale of values and duties that were appropriate for family life.[74] The education of children offered every man a vocation as politician, teacher and priest as important as the means by which he earned a livelihood. Private possessions he held to be 'morally neutral' while true wealth was freedom from immoderate anxiety as in Andreae's Christianopolis where the artisan was an educated man with ample leisure and security.[75]

Seventeenth century utopias were, of course, male-centred. For the woman the emphasis was on industry, prudence and chasteness, with the Book of Proverbs as guide to conduct, and the domestic scene as sphere of activity, but yet in the Church of the Brethren women played an honourable part.[76] They were expected to be familiar with the Bible and to share equally with their husbands in family devotions.[77] Comenius shows some sympathy with their complaint that 'they had to live under the rule of the men' since they formed 'one half of the human race'. His solution showed some perspicacity – that men should tacitly grant superiority to women in the home . . . the great secret being that men rule the community and women rule the men'.[78] The radical reform of sex relations was that neither should try to dominate the other and of women's education that she should develop in the image of God as much as the man. The 'folly that arises from emptiness of mind' is just as dangerous in one sex as the other while the intelligence is just as 'ready' in both.[79] If all would live simply, work industriously, and avoid contention there would be 'no prerogative except that of virtue'.[80]

For the initiation of radical reform Comenius looked primarily to an international body which he called the Universal College of Light. Its function was 'to seek whatever will be beneficial to men', to 'promote the light of wisdom among all men', and 'to protect what they have developed against corrupting influences'[81] that is to say Research, Communication and Maintenance.

Inspiration for such a body came from various sources. There was Salomon's House in Bacon's New Atlantis where the learned Fathers sought out the 'knowledge of causes and secret motions of things' and 'enlarged the bounds of human empire, effecting all things possible'. The laboratories, observatories, experimental stations and sanatoria of Bacon's fertile imagination stirred men to put forward plans for collegiate foundations through private benefaction or royal patronage. Chelsea College was an example of the first, made possible by the will of Matthew Sutcliffe (1550-1629) as a 'spiritual foundation'[82] while James I took an interest in the Academy Royall suggested by Edmund Bolton (1575-1663) for the 'superintendence of secular learning'.[83]

The arrival of Comenius in England was a flash-point in the junction of Baconism and Puritanism and the Parliament, seeking to undo the system of ecclesiastical privilege, resolved that 'all lands taken from Deans and Chapters should be employed to the Advancement of Learning and Piety'.[84] This was in June 1641 and Comenius arrived in September and his friend and supporter, Samuel Hartlib, published 'A *Description of the Famous Kingdom of Macaria* . . . wherein the inhabitants live in great prosperity, peace and happiness; the King is obeyed, the Nobles honoured, all good men respected and Vice is punished'. The instrument for this much-to-be-desired state was a College where 'such as shall be able to demonstrate any experiment for the wealth or health of men' were to be 'honourably rewarded at the public charge'.[85] When Parliament reassembled they agreed to assign 'a college, with its revenues, for a number of men called from all nations' though the actual details were to wait until they had 'sufficient leisure from other business'.[86] In readiness Comenius wrote the *Via Lucis* outlining plans that 'men whom God had equipped with appropriate gifts' should be maintained 'out of public funds' but given 'no definite duties except to communicate with their brethren any intimate mystery'.[87]

Whereas in Bacon's Salomon's House the emphasis was on marvellous contrivances of science, Comenius laid most stress on universal education through schools which 'truly enlightened men's minds'[88] and pedagogical methods which were not for 'the torment of souls'.[89] His Pansophic College was to protect mankind 'against corrupting influences' and its 'principal business' was 'to call men back to the ancient ways of God'.

The scheme came to nothing because of the war but the Long Parliament fully justified the claim which it made in 1649 that it 'had ever been zealous to continue and establish all Works and Foundations tending to the advancement of learning'[90] while Hartlib and his friends never ceased to keep the issue alive. It has been said that the educational impulse has never been 'so deep and warm' as in the days leading up to the Commonwealth[91] but the remarkable thing was that this enthusiasm tried to embrace utopianism, higher learning and popular education. It was to find 'Ways and means to make a kingdome happy by setting up of Schoole-masters in every parish'.[92] According to Hartlib 'schools should be looked upon as the ordinary and natural fountains of a settlement of society'[93] and the argument for equality of opportunity could not have been put more clearly than by William Petty since, as he put it, but for poverty 'many now holding the plough might have been made fit to steer the state'.[94] But it was not a sufficient argument for universal education that it might assist social mobility for the few and an anonymous description of the ideal republic written in 1648 is closer to the thought of Comenius where it says, 'Nor are the less gifted reckoned unworthy of educational care; indeed we use special endeavours in their case, that they may be able to rise to the full height of their capacity, and in due course perform their duties to the state'.[95] A little later in 1656 James Harrington put the case for equal provision of education 'to the end that there should be no detriment or hindrance to the scholars upon case of removing from one place to another'.[96]

To this very lively movement Comenius made what contribution he could by correspondence but it was in the writing of the *General Consultation* that he tried to sketch out his pansophic schemes in detail. What is so noticeable is the importance he ascribed to the College of Light in the government of an ideal world and the importance of its function in regard to schools, 'the workshops of light'.[97] The utilitarian responsibility of the members of the College for the dissemination of knowledge was 'so that whatever new light on the new sciences, arts, crafts, and inventions may arise in any corner of the world whatsoever, may become the common property of all peoples and nations'.[98]

IDEOLOGICAL REFORM

It was always the conviction of Comenius that reform required an ideological dynamic. Men would not stop heaping up treasure on earth until they set their sights towards heaven nor would they play 'the drama of life till the sunset'[99] until they looked upon death as 'the hinge to eternity'. Only an ideological revolution could make the end of life become its fulfilment so that preparation for death became the ultimate gift to life.[100] Only a strong belief in Paradise Regained could enable men to see the end of learning as the 'repair of the ruins'.

To say that Comenius believed in the Millenium does not mean that he was waiting for some future event in time. He was the true Chiliast, believing that men could force their way at once into a transformed world and that the present was always an incidental point in time and space from which the eternal world could immediately be realized. His cry was always in the present – Not 'Thus said the Lord' but 'Thus saith the Lord'. Karl

Mannheim describes the attitude of seventeenth century believers in the Millenium thus:

'He (the Chiliast) expects a union with the immediate present. He is not preoccupied with hopes for the future or romantic reminiscences. His attitude is characterized by a tense expectation. He is always on his toes awaiting the propitious moment and thus there is no inner articulation of time for him. He is not actually concerned with the Millenium to come . . . The promise of the future is not for him a reason for postponement, but merely a point of orientation . . . from which he is ready to take the leap'.[101]

There were grave dangers in this belief and it tended to make its devotees fanatical visionaries[102] but it also gave an enormous drive beyond the reach of the liberal-humanitarian movement. Jeremy Bentham's 'fabric of felicity raised by the hand of reason and of law' certainly achieved more but Comenius believed that something of an ecstatic hope 'of an age golden in a higher sense than the age of Solomon' was an essential preliminary to the age when 'men would live indeed and devote themselves, as men, to a life rational, spiritual, divine'.[103] Granted the premiss that God was present in every aspect of life it was reasonable to accept a theocratic basis for democracy and to make this a universal principle, not a matter of private judgment.

Therefore, Comenius believed that world evangelization was incumbent upon all Christians. They must be 'at pains to convince and convert Jews, Mohametans, idolaters and others'[104] and must bring into the fold 'any neighbouring people, or any men in their own midst, who had not yet come to Christ'.[105] It was the Gospel that should follow trade particularly in the case of the many 'barbarous uneducated people' of America[106] who were 'white for harvest'.[107] Comenius knew of the Catholic missions through the writings of Joseph D'Acosta and he felt 'some affection' for Moslems[108] He believed that the appeal of universal reform would be strong enough to overcome all cultural or sectarian differences. If the case could only be put clearly enough 'nobody who had a healthy reason could refuse it'[109] until 'nothing would remain without reform'.

The initiative for ideological reform lay, therefore, with the church, and it must be taken at two levels – the local and the universal.

At the local level Comenius envisaged a single place of meeting for each community, large enough 'to hold all the people, neither more nor less, even if no greater than a private cottage'.[110] Its function was simply to foster piety – 'to seek God everywhere, and to follow Him, and, when we have attained Him, to enjoy Him'.[111] Without piety men would be as 'squirrels imprisoned in a cage',[112] but this placed a frightening responsibility on the minister whose solemn duty it was 'to present his flock perfect before God'[113] so that Comenius could say, 'O Pastors! You are the schoolmasters to bring them to Christ. Are you not afriad lest the heavenly Diogenes, beholding the abominable manners of your scholars, should fall upon you with his Strokes?'[114] Comenius saw no necessity for unanimity which 'by itself is no sign of the Church'[115] and he believed that within the unity of the 'single house of God'[116] there could be unlimited variety. Local churches must not 'shut themselves up within boundaries and separate themselves from their fellows . . . so that the good ceases to be for the common benefit and becomes the private possession of a certain group'.[117] Each local group must be ready 'to share the treasures which God has entrusted to them'.[118] Comenius had experience of such a situation in his first pastorate at Fulnek. The walls of the old church still remain and reveal it to have been a place of considerable size. It lies at the foot of a hill on top of which can be seen the old castle of Skrbensky under whose protection the congregation met. The majority were Czech-speaking peasants from the surrounding villages but there were enough Germans to warrant a separate service for them. Attached to the church was a primary school for about 100 to 150 boys and girls and the place is pointed out on the well-wooded hill where by tradition Comenius taught.[119] Until quite recently the Moravian Church at Herrnhut presented a striking example of a community wholly centring its activities upon the church and this was a model of what Comenius had in mind.

Nevertheless beyond the local church there must always be the church universal and here Comenius utterly rejected the

Papacy because of its associations with power politics. The efficient study of universality 'against all particular sects'[120] was necessary to avoid the 'stupidity' of hating 'a man because he is born in another country, because he speaks another language, because he thinks differently, because he is less well educated'.[121] The maintenance of this unity within diversity Comenius felt should be undertaken by a universal body – 'the Consistory of the Church'. The aim of this tribunal would be that 'the whole garden of the Church should blossom with voluntary piety without coercion' and for this purpose they should have their agents everywhere to promote and secure knowledge and piety and to keep watch 'as from a high tower' against abuses and injustice. They had two particular duties – the first to make available in every language the text of Scripture and the second to 'keep watch that the poor were properly taken care of through almshouses'.[122]

In welcoming Comenius to England John Gauden spoke to the assembled Houses of Parliament of his 'faire design and foundation for the raising up of a structure of Truth . . . and for the exquisiteness of attaining true knowledge of things'. For twenty years the people of England listened to promises of the Millenium. They looked carefully at Levellers, Diggers, Fifth Monarchists and Quakers but in the end they liked them not and chose – the Restoration. In Germany the ideas of Comenius found their clearest expression in the educational and philanthropic institutions of Franke but they never over-stepped the bounds of Halle. In America isolated settlements tried to unite church, state and school in ideal communities[123] but there was no universal reform and even the plans for educating the Indians fell away.[124]

It must be admitted that mankind as a whole failed to respond to the great Awakening or to accept the Universal Reform.

NOTES

1. *Panorthosia* VI.9.
2. *Via Lucis*: Dedication 32 I Kings XIX.11.
3. *Via Lucis*: IV.1.

4. Čapkova and J. Kyrášek : J.A.K. 24.
5. *Labyrinth* XIX.
6. *Panegersia* V.25 speaks of the war as lasting thirty years which places it at about 1648. Panorthosia XXV mentions the year 1655.
7. *Gentis Felicitas* (Kvačala : *Korres.* II.283).
8. *Pampaedia* IV.6.
9. *Labyrinth* XIX.
10. *Pampaedia* IV.2.
11. *Angelus Pacis* : p. 55 (Tr. W. A. Morison) cf. *Via Lucis* : Dedication 27.
12. *History of Bohemian Persecutions* : p. 253.
13. *Labyrinth* : p. 251 (Tr. Lutzow).
14. Seton Watson : *History of Czechs and Slovaks* p. 14.
15. cf. E. Denis : *Fin de l'Indépendence de Bohême* – 'En prêchant aux paysans l'obéissance et le sacrifice, n'a-t-elle pas enervé leur force de résistance'.
16. Letter from P. Figulus (Kvacála : *Korres.* I.187).
17. *Via Lucis* XIV.16.
18. *Panorthosia* XV.8.
19. *Pampaedia* II.22.
20. *Labyrinth* p. 36.
21. T. Hobbes : *Leviathan* Ch. 17.
22. *Via Lucis* XIV.18.
23. *Via Lucis* III.14.
24. H. Grotius : *De Jure Belli ac Pacis* 21.
25. *Panorthosia* XVII. 5.8.
26. H. Grotius : *Prolegomena* 12 Quoted by F. Copleston : *History of Philosophy* (Vol. 3) p. 330. Grotius approved of the Prodromus cf. Turnbull : *Hartlib, Dury and Comenius* p. 348.
27. *Angelus Pacis* 19.
28. *Pampaedia* IV.6.
29. *Panorthosia* XV.
30. *Panorthosia* XV. 3.7.
31. *Panorthosia* XVII.11.
32. *De Bono Unitatis* : 19.
33. *De Bono Unitatis* : 5.
34. *De Bono Unitatis* : 37.
35. *Panorthosia* XVII.7.
36. *De Bono Unitatis* 18.
37. *De Bono Unitatis* 26.
38. *Panorthosia* XII.7.
39. *De Bono Unitatis* : Introduction.
40. *Methodus* XXX *Panorthosia* XV.2.
41. *Bequest* XVIII.
42. *Retuňk.* (Ed. B. Souček 1924) p. 236.
43. *Pampaedia* II.22.
Radical Reform
44. *Panegersia* IV.22.
45. *Panegersia* I.8. cf. *Via Lucis* : Ded. 31.
46. *Panegersia* VIII.14.
47. *Via Lucis* XIV.19.
48. *Via Lucis* XIV.18.
49. *Via Lucis* XIV.16.

REFORM

50. *Unum Necessarium* VI.
51. *Pampaedia* II.10.
52. *Labyrinth* p. 230.
53. *Panegersia* IX.24.
54. *Labyrinth* p. 185.
55. cf. R. Alt: *Der Fortschrittliche Charakter der Pädagogik Komenskys* (1954) J. Popelová: J.A.K. *Cesta k Všenápravé* (1956).
56. *Angelus Pacis* 25.
57. *Panorthosia* VIII.
58. *Pampaedia* III.22.
59. *Angelus Pacis* 29.
60. *Angelus Pacis* 73.
61. *Labyrinth* p. 61.
62. *Angelus Pacis* 73.
63. G. H. Turnbull: *Op. cit.* 300.
64. O. Odložilík: *Slavonic Review*, June 1930.
65. *History of Lasitius*: Conclusion.
66. Seifferth: *Church Constitution of Bohemian Brethren* p. 187.
67. *Panorthosia* VIII.
68. *Panegersia* XI.
69. *Angelus Pacis* 16.
70. *History of Lasitius*: Conclusion 36.
71. Seifferth: *Op. cit.* 159-60.
72. *Panorthosia* V.
73. *Pampaedia* XII.
74. *Regulae Vitae* (Tr. Edw. Synge 1736).
75. J. V. Andreae: *Christianopolis* Ch. XVIII (Tr. F. E. Held 1916).
76. Anna Cisařová Kolářová: Žena v Jednotě Bratrské (1942).
77. D. Čapková and J. Kyrášek: J.A.K.
78. *Labyrinth* Ch. 32.
79. *Great Didactic* IX.5.
80. J. V. Andreae: *Op. cit.* XVIII.
81. *Via Lucis* XVIII.2. *Panorthosia* XVI.1.
82. Fuller: *Church History of Britain* X.51.
83. R. F. Young: *Comenius in England* p. 4.
84. J. W. Adamson: *Pioneers of Modern Education* p. 90.
85. S. Hartlib: *Macaria* p. 5.
86. ODO Intro. Pt. II.
87. *Via Lucis* XVIII.5.
88. *Panorthosia* XV.7.
89. *Panorthosia* XVI.7.
90. W. A. L. Vincent: *The State and School Education 1640-60* p. 46.
91. Foster Watson: The State and Education during the Commonwealth (*English Historical Review* 1900) p. 72 cf. A. F. Leach: *Educational Charters and Documents* (Introduction): 'The Great Rebellion and its child the Commonwealth, so far from being adverse to education, was just the reverse'.
92. Samuel Harmer: *Vox Populi or Glostershere's Desire* (1642).
93. S. Hartlib: Preface to John Dury's *Reformed School* (1650).
94. William Petty: *Advice for the Advancement of some particular Parts of Learning* (1648).
95. *Nova Solyma* (1648) Quoted by W. A. L. Vincent: *Op. cit.* p. 35.

96. J. Harrington: *Oceana* (Ed. H. Morley 1887) p. 204.
97. *Panorthosia* XVI.5.
98. *Panorthosia* XVI.12.
99. *Pampaedia* XIII.10.

Ideological Reform

100. One of the few moderns able to take this view was Dag Hammarskjöld.
101. K. Mannheim: *Ideology and Utopia* (1936) p. 195.
102. cf. Zwickau Prophets of 1521.
103. *Via Lucis* XX.14.
104. *Via Lucis* XVIII.13.
105. *Panorthosia* XVIII.13.
106. *Angelus Pacis* 44.
107. R. F. Young: *Comenius and the Indians of New England* (School of Slavonic Studies 1929).
108. R. F. Young: *Comenius in England* p. 89. *Labyrinth* Ch. 17.
109. *Panorthosia* I.
110. *Panorthosia* XVIII.5.
111. *Great Didactic* XXIV.2.
112. *Pampaedia* III.27.
113. *Colossians* I.28.
114. *De Bono Unitatis* 17.
115. *Retuňk* (Ed. B. Soucek) p. 236.
116. *Bequest* XVIII.
117. *Via Lucis* III.14.
118. *Bequest.* (Tr. M. Spinka).
119. Professor Menel is engaged in reconstructing the establishment at Fulnek.
120. *Via Lucis* XVIII.8.
121. *Panegersia* XI.22.
122. *Panorthosia* XVIII.4.14.
123. J. K. Clauser: *Pedagogy and the Moravian School Curriculum* 1740-1850 *in East Pennsylvania* (Penn. University 1961).
124. R. F. Young: *Comenius in England* p. 94.

CHAPTER 9

THEORY AND PRACTICE OF EDUCATION

THE basic principles of education according to Comenius were enunciated in the Czech *Didaktika* written between 1628 and 1632 and he did not alter them materially in his later writings. The development which was considerable came from his constant effort over forty years to bring each aspect into harmony with every other.

His immediate concern was 'For the renewal of schools in the Czech Kingdom'[1] and the rebirth of Paradise in Bohemia[2] but as this possibility receded he turned to the wider aim of a didactic for all nations and people. The Latin translation of the *Didaktika* was finished in 1636 and instead of the precise arrangements for the reorganization of Czech education in ChapterXXVIII the appeal was to all 'Christian kingdoms and states'.

He was not an educational philosopher escaping from the class-room but one anxious to lift the 'Sisyphus-labour of schools'[3] by providing suitable text-books for every stage of education. Yet on the other hand he did not regard class-room efficiency as an end in itself. The 'culture of the entire human race' which he proclaimed as his objective in the *Great Didactic* extended much further than methodology or programmed learning. He hoped for a 'universal antidote to ignorance'[4] and therefore began a preliminary survey of pansophy to prepare the minds of men to accept true wisdom. This was finished by 1636 but never published probably because Comenius was not satisfied that he had in fact integrated his didactic theory successfully.[5]

With all the emphasis that Comenius put on the provision of schools he was far from thinking that education was limited to formal schooling. Therefore he wrote his book of advice to mothers (*Informatorium Školy Mateřské*) which was intended as a kind of Intelligent Parents' Guide for the up-bringing of young children and he included in his programme everything fitting for Christians in this life and the next. This was the theme of the *Via Lucis* which he wrote in 1641 in which he agrees that his 'whole hope of restoring the world to better ends hangs upon the instruction of the young'[6] but stretching beyond school education is the style of life where 'all who choose would be free to travel in every clime to teach and to be taught'.[7]

The argument of the *Great Didactic* is based on analogies from nature and art. 'Nature' is the 'immovable rock' on which educational principles must be built[8] but Comenius came to see that language is also a part of human nature. So he wrote the *Newest Method of Languages* (*Linguarum Methodus Novissima*) some time between 1643 and 1647, although he was still in a state of some confusion as is clear from his correspondence with his collaborator, Cyprian Kinner. Thus in 1645 he wrote to Kinner praying that God would give them strength to complete the work but in the following year Kinner submitted an Outline of Method (Diatyposis) which Comenius could not accept although it was subsequently published by Samuel Hartlib as a *Continuation of J. A. Comenius' School-undertakings*.[9]

The 'Analytical Didactic' is a title which has come to be applied to the tenth chapter of the *Methodus* and Comenius himself claimed that it represented a new approach to the problem of didactic theory.[10] He still uses analogies from nature and from art but the treatment is deductive. In the first eight paragraphs certain key propositions are set out and from them 187 Axioms are deduced each of which is supposed to be a link in a logical chain or a particular instance of a general rule already established. The analogies are contained in the interpretative paragraphs but they only illustrate the propositions which are assumed to be incontrovertible. Thus the 'immovable rock' of nature becomes a storehouse of examples and the 'Newest Method' is 'firmly constructed on didactic foundations . . . adapted with utmost precision'. Whereas the Great Didactic might be regarded as a guide to method in imitation of nature the Analytical Didactic is a shift towards logic by which 'the general and particular activities of teaching, learning and knowing can be determined'.[11]

Already, however, Comenius was engaged upon the supreme

tack of integrating all the aspects of his philosophy into a General Consultation in which education was a central theme. Even in 1639 he was seeking for a broader and firmer foundation for educational theory and practice than he had given in the *Great Didactic*.[12] This he elaborated in the Fourth Part of the *Consultation* to which he gave the name *Pampaedia* or Universal Education. It seems that he was working on this in 1645[13] though when it was completed is not certain. From some points of view it is a development of the Third Part on pansophy but it could also be regarded as 'the central part of pansophy'.[14] It is without doubt an attempt to make education truly universal by linking it with every aspect of reality. It deals with the educative process in the individual even before his conception and it continues it beyond the dissolution of his earthly body. Its terms of reference cover everyone 'who partakes of human nature' and everything that 'can make man wise and happy'. The two works which were written at the end of his life and published posthumously – the *Spicilegium* and the *Triertium Catholicum* – may be regarded as elaborations of themes already given in the *Pansophia*.[15]

IMITATION OF NATURE

The chameleon word 'nature' has frequently been used as a foundation for the most varied arguments and Comenius is often guilty of inconsistencies in this respect.

The main interpretation of nature according to Comenius may be illustrated by the following words from the *Via Lucis*: 'Let it, then, be taken as established that the more clearly and fully nature is revealed, the more clearly and fully will the majesty of the Creator of Nature shine forth'.[16] According to this view there is complete accord between the theologian and the scientist and T. H. Huxley is expressing almost the same thing when he says: 'Education is the instruction of the intellect in the laws of Nature . . . and the fashioning of the affections and of the will into an earnest and loving desire to move in harmony with these laws'.[17] The essential characteristic is the orderliness and regularity – one might even say the inevitability of nature. Huxley speaks of it as a game of chess which we play with an opponent who is hidden from us while Comenius speaks of 'the regular order by which Nature preserves her own laws, and the variations and exceptions which she playfully allows herself'.[18] The argument is that the visible world of nature is 'created for the training of the human race'. It is 'the first and greatest book of God' – 'the brightly lit theatre in which we can watch the course of all things' and since the time of Adam man has been commanded to observe, classify and distinguish all its phenomena.[19] The great lesson of nature according to Comenius is that 'all-ruling force of order' which 'really holds together the fabric of this world of ours'.[20] In places Comenius treats 'order' as a purely mechanical principle – it is 'derived from arranging all the parts according to their number, size and importance so that each performs its own proper function'. Thus he explains the working of the heavens and the organization of insects as nothing but 'natural talent for harmoniously combining order, number and mass'.[21] This emphasis upon inter-locking harmony leads him dangerously near a mechanical theory of education parallel with nature. Thus he speaks of education as 'an automatic machine' by which 'it will be no harder to teach schoolboys, in any number desired, than with the printing press to cover a thousand sheets daily'. Lewis Mumford strongly criticizes this 'rigorous control of the process of teaching'[22] which he says 'has helped to ruin modern education'. There are many other places where Comenius takes a less mechanical view and approaches more to a Gestalt interpretation of the principle of order. It is true that his favourite analogies of clocks and printing presses emphasize structural rigidity and Comenius makes it clear that the teachers initial task is to 'present the subject to the pupil as a whole, skilfully in order to make patently clear what is to be taught'.[23] The natural order is the true principle of teaching which cannot be violated without loss of symmetry and continuity. Nevertheless it is not mechanical. It is often a-symmetrical, discontinuous and complex and the harmony of the 'good' pattern (its 'Prägnanz') has to be imputed by a creative mind. The teacher has to remove the impediments which stand in the way'[23] but then, as Piaget says, 'the sequence is dynamic, and the educator can carry out his task only if he remains a tool in nature's hands'.[24] The teacher must adjust himself to the harmony innate in nature but he cannot convey it to the pupil directly. The pupil must make his own meaningful pattern out of what must seem to him at first vague and confused and he must do it in his own way. He is not a 'block of wood' from which the teacher can 'carve a statue subject to his will'[25] nor can the teacher 'handle' him except 'according to his nature'.[26]

Comenius offers 'a method of teaching and of learning with such certainty that the desired result must follow'. Without method the teacher will be like 'an unpractised gardener' who plants trees but 'the few that prosper do so rather through chance than through skill'. He admits that 'even an experienced man meets with failure occasionally' but sums up, 'it is not an abstract question of circumspection and chance, but the art of doing away with chance by means of circumspection'.[27] This basic principle is common ground for all who have thought about the problems of education and the analogy of the gardener underlies most definitions. Thus Pestalozzi says, 'If men would only realize that the aim of all instruction is, and can be, nothing but the development of human nature by the harmonious cultivation of its powers and talents'.[28] Comenius uses it explicitly in the *Great Didactic* and the *Pampaedia*.

The most important aspect of all living things is that their pattern of growth seems to be determined by an innate force. They are autonomous. Comenius gives the example of a bird hatching out its young where the entire process is apparently unpremeditated and yet it conforms to a logical sequence – the preparation for mating, the whole process of incubation, the parental care and protection. And yet, although the creation of a fledgling is a unique and autonomous event in nature it is after all only a reproduction of a pattern repeated millions of times before. Each particular event in life is spontaneous and individual but in another sense it is general and universal. Creative activity is marked by self-enjoyment on the one hand but by a purpose which goes beyond the self on the other. A. N. Whitehead maintains, indeed, that this is true of inorganic matter as well and Comenius would agree because in his view all nature is of a piece and differences are only of degree. The child exhibits the same marks of life as the seed in the ground or the bird in the nest – enjoyment in activity, creativeness and a sense of purpose – only more strongly. The child is 'lively, rejoicing in movement'.[29] It is 'so formed that it wishes to act according to its own will and not to be forced'.[30] Yet behind the random movements there is a sense of purpose, even if unconsciously held, and the stages of development are orderly. Innate in the child there is the potential of the man and in striving to be 'of worth', to be secure in relationships, to achieve stability the child is following the laws of its nature.

The Comenian method of education was therefore an 'assimilation of the processes of nature' and its validity arises from observation. In essence it was not dissimilar from the methods of modern educational psychology and Comenius' chick is as valid an example as Thorndike's cat or Köhler's ape.

Comenius starts with the proposition that man is 'very suitable for education' because the processes of nature, spontaneously at work in him, can be brought to a higher peak of perfection by cultivation. He gives as his frontispiece picture for the *Pampaedia* a gardener transplanting shoots on to a young tree and the implication is that the young tree, if left to itself, would grow wild and imperfect. The teacher is therefore, by analogy, one who grafts shoots from the tree of knowledge on to children and thereafter takes all necessary steps to assist growth. Thus he removes impediments, gives as rich an experience as possible, encourages the child's faith in his own powers, provides opportunities for self-expression.[32]

His next proposition is that in nature there is a norm for each species so that the resemblances between one member and another are more important than their differences. Thus he says, 'Whatever one man is by nature, whatever he has, wishes, knows or can do, the same is true of all other men – If you know one you know all' and, therefore, 'if we can show one single man the true path of wisdom, virtue and salvation, then this one art will suffice for all'.[33] Thus nature itself gives the foundation for the 'levelled road' for 'all peoples, conditions, families, persons, never omitting anyone'.[34] Several reasons are given for an egalitarian education all of them based on some aspect of nature. The first is that individual ignorance is a threat to the body politic – 'it cannot go well with the whole body if it does not go well with all its members together and singly; for they are so bound together that if any one of them, even the smallest, is affected, it is immediately felt by all'. The second is that without education man inevitably deteriorates and 'it is certainly desirable that this should not happen'. The third is that the identities that make men equal are more important than the differences that divide them and since God does not wish to have 'too great differences' inequality in educational opportunity is 'lamentable, unjust and utterly insulting'.[35] Thus Comenius maintains that the great majority of people cluster around the average and are therefore equally capable of motivation and can 'achieve eminence, if only they know the real meaning of eminence'. Only 'eminence' does not mean higher status or authority. In that sense Comenius is no egalitarian but he believes that 'where God makes no distinctions, it is undesirable for man to make them' and that 'any man who has been given a sound mind, a tongue and ears, can become eloquent'. There must be a hierarchy of office and responsibility but in a good society there should be 'no man who is not a philosopher; no man who is not a king; no man who is not a priest'.[36] Education is not a preparation for a function of living but for living itself.

Comenius regards individual and group differences as a challenge to the principle of equality which must be met by greater effort. Thus 'it is to be desired that even utterly barbarous people should be liberated from the shades of their barbarity, for they are part of the human race'. The under-privileged child needs to be 'raised from deadening conditions and transferred to where he can perceive differently'. Only education can ensure that 'brutes become men'. The handicapped child needs 'more external help since nature on account of his internal defect, can help him less'. The only exception to this humane rule is the case of 'such a wooden block that there is not any window to look out of' who 'must be left in the hands of his Architect.'[37]

Comenius cannot see 'any sufficient reason why the weaker sex should be excluded from the pursuit of knowledge'. Women are 'often endowed with more sharpness of mind and capacity for knowledge than the opposite sex and they are able to attain the highest positions and to give sound advice to kings and princes' and he concludes, 'the more we occupy their thoughts, so much the less will the folly that arises from emptiness of mind find a place'.[38]

There is some recognition of the importance of temperamental differences which Comenius classifies according to excess or deficiency in one of the three major psychological categories – mind, will and emotion. Thus 'some men are sharp, others dull; some soft and yielding, others hard and unbending; some eager after knowledge, others more anxious to acquire mechanical skill'. He tries to link these differences up with physiological factors as, for example, by explaining stupidity as a 'clammy viscosity of the humours of the brain' but he regards these weaknesses as capable of manipulation – 'the best remedy against the errors of the human mind is a didactic method of such a kind that by its means excess and defect may be neutralized in the natural disposition'.[39]

The case for universal education derives its strength not simply from the nature of the individual but also from the nature of society. The essence of society is its educative function – 'Go into the shops of the workmen, the cottages of country folk . . . wherever men are to be found there you will find them occupied in teaching and learning'.[40] The justification for vocational education is not simply economic but because work is in itself therapeutic and 'wherever honest labour flourishes, there vice does not share the throne'. To learn the 'art of being rich' is not to compete for material rewards but to enjoy 'sufficiency and safety' in his own sphere.[41] As the whole world is a 'school for mankind' and the whole of life a school for the individual so the public school is really a workshop (officina) set up by society in which thought, speech and action are cultivated in all the 'young people of the whole village, town or province'[42] and no person is left to live as a beast. Society cannot afford 'the one sick limb which easily affects the others'.

THE IMAGE OF GOD

The insuperable optimism of Comenius derived from his confidence in the divine origin of man. God made man in His own image as a rational creature to have dominion over the earth and 'with the knowledge and ability to govern himself as well'.[43] Therefore a man 'defaced' injures 'the glory of God' but he still remains potentially an image of God just as a seed is potentially an image of the plant. Comenius is not unaware of the obstacles. Man tends to be intractable and 'will not easily be ruled'. He is subject to the evil influences of a society, not yet redeemed by education, which he seems 'to suck in with his nurse's milk'.[44] Yet the desire for perfection is so deeply imprinted in human nature that universal education is not something 'snatched in bold usurpation but granted by the divine will'.

When Klaus Schaller speaks of universal education as being the cardinal point (*Angelpunkt*) of human salvation and Halliday calls it a 'vast scheme of religious education'[45] they are drawing attention to the infinite width of the concept of Comenius. In the *Pampaedia* he is only incidentally concerned with school methodology.[46] The real purpose of education is 'to instil pansophy into the soul' – 'to give man, the image of God, whatever is possible for the greatest glory he can attain beneath heaven'.[47] In his present state man is an educable animal (not a true man at all) but he could be transformed into a rational animal (which is his potential self).

Comenius was well aware of the incredulity with which his ideas would be met even by 'friends of the truth . . . who whisper, as Peter did to Christ, 'Be it far from thee'.[48] He realized that universal education, in his sense, was only possible if men would awaken and realize their position in the circle whose centre is God and whose circumference is nature. His dying conclusion is that without Christ reformation is impossible,[49] but even Christ can only release powers already present so that 'man should know himself, govern himself, employ his faculties usefully, and be content to find his happiness in himself'.[50] The imitation of Christ is compatible with all human desires for life, power and health provided man knows how to exercise them – 'Cease to look for what is not necessary. Be content with things appropriate to secure well-being. If things fail be satisfied with essentials. Even if deprived, guard yourself . . . He who possesses God can forego everything, for he has the supreme good – life in God and with God'.[51]

This emphasis on spiritual contentment was not in Comenius' view incompatible with keen awareness of the most mundane consideration of physical health. Fitness of the body may not be essential for spiritual awareness but Comenius believes it to be conducive, and furthermore he believes it to be attainable by a regime of moderation and regularity. The body must be protected from disease and accident because it is 'the dwelling place of the soul' and because it is the 'instrument of the soul' and any man who observes the rules of natural therapy 'cannot fail to preserve his health'.[52] A man is defined as 'that one who has attained the full limits of his growth and strength and so is capable of the tasks of life for which he has prepared himself'[53] and the most important task is to learn how 'being corporeal, he can live outside the body'.[54]

No earthly treasure can exceed in value good health and therefore it must be safeguarded at every stage. The foundations are laid in infancy and Comenius wisely lays stress upon the mental hygiene of the mother and upon freedom of movement in the baby.[55] During youth and manhood he emphasizes the interdependence of body and soul provided it is always recognized that the body is the instrument of the soul. He would support Plato's dictum – 'My belief is that the good soul by her own excellence improves the body' and he almost assumes that old age should be nothing more than a 'gradual weakening in strength' to which man can look forward as the evening rest of a workman.[56]

PRINCIPLES OF PEDAGOGY

Dr D. Čapkova has made an analysis of the basic concepts underlying the principles of pedagogy adopted by Comenius (*Acta Comeniana* XXI (1962) p. 12-13). He kept three ideals before his mind which were to be in correspondence with each other – first the essential harmony of all things, second, the original perfection of man unhappily lost, and finally the unlimited possibilities open to him. The process of bringing these ideals into line with each other Comenius called 'syncrisis' and he believed that it could be achieved in three fields – first, in the created world of visible things – second, in the world of human thought and behaviour, and lastly in the world of cause and effect operating according to inherent and unalterable laws.

Comenius maintained that man had at his disposal certain tools which he could employ in this syncritic process. To begin with he had his sense faculties but no less important was his natural capacity for reasoning. Finally he had a capacity for faith and when these three capacities were brought into harmony with each other man was on the road to wisdom and this, being a possibility for every person created, constituted a legitimate ground for belief in universal education.

The imitation of nature, the recovery of the divine image, and unlimited progress are within human powers if well-directed efforts are made. Comenius indicates the source of a right didactic method thus: 'It is quite clear that that order, which is the dominating principle in the art of teaching all things to all men, should and can be borrowed from no other source than the operations of nature'.[57]

Thus there is a time factor to be considered. 'Nature observes a suitable time'. For every stage of life there is an appropriate type of educational activity. The opportunity must be seized when it appears and, once lost, is hard to recover. Therefore from infancy onward childhood 'being malleable, must be utilized for education'[58] and 'the foundation of wisdom is to manage one's time wisely'. Moral education, particularly, depends on 'first impressions which adhere most strongly' and 'although God can make a bad man useful, yet in the regular course of nature this scarcely ever happens'.[59] The effectiveness of education depends upon having a sufficient time to pass all stages but since (according to Comenius' reckoning) there are 2,495 hours per year available for 'the serious work of life' a 'vast stock of learning' could be acquired with a careful time organization.[60] Readiness to learn is the best remedy against abortive learning and the teacher will find it difficult to teach one unripe for instruction or incapable of being taught or uninterested.

Therefore Comenius concludes: 'The pupil who is unripe lacks discernment, the one who is incapable lacks aptitude, and the one who is uninterested lacks diligence and, without these, learning prospers little or not at all'.[61] He admits there are some cases where readiness is so completely lacking that the task is hopeless but such are very few and for the majority we must 'await the opportunity and avoid undue haste'. As an example of this waiting for the right moment he counsels the teacher, 'Do in front of their eyes what you would like to have them imitate. If they are attentive, let them try. Correct them. If they persist you will know that natural talent is asserting itself'. The assumption is that the pupil is naturally drawn towards learning but cannot be forced. Any apparent unwillingness is simply a challenge to the teacher's patience and an opportunity for didactic skill.

Concern for correct timing must also be shown in the organization of progression which may be compared to the steps of a ladder. It can be done 'in no other way than by advancing from the step on which the pupil stands to the next'.[62] Comenius admits that there may be some 'exceptionally gifted natures that stimulate, admonish, guide, correct and reprove themselves but they are rare'. The good teacher is the one who can make a difficult concept or skill seem easy to the pupil because he approaches it in such easy stages that the pupil is not confused or discouraged.

Nevertheless in one sense there is no finality in learning. Anna Heyberger speaks of a 'lacuna' in the pedagogy of Comenius in that he failed to appreciate the gap that so often occurs between the child's capacity for action (which he goes for eagerly) and his capacity for understanding abstractly what he is doing. It is more difficult for him to think than to act.

Comenius recognized this by his concentric method in which the same concepts are brought to the child at every stage of his development but at different levels; pansophic education is essentially the same from the school of infancy to the university with the presentation changing but 'no difference except in degree'. The first exploration of space relationships may be 'to distinguish the cradle from the mother's bosom'[63] but the 'inner meaning' changes with every fresh experience. Thus the formation of an abstract concept is never complete. It begins with sensori-motor activity and gradually acquires meaning as the individual assimilates the universe to himself and accommodates himself to it. In Piaget's terminology the action is internalized and eventually detached from concrete situations and 'thought

in all realms starts from a surface contact with external realities
. . . and gradually expands into a system of logical relationships and adequate representations'.[64] Consequently the only
'lacuna' is a necessary process that takes time between the
playful activity of the child (Piaget's pre-operational thinking)
and the more abstract concept of the adult. In fact a time lag
is required for every type of learning – 'No artisan lectures his
apprentice on the abstract rules of his craft. Instead he sets to
work, with the apprentice looking on. Thereupon he puts tools
in the boy's hands and teaches him how to handle them'.[65]

The second factor which must be considered in pedagogy is
the stimulus-response situation. Comenius puts it in these words,
'if you are to know anything, you must find something to which
you can adapt your senses and through them your mind, hand
and tongue. Knowledge and skill must have a model'.[66] In the
Great Didactic he interprets this principle somewhat narrowly –
'Those things, that are placed before the intelligence of the
young, must be "real" things and not the shadows of things . . .
and by the term I mean determinate and useful things that can
make an impression on the senses and on the imagination'.
Realism would demand that knowledge of the human body
should be obtained by dissecting it but necessity may require 'a
skeleton on to which models of all the various organs have been
fastened (which will amply repay the expense and labour)'.[67]
Comenius was well aware of the problem of bringing realism
into classes of a hundred or more and therefore he accepted
visual aids as the best alternative to actual objects for providing
sensory experience. The function of the teacher is to present
the object or some representation of it first of all as a whole and
then to 'analyse it by the questions – What? Of what kind? and
Why?' so that it is broken up into its 'smallest parts by reference
to their order, position and connection with one another'. Sense
experience is 'the gate through which anything outside man can
find a way into the soul'[68] but it is also the assurance of validity
since it gives 'the equivalent of proof'.[69]

Comenius shows his practical background in the criteria
which he gives for effective stimuli for learning – a good
stimulus stands out clearly from its background, engages as
many senses as possible, allows for a sufficient span of attention,

gives contrast and variety, and awakens pleasant associations.[70] Even when all these factors are present the teacher needs to amplify as much as he can by dramatic emphasis (as with gesture)[71] or by artificial illumination (as by mirrors).[72]

Nevertheless the effectiveness of a stimulus must in the end be judged by the response it evokes. At times Comenius seems to see value in any active response since 'activity is an excellent remedy against weariness'[73] and an 'industrious disposition' can by itself make 'sluggish ease intolerable'.[74] The formation of habits of industry is, therefore, a form of conditioning and 'it makes no difference what is done, if only the boy be occupied'.[75] The child may accept a habit without any immediate understanding of its purpose and the earlier he does so the better before other less desirable habits take hold. Thus little children should be 'like ants, continually occupied in doing something – carrying, drawing, constructing and conveying' and they should be led 'upwards in exercises of piety'. Even rote-learning at an early age has some value and Comenius cites as 'worthy of note' the Mohammedan custom of teaching the Koran in an unknown language and advises the Apostles' Creed 'in little portions' up to the third or fourth year.[76]

Nor does Comenius confine the law of frequency to early childhood – 'no one has ever succeeded in learning anything without practice or exercise'[77] and the exercise he has in mind seems at times little more than a reflex response, which will presumably strengthen association bonds, even when it concerns piety – there must be constant consideration of God, especially in old age, when it must be 'at the highest degree'.[78] Habit is important in every learning situation and the advice to the teacher is: 'Whatever the subject of study insist on practice until the student imitates his model with the utmost faithfulness'.[79]

Nevertheless Bovet makes a fair comment when he says, 'We must render him (Comenius) the justice to admit that he was less concerned with mechanizing education than with psychologizing it'.[80] Comenius certainly did not think that a stimulus/response habit structure was more than a condition for the development of a cognitive structure. Nor does he believe that perception is only crude sensory experience. Cognition and perception begin with the formation of images.[81] Images are the furniture of the brain and if they are obliterated 'the mind will no longer know anything'. Comenius was in no position to discuss the psycho-physical problem of the connection between sensory nerve impulses and the psychological perception of images and he fails to appreciate the range of sense-illusion in his conviction that 'ocular evidence is the equivalent of proof'. His theory is largely based on association and he defines learning as 'a sort of motion from a given landmark (something already known) to another landmark some distance away . . . whatever we learn, we learn through what we knew before'.[82] He distinguishes the factors concerned in memory – recognition, retention and repro-duction – as follows: 'Memory is the supplying faculty of the mind, which receives whatever is grasped by the senses, pre-serves it and then produces it when there is need'. He emphasizes also the need for assimilating each new percept into a total apperceptive system since 'no one knows a thing perfectly if he knows only that one thing' and each new concept must be grasped in its context and in its total relationships. Thus he speaks of 'particularization' by which one can 'grasp a thing and hold it more firmly through its cause, effect, place, time and similar handles'.[83]

From his theory of perception and memory Comenius drew his principles of pedagogy. Thus 'the highest law and guiding light, the centre and circumference, the foundation and summit of teaching is this alone: Teach everything through examples, precepts and imitation. Thus precept (or instruction) is the mediating factor between stimulus and response. The stimulus leads to a restructuring of the existing apperceptive system since 'all matters should be presented to the senses so that the pupil will learn that this, that or the other exists and develops in this, that or the other fashion' but then the pupil accommodates him-self to the external world and thus gains mastery over it. Comenius puts it thus: 'Human nature delights in working with things because, being the ordained mistress of things, it believes that to be always forming, transforming or building something is to exercise mastery'.[84] Thus the imitation which Comenius insists on is not mechanical but a means whereby man 'can create and transform at will'.

The function of pedagogy, as Comenius sees it, now becomes a little clearer. It might be defined as such a refinement of the mechanical stimulus/response relationship that aversion – 'the most insidious poison in studies' – is avoided, while the pupil is encouraged to form his own meaningful patterns (or Gestalten).

In a sense it is a mechanical operation. Comenius freely admits this and, in fact, boasts of it – 'Hitherto the method of instruction has been so uncertain that scarcely anyone would dare to say: "In so many years I will bring this youth to such and such a point; I will educate him in such and such a way . . . we must see if it be possible to place the art of instruction on such a firm basis that sure and certain progress can be made".'[85] A mechanical element in learning is necessary to build up a family of stimulus/response combinations and it gives a basis of facility, thoroughness and rapidity for a later development of creative and cognitive thinking. Thus a suitable environment must be provided and materials prepared, impediments must be removed, difficulties avoided and assistance given where required. Then the timing must be right and the programme must advance through the simplest steps possible, with everything necessary for success and nothing irrelevant'.

The axioms laid down by Comenius in the *Analytical Didactic* anticipate in many ways the modern device of the teaching machine. The machine itself is simply a technical instrument for supplying a learner with a programme of carefully graded information and questions so that he passes from one stage to the next as soon as he makes the correct response. If he makes a wrong response the machine helps him by further questions to understand his error and regain success. Thus correct responses are reinforced by success and incorrect ones are inhibited by being quickly replaced by more successful ones. The chief problem lies in the construction of the programme because it has to be adjusted to the learner's background and because it has to maintain a diagnostic record of his performance. In particular there is the problem of dealing with incorrect responses by providing additional information or presenting the same question in a different form or breaking it down into parts. Automated teaching must go beyond merely encouraging right answers; it must establish right concepts.[86]

Robert M. Gagne and B. F. Skinner have laid down certain principles which should guide the makers of automated programmes as follows: –

1. Introduce new knowledge by associating it with what is already familiar.
2. Concentrate on the main feature of a problem.
3. Concentrate on formation of the concept involved and help the learner to use it subsequently.[87]

John D. McNeil has shown that modern programmed learning was anticipated by Comenius except that he could not provide a self-instructional device such as the teaching machine. On the other hand he opened up critical questions of the long-term purpose of learning and the selection of content which the programmers have still to consider.[88]

Two quotations from the *Analytical Didactic* will serve to show the Comenian teacher as a living machine: –

'Imitation is the task of the student, but the teacher should ever lead the way, correct the faults, and constantly urge the student to express himself with greater precision . . . since no one learns without making mistakes and errors, we must not leave the student to his own devices . . . finally since the advance from the rudimentary to the perfect is never sudden, we can insist only on a gradual progress towards perfection'.[89]

'There are three methods of reinforcing instruction. In the first place, whatever the subject of study, insist on practice until the student imitates his model with utmost faithfulness. Second, introduce fresh material, not as if it were something entirely new, but as if it were a continuation of previous endeavour. To that end it is desirable to arrange the system of every science into a chain linking all parts. Lastly, sprinkle your teaching with constant repetition of earlier matter'.[90]

Comenius realized the need for immediate correction, though he could not implement it by a machine. He frequently emphasises the need for vigilance that 'no error become a habit' and therefore 'correction should be during the very act . . . before error becomes strengthened by habit'.[91] It is because 'man unlearns with greater difficulty than he learns' that undesired responses must be held at low strength while more desirable responses are established by reinforcement.[92] This principle is just as applicable in the field of morality as of academic learning and Comenius maintains that the child needs to be provided with 'barriers of reason' to protect him from insidious bad habits but since situations will arise when the most reasonable command (from the teacher's point of view) will seem unreasonable (from the child's) it is best 'if things can be so arranged that whatever the child has to do he can do *as if* it were his own accord'.[93] There is a 'mystery of reasonable obedience' which cannot be explained to children but the art of teaching is to prevent it from appearing as an authoritarian dictate.

A mechanical programme of learning seemed to Comenius infinitely preferable to the 'complicated riddle'[94] that he found in the schools of his day and which he believed would 'afford amusement to succeeding generations'. By the application of his principles how easy it would be 'to teach a boy to read and write if the matter is mechanically and systematically arranged from elementary beginnings and spread out gradually after the manner of steps'.[95] But he went further than the mechanics despite some preoccupation with them. Underlying all theories of stimulus/response learning or cognitive learning there is the problem of the will and this goes deeper even than motivation, and the 'executive faculties' cannot but 'busy themselves with carrying out the thoughts and decisions of the free will.[96]

McCallister suggests that the contribution of Comenius to freedom has little of distinctive value but is merely a synthesis and elaboration of the views of his predecessors,[97] and this may have been true of the *Great Didactic* but in the *Analytical Didactic* and the *Pampaedia* the subject is treated more significantly. There is in the first place the factor of imagination. Comenius shared the general view that mental images were imprinted on the brain from sense experiences. Aristotle said they were the same except that the image contains 'no matter'[98] and Comenius accepts his authority. Later David Hume and Hartley took the view that images and sensations differed only in intensity and that ideas were 'the faint images of impressions' and the experimental psychologists, such as Wundt, started their work on psycho-physics from this premiss. The break from this somewhat sterile approach took place with William James who found in image-formation the key to problems of habit, will and freedom. James maintained that habit was established by the nerve pathways of strong images and that will was an 'effort of attention' to these images, only consciously exercised when there was a conflict of images struggling for expression. Starting from a physiological explanation he came to see the close connection between imagination and a sense of purpose and thus he offered some prospect of bridging the gap between sensation and perception, between the conditioned reflex and consciousness, between instinctive motivation and free will. When McCallister concludes his study on freedom in education by saying 'the wider the educator's ken the deeper his concern for liberty'[99] he is indicating the contribution of Comenius which, though externally mechanical, was inwardly very much akin to that of William James. On the one hand Comenius stood stoutly for freedom - 'the will, being by its very nature completely free, neither desires to be nor can be forced; it obeys only its privy councillor - reason'.[100] The educator's function is to ally himself with the natural tendency towards imitation. By providing the right stimuli and preventing the wrong he can ensure that the child will form images by which he will then freely choose the good and reject the evil. It is because 'the little monkey loves to imitate'[101] that the educator can with reasonable confidence present to him 'the greatest things in the world' so that 'lesser parts will follow the will like captives'.[102] Without proper education the mind would 'create vain imaginings to deceive itself . . . and the power of the will, if not directed towards what would provide healthy pleasure, seizes on whatever is false, and rejoices in harmful instead of useful things'.[103] The educator does not attempt to coerce the will directly since to do so would 'violate nature'[104] but to induce through examples a favourable mental 'set' which would then act as a hidden determinant of choice and purpose. This is very similar to Kant's theory of freedom through obedience - 'The child must be so trained that he will choose none but good ends - good ends being those approved by everyone and which may at the same time be the aim

of everyone'[105] except that Comenius has a wider justification –
'The general aim is to restore man to the lost image of God,
i.e. to the lost perfection of the free will which consists in the
choice of good and the repudiation of evil'.[106]

Comenius does not even consider the charge that this manipulation of the human will is, in itself, an interference with
human freedom. He is more concerned with two other problems.
The first is the universal awakening of mankind which is necessary before a new generation in the image of God can be
educated. He seems to be asking men to act the part of Baron
Münchhausen who pulled himself from the swamp by his own
hair.[107] The second is to induce the child to accept adult control
willingly until the desirable images have been formed in his
mind. The answer of Comenius to this question is contained in
the principle of agreeableness according to which the desirable
images must always be associated with positive feelings – love,
admiration, encouragement, etc. Since 'our feelings are half our
being'[108] we 'must strive in every way to make the pupil regard
his task as worthy of admiration. This admiration will arouse
love and love will arouse desire'.[109] Thus wise guidance is far
more than cognitive interpretation. It is to awaken 'natural
desire' for the possibilities of the divine power which makes
nothing impracticable.[110] No theory of learning can ignore the
factor of purpose and no theory of freedom can ignore the factor
of conditioning and Comenius cannot be accused of failing to try
to integrate the two. His pedagogical principles provide a field of
freedom in which effective learning can take place but they also
provide the cues by which wise choice can be exercised.[111]

NOTES

1. *Brief Proposal regarding the Renewal of Schools in the Kingdom of
   Bohemia* (1632 Published 1849. English Tr. 1965).
2. Original title of Czech Didactic was *Paradisus Bohemicae* or *Paradisus
   Ecclesiae Renascentis*.
3. *Great Didactic*: Greeting 1.
4. *Continuatio*: 45.
5. G. H. Turnbull: *Two Pansophical Works* p. 23.
6. *Via Lucis* XVII.5.
7. *Via Lucis* XX.7.
8. *Great Didactic* XIV.1.

9. G. H. Turnbull: *Hartlib, Dury and Comenius* p. 403.421.
10. *Methodus* IX last paragraph.
11. *Analytical Didactic* 5.
12. Letter from J. Hübner (Kvačala: *Korres*. 73-82).
13. Letter to Hotton (Patera: *Korres*. 102) Quoted by K. Schaller: *Pan* p. 9.
14. K. Schaller: *Die Pädagogik des J.A.C.* 204.
15. The Dedication of the Triertium Catholicun was dated only six weeks before his death.
(a) *Imitation of Nature*
16. *Via Lucis* XIV.7.
17. T. H. Huxley: *Science and Education* (Collected Essays Vol. III) p. 82.
18. *Via Lucis* XVI.12.
19. *Pampaedia* III.2.
20. *Great Didactic* XIII.1.
21. *Great Didactic* XIII.3-5.
22. Lewis Mumford: *Condition of Man* p. 258.
23. *Pampaedia* II.22.
24. J. Piaget: *Intr. to Selections* p. 14.
25. *Analytical Didactic* 24.
26. *Pampaedia* III.28.
27. *Great Didactic* XVI.3.
28. Pestalozzi: *How Gertrude teaches her Children*. (Tr. Holland and Turner) p. 79.
29. *Pampaedia* III.41.
30. *Pampaedia* III.40.
31. *Pampaedia* III.11.
32. *Pampaedia* II.22-30.
33. *Pampaedia* II.19 and 27.
34. *Pampaedia* I.11.15.
35. *Pampaedia* II.8.10.11.
36. *Pampaedia* III.27.29.31.
37. *Pampaedia* II.10.30 and III.27.
38. *Great Didactic* IX.5.
39. *Great Didactic* XII.18-30.
40. *Via Lucis* I.4.
41. *Pampaedia* III.21.
42. *Pampaedia* V.8.
(b) *The Image of God*
43. *Pampaedia* II.4.
44. *Pampaedia* III.8-11.
45. K. Schaller: *Die Pädagogik des J.A.C.* p. 177. J. C. Halliday: *Pampaedia* p. 64.
46. cf. *Pampaedia*: Ch. IX on Reading and Ch. X on Writing.
47. *Pampaedia* I.5 and III.19.
48. *Pampaedia* II.1.
49. K. Schaller: *Die Pädagogik des J.A.C.* p. 214.
50. *Unum Necessarium* I.21 and VI.14.
51. *Unum Necessarium* X.
52. *Great Didactic* XV.7-13. *Pampaedia* III.37.
53. *Pampaedia* XIII.1.
54. *Pampaedia* XIII.10.
55. F. Ninger: *Zdravotnichó výchovné snahy J.A.K.* (1957).

56. *Pampaedia* XIV.22.
(c) *Principles of Pedagogy*
57. *Great Didactic* XIV.7.
58. *Pampaedia* V.14.
59. *Informatorium* Ch. IV.
60. *Great Didactic* XV.16-17.
61. *Analytical Didactic* 16.
62. *Analytical Didactic* 10.
63. *Informatorium* p. 87.
64. J. Piaget: *The Construction of Reality in the Child* p. 383-386.
65. *Analytical Didactic* 28.
66. *Analytical Didactic* 8.
67. *Great Didactic* XX.10.
68. *Analytical Didactic* 52.
69. *Analytical Didactic* 54.
70. *Analytical Didactic* 55.59.60.138.145.
71. *Analytical Didactic* 155.
72. *Via Lucis* XII.
73. *Pampaedia* VII.29.
74. *Great Didactic* XXIII.11.
75. *Great Didactic* XXIII.11.
76. *Informatorium* Ch. VII Ch. IV *Pampaedia* V.16.
77. *Analytical Didactic* 27.
78. *Pampaedia* XIV.15.
79. *Analytical Didactic* 34.
80. P. Bovet: *J.A.C. Un Patriote Cosmopolite* p. 15.
81. *Analytical Didactic* 8 'Wissenschaft und Kunst muss Vorbild haben'.
82. *Analytical Didactic* 10.
83. *Analytical Didactic* 79.
84. *Analytical Didactic* 143.
85. *Great Didactic* XVI.4.
86. B. F. Skinner: *Science and Human Behaviour* (1953). E. R. Hilgard: *Theories of Learning* (1958) Ch. III.
87. Robert M. Gagne: *Teaching Machines and Transfer of Training* (1959). B. F. Skinner: 'Teaching Machines' (*Science* Vol. 128 1958).
88. John D. McNeil: *A Great Didactic and Automated Learning* (Education. Indiana, 1961).
89. *Analytical Didactic* 33.
90. *Analytical Didactic* 34.
91. *Analytical Didactic* 41.42.
92. E. R. Hilgard: *Theories of Learning* Ch. III.
93. *Pampaedia* III.14.
94. *Great Didactic* XII.
95. *Pampaedia* VII.26.
96. *Pampaedia* III.41.
97. W. J. McCallister: *Growth of Freedom in Education* p. 173.
98. Aristotle: *De Anima* III.8.432.
99. W. J. McCallister: *Op. cit.* p. 537.
100. *Analytical Didactic* 97.
101. *Pampaedia* VII.29.
102. *Pampaedia* IV.18.
103. *Pampaedia* II.8.

104. *Pampaedia* III.40.
105. I. Kant: *Über Pädagogik* c.4.
106. *Pampaedia* VII.7.
107. K. Schaller: *Pan* p. 29.
108. *Analytical Didactic* 138.
109. *Analytical Didactic* 22.
110. *Pampaedia* III.34.
111. Kurt Lewin: *Dynamic Theory of Personality* (1935). E. C. Tolman: *Purposive Behaviour in Animals and Men* (1932).

PART III

INSTRUMENTS OF UNIVERSAL
EDUCATION

CHAPTER 10

SCHOOLS

COMENIUS accepted without question the tradition of the Unity of Brethren that the responsibility for the education of children was primarily with the home and church but that special provision in schools was essential. He himself had the normal experience of a son of a devout member of the Brethren although his schooling was interrupted by the death of his parents. He commends 'the wise habit of giving over children to select persons' and the collecting of children for common instruction in places destined for this purpose. Formal schooling is justified on grounds of expediency 'since human occupations have multiplied so that it is rare to find men who have either sufficient knowledge or sufficient leisure to instruct their children'. In fact formal schooling has a very long history and Comenius cites the patriarch Shem as being its founder and the Emperor Charlemagne as an example of one who saw the value of schools for establishing Christianity.[1] There is also a positive value in bringing children into contact with each other 'since they will mutually stimulate and assist each other'[2] and 'although parents can do much, children of the same age can do more'.[3] The analogy of agriculture was a common one in the seventeenth century as an argument for the institution of schools 'as fishponds are dug for fish and orchards laid out for fruit trees'.[4] It was used in England in 1642 in support of universal education by a pamphleteer who urges Parliament 'carefully to plant Orchards of young stockes, meaning nurseries of general Schooling throughout the land'.[5]

Comenius gives strong reasons for 'never omitting anybody' from school education:

1. There is the religious argument that all are 'made in the

image of God' and if anyone fails to achieve this 'instead of God's glory ignominy results'.[6]

2. There is the argument of natural equality as being more important than natural inequality – 'where God has made no distinctions it is undesirable for any man to make them'.[7]

3. Social expediency demands that there should be no discrimination because it is impossible to forecast that any particular child is unfit for education and 'out of the poorest God has produced instruments for His glory'.[8] In any case the 'world would be blest if all men were schooled in earnest industry'.[9]

4. Social justice demands that the handicapped should be compensated, 'all the more so since they have greater need of external help'. Light 'must be instilled by whatever path is provided'.[10]

5. Each man's conscience must be convinced that universal education is 'no impossible recommendation' and each should 'judge the whole human race by his own self'.

Comenius believed that a decisive hour had arrived in history. 'The comedy which God plays with the sons of men' was approaching 'a happy ending to all the tangled fortunes and adventures' and Comenius asks: 'Is it fit that we should expect less from the heavenly artist?'[11] But he was convinced that the Millenium would not come without active human participation. Man himself must 'make the breach through which what was previously inward bursts out suddenly and takes hold of the outer world and transforms it'.[12] Yet the breach could not be made by violence and here Comenius rejected the desperate fanaticism of down-trodden peasants. That way lay more and more violence and so his appeal was to those in any class who shared the ideals of industry, discipline and self-cultivation. The discoveries of explorers and scientists and the prospect of greater conquests still, coupled with rising social forces of the bourgeoisie, gave to men completely new notions of human potentiality. Comenius tried to interpret these changes in terms of fulfilment of biblical prophecy but his hopes were entirely conceived in terms of educational reform. It was the idea of a Nuremberg funnel, through which all desirable knowledge and wisdom could be transmitted to everyone, that seized his imagination and his vision of universal schools was of a 'well-arranged and well-devised disposition of parts'. The world could be transformed by schools – 'Let us, therefore, endeavour, in the name of the Almighty, to organize schools in such a way that they may bear resemblance to a clock which is put together with the greatest skill'.[13]

SCHOOLS OF LIFE

For all his enthusiasm for the institution of schools Comenius does not regard them narrowly as ends in themselves. They have a special function towards the young 'before they are corrupted but are still susceptible to influences which shall refashion them'.[14] But schools must 'necessarily be preparatory to the greater School of Life itself, and their one purpose must be to bring it about that every man who is in the world shall be nothing but a pupil'.[15] The formality of schools as institutions is that young people 'exercise themselves under the supervision of the most respected men or women', but informal schools exist wherever there is a 'company of persons who teach and learn what is useful'. In fact, the world is made up of 'an order of teachers, learners and disciplines' and 'every age is destined for learning, nor is man given other goals in learning than in life itself'.[17] There are times when man is incapable by himself of arranging 'all the tasks of life' from an educational point of view and, for these, formal direction is necessary but the ideal is that each should be 'the maker of his own fortune'.[18]

There is one period of life which is of vital significance but in which the individual cannot consciously play any part and Comenius calls this the School of Birth. The moment of conception is clearly outside the control of the fertilized cell and, therefore, Comenius is very concerned that procreation should be 'done holily'. Mistakes here are 'hardly possible to be repaired' and therefore children should only be conceived through the parents' resolution 'to take over the divine act of creation' and with 'pure and holy intention'. Therefore 'people who are well advanced in years or infected in any way or so poor and indigent that they could not provide for their posterity' should avoid marriage. There is, of course, no mention of contraception but Comenius was certainly in favour of marriage preparation according to the Brethren's rule that 'those who intend to get married should do nothing in that respect without consulting their parents, relatives and the pastor'.[19]

The nine months period of gestation in which the forces of heredity interact with the forces of environment is, on another plane, a process of adjustment between two persons, both of them acting unconsciously. Nevertheless the mother's state of mind will powerfully affect the development of the unborn child and Comenius speaks of the womb situation as two circles with a common centre. Pregnancy is not an illness and it is best treated as a natural experience. The mother should avoid 'effeminacy and extremities' but 'accustom herself' to contrarities of food and activity. Every aspect of life in thought, word and deed is part of the parents' care for children earlier than they are born.[20] Anna Heyberger speaks of the ideal of motherhood as a mixture of simplicity and grandeur with which Comenius would be familiar in the life of an exiled religious community.[21] He speaks with scorn of those mothers who for selfish reasons avoid breast-feeding their own children.

The School of Birth is followed by the School of Infancy up to the age of about six years and Comenius is inclined, with Plato, to regard it as the most important part of education.[22] This is the stage of life at which the educative functions of parenthood devolve upon every man and woman with most urgency and no one should exempt himself on the ground of professional pre-occupation or unsuitability – 'The one who will not act according to this aim will not understand his profession and will not use it rightly'.[23] Because infant education is necessarily informal it is in some ways the most difficult stage of all and the parents must seize every opportunity of training the child in the whole range of activities required to make man in the image of God. Comenius recognized that parents themselves need guidance and training for this function and that the means of instruction must be simplified so that even the ordinary man and woman could teach their own children.[24]

The instruction of parents is not, however, an easy thing because so much depends upon the intuitive factor and any laying down of rules of procedure can lead to anxiety and lack of confidence. Comenius did, indeed, speak of a 'hand-book for parents and nurses, that they may have their duties in black and white before their eyes'[25] but his appeal is always to natural development and to the inherent tendencies towards good in the child himself. The parent participates in the work of nature as a creator of forms. Thus 'External music begins to delight children in their second year, such as singing, rattling and striking musical instruments. They should be indulged in it so that their minds may be soothed by concord and harmony'. Comenius states his aim as follows: 'to show that the roots of all arts and sciences, though we seldom do anything about it, begin at this tender age'.[26]

The mental processes appropriate to the School of Infancy are basically the same as those for any other stage of life, differing only in level. They are creative in that they proceed from relative obscurity to relative clearness. Thus the remembrance of 'what was done yesterday, what recently, what a year ago' though it may be 'obscure and, as it were, through a cloud' is yet the 'beginning of history'.[27] Similarly 'the seeds of Arithmetic are planted if the child understand what is meant by 'much' and little'.[28] Comenius realized very well the importance of verbalization as a series of acts of apperception, each of them having a creative character. First there is the stage of babbling in which 'we learn mutually to understand by gesture' and establish emotional rapport. But the loving relationship between mother and child is more than a prophylactic against later maladjustment. It is the tentative beginning of pansophic wisdom. The second stage is the association of symbols with things and to this Comenius attaches great importance and his advice is that children must 'make it a habit to name whatever they see'. Between birth and five years old the child has to learn more than in any other similar time span and this learning takes place mainly through a modification of 'baby talk'. At the same time baby talk only becomes perceptive when it is associated with baby activity and when thought, word and action are integrated. The third stage is the co-ordination of words to express meaning, and this gives rise to sentence formation and eventually to abstract thought. Here Comenius realizes the importance of listening as well as speaking so that 'when children have acquired the use of speech it is of the highest importance that they should learn to keep silent'.[29] In fact 'the elements of the process of reasoning are learned when the child observes that conversations are carried on by means of question and answer'.[30]

The objective of the School of Infancy was that the child should be perfectly adjusted (at his own level) to the worlds in which he lived of Nature, Man and God and therefore the adult function was so to modify the child's environment that this should happen spontaneously. Thus the child should be encouraged 'to express the efforts of an active mind in mechanical production'[31] – to learn 'spontaneously and imperceptibly and as it were in play'[32] since 'the more he is active, runs about and plays, the more quickly does he grow'. The child must live in a child's world with 'little seats and carriages'[33] and the company of those of his own age 'who can do far more for him than adults'.[34] Yet he must also be initiated into the adult world, 'to working places in the fields and granaries', so long as his activities 'correspond to his possibilities'.[35]

Comenius found a certain connection between health of the body and health of the soul. The 'well-ordered life in respect of food, exercise and sleep' corresponds to the 'second part of celestial wisdom', which is 'to regulate carefully and wisely one's self and all external and internal actions'.[36] The first part is 'a clear knowledge of God' and Comenius believes that no time can be too early for this 'even if the child cannot speak'. He admits, 'We cannot teach godliness to new-born babies but we can, by being godly, lay the foundations of piety'.[37] The child's natural tendency to imitation can be encouraged 'if immoderate softness be avoided'.[38] Therefore Spartan hardening to endure changes of weather and to 'accept difficulties which require effort' has both moral and physical justification; it inclines the child towards obedience so that he 'may learn to do what subsequent experience will teach him to be right'.

Comenius had a genuine horror of the ill-disciplined family where children 'scream, squall and stink'[40] and he is quite sure that 'wilfulness should not be excused on the grounds that the child does not understand'. It is not punishment but regularity of conduct that will 'bridle impatience and discontent'. The child needs a strong super-ego if he is to hate what he ought to hate and love what he ought to love and he must be inured to the whole of reality even to the point of 'speaking about the other life when someone dies and is taken to the tomb'.[41] On the other hand Comenius was free from the harshness so often found in Puritan writers and, in spite of his passion for systematizing, he recognizes woman as the natural and universal teacher of man.[42] Since 'one cannot give profit without at the same time giving pleasure' the child should not be refused whatever is agreeable to it.[43]

The School of Childhood extends from the age of six to twelve. It is too early to determine vocation and too 'slender' for artisan's work but it must be treated in all seriousness. Comenius says that 'the main emphasis must be towards the inner faculties' by which he means the power to differentiate and remember.[44] Although children must be treated 'according to their age' their capacity must not be under-estimated and no time must be wasted since 'one year in childhood is worth ten years later on'.

Then comes the School of Adolescence from twelve to eighteen in which the reason is able to grasp the purpose of all things, the hand is able to turn all things to use and advantage, and the tongue is able to communicate inner imaginations to others.[45] If good foundations have been laid the adolescent should be able to manipulate the world of reality surrounding him with these instruments – the mind 'with which to invent what is necessary', the hand 'with which to carry out all that he has learned from others', and language 'as a helper'.[46] Adolescence is also the period when the three aspects of human knowledge must be brought into harmony with each other – knowledge through sense experience, through inner reason and through faith.[47] Comenius finds no justification for the theory that youth is a time for sowing a few wild oats. On the contrary he believes that bad habits are easily learned but cured with very great difficulty and some 'cannot be recompensed even through the omnipotence of God'.[48]

Comenius believes that a man does not reach maturity until about the age of twenty-four and therefore the School of young manhood is the necessary stage for everybody before he passes 'to his tasks either public or private in the world'.[49] In particular it is the school in which a universal point of view is acquired so that all knowledge is brought into one compass and every single item of knowledge is seen in its relationship to the rest.

The attainment of maturity is not the end of the educative process of life and in the School of Manhood the individual must learn the art of how to live well. Comenius says of this stage of learning 'not to proceed would mean to go back' and the 'bustle of life' must not be allowed to bring to waste the 'education of earlier years'.[50] The special task of the school of manhood is to keep a balance between active service to the community, 'to do always what we would like to have done at the end of life, and individual study using books 'not as couches or easy chairs but as cars or ships to help us get somewhere'. Progress depends upon a proper sense of vocation so that everyone should say, 'If I am a priest, physician, servant, artisan or tradesman I am prepared to do service to people and to God'. But at the same time Comenius is aware of the temptation of over-busyness and therefore he warns against a dissipation of effort on outward affairs.

Old age Comenius calls 'the highest school of human life' in which man should be 'zealous to finish what remains to be done'. Though it is 'the evening of man's day, the sabbath of his week, the vintage of his year' it has great significance in the drama of life as an opportunity for self-examination and the purification of desire. Age should add a certain 'stateliness' to life as the bonds of business are loosened and man learns 'to walk in the garden of his conscience'.[51] Retirement has, as its special task, the search for the soul.[52]

Finally comes the School of Death which Comenius regards, not as a pitiful petering out of life, but as its renewal. He likens it to the experience of Moses on Mount Nebo when he viewed the Promised Land so that death adds a new dimension to life and partakes of the culture established in living. For Comenius a school of life which ended in dust would be to defraud man of 'the infinity of his desires'.

SCHOOLS FOR YOUTH

For the stages of Childhood, Adolescence and Young Manhood

SCHOOLS

Comenius advocates what he calls public schools under the care of the Church and the civic authorities, and he defines them as 'public assemblies for the young people of the whole village, town or province.[53] Each of these public schools should be like 'links in a chain', consolidating the work of the previous stage and preparing for the work of the next. Thus mothers could organize 'nursery schools' for children under the age of six 'to play, sing, say numbers, and cultivate good manners'. There should be no formal instruction but letter games and picture books might help to give 'school readiness'.[54] Parents should try to inspire their children with joy at the prospect of school and should cultivate the friendship of teachers even to the extent of sending 'an occasional present'. At the other end of the educational system all instruction should be 'with the aid of objects ... so that when they come to the real business of life they will think they are not seeing anything new'. Every school should be a mirror of society – 'a little economic unit, a little state, and finally a little church'.[55]

Schools are also defined as 'places destined for common instruction',[56] 'delightful playgrounds of the spirit'[57] but most commonly 'workshops or forging places of humanity'.[58] In the *Methodus* Comenius makes an acrostic of the word to express its purpose:

1.S.	Sapienter	Wisely
2.C.	Cogitare	To think
3.H.	Honeste	Honestly
4.O.	Operari	To act
5.L.	Loqui	To speak
6.A.	Argute	Sagaciously

Thus the school is a place where children learn to think wisely, to work honestly and to speak sagaciously and Comenius gives the following characteristics:

1. It combines instruction with play.
2. It gives full scope for intellectual and physical activity.
3. It encourages spontaneous effort.

221

4. It demands co-operative effort and yet nourishes honest rivalry.

5. It requires constant practice with a minimum of theory and abstract discussion.

6. It lays stress on direct observation and learning through sense impressions.

7. It provides sufficiently varied occupations to prevent weariness and boredom.[59]

In speaking of schools Comenius is constantly trying to adjust the principles of pleasure and of thoroughness. On the one hand he speaks of them as 'gardens of delight'[60] or 'retreats of ease and of literary amusement'.[61] On the other hand the utilitarian element frequently obtrudes – 'The Pansophic school must adopt as its foremost goal that nobody admitted to it should be dismissed until he has received a thorough training'.[62] At times there is a compulsive note – Schools are places where children are 'seized and subdued for strong draughts of wisdom (before the world take possession of them or they fill themselves with idle and vaporous notions)'.[63] Schools are 'a panacea against idleness, inertia and confusion'.[64] It may be that, like his friend and collaborator John Dury, he would have liked to imitate Jesuit efficiency and avoid its rigidity,[65] and this comes out in his attitude towards inspection. Although 'schools should be like monasteries subject to constant supervision and to perpetual exercises',[66] they should also 'achieve everything without coercive discipline'.[67] And if Comenius often uses the analogy of a clock[68] he also urges 'let mechanical imitation cease in all schools and let a beginning be made with live observation'.[69] His ambivalence towards joy and efficiency is well shown by his rhetorical question – 'How could it be anything but pure joy to change schools into mills running only at the urge of nature?' But it is not the joy of Vittorino's famous school at Mantua. Four hours a day and two on Saturday and making allowance for holidays gives about a thousand hours for instruction in each year and Comenius asks, 'How much might be learned in this time were it only methodically employed?'[70]

His own experience indicated to Comenius that inefficiency was the foe of freedom in schools – 'I, unfortunate man that I am, am one of thousands who have miserably lost the sweetest spring-time of life on scholastic trifles'.[71] Nevertheless curriculum reform was only one aspect of the positive gearing of the school to efficiency and no effort should be spared to encourage health, play, culture and work. The school should be 'in the centre of a town, and if possible near the Church . . . in a pleasant spot, green and shady with trees and decorated with pictures . . . and big enough for the whole number of pupils'.[72] The school established by Prince Sigismund Rákóczi at Saros Patak seemed to Comenius almost ideal. There was a large house and a number of smaller houses adjacent, each with spacious garden, the whole forming a campus surrounded by a continuous wall. Nearby were woods, fields and a quarry and the settlement included a number of families setting a 'vivid example' of good living.[73] As in the School of Infancy Comenius finds a close connection between the simplicity that leads to physical health and the exclusion of harmful moral influences. Thus the pupils who 'abstain from wine and beer if there is no lack of pure water'[74] will also contract the 'habit of virtue gradually and unnoticeably'.[75]

A cardinal principle of school organization according to Comenius is the acceptance of large class units both on grounds of economical use of teachers[76] and of social stimulation for teachers and pupils.[77] In the education of the family account can, and should, be taken of individual differences according to the 'prudence' of the parents,[78] but with large numbers being taught simultaneously this is impracticable. In any case he feels that there are inherent disadvantages in ability streaming and that the teacher should put his emphasis on motivation. He should 'tempt the student to plunge willingly into work' and devise his instruction so that 'it offers no task for which there is insufficient time'.[79] Comenius rejects the idea that education is only, or even chiefly, concerned with intellectual accomplishments; man is 'the most complex of creatures' but gifted with 'ability to turn to an infinite number of things and to transform himself in an infinite number of ways, if occasion arises'.[80] Therefore the teacher must hold fast to the principle of infinite potentiality to become 'truly rational and wise, truly active and spirited, truly moral and honourable, truly pious and holy'.[81]

Group homogeneity is provided on a chronological basis first by dividing schools into stages – six to twelve, twelve to eighteen, and eighteen to twenty-four – and second by dividing the school into year groups each with its own room and teacher. Each class must be 'free from distraction' and undisturbed by the sight or sound of others'.[82] The yearly task must be 'proportionate to pupils of average talent so that they can go through it comfortably' and with no change of teacher or pupils 'every class will advance in a body from year to year'.[83] There is a parallel in the training of an artisan through the stages of apprentice, journeyman and master workman which is appropriate to a 'forging-place of humanity'.[84]

The management of large classes appears to Comenius to be possible 'without the slightest inconvenience' if group leaders are appointed either 'one that stands out owing to his age, talent or diligence' or 'one that has already passed through the class and knows what is to be done'. The group leader's duties are:

'1. To see that the pupils arrive in time and occupy their places.
2. To supervise everyone at his work, and
3. To help anyone who is weaker or slower or to inform the teacher'.[85]

The group leader can even help with that bugbear of all teachers – the correction of written work – so that 'one teacher can instruct a hundred scholars with as little labour as he would expend in teaching a few'.[86] Comenius maintains that the practice of making pupils act as teachers is 'not sufficiently well known, nor is it commonly put into practice' and he concludes his *Analytical Didactic* with the axiom: 'Every pupil should acquire the habit of also acting as a teacher'.[87]

As might be expected from his addiction to the simile of a clock Comenius is an inveterate time-tabler. The school year should follow the pattern of the seasons so that 'all may be in harmony', and the beginning and end should be in the winter when 'the contrast of the air itself makes the force of nature in each living body more concentrated'.[88] He is particularly concerned that fatigue should be avoided so that the time available should be used to maximum advantage and therefore prescribes a rest-pause of half-an-hour after each hour's instruction and a full hour's rest after each meal. His conception of school holidays is that they should be long enough for relaxation but not so long that they produce forgetfulness and boredom and that they should have some regard for the exigencies of community life. Thus he proposes for the Pansophic school two half-days holiday per week and two weeks at Christmas, Easter and Whitsun, plus four weeks for the harvest work. On the other hand he advocates a time-table free from the fragmentation of short periods or frequent change of subject as may be seen from the following plan:

6.0 a.m. to 7.0 a.m.	Hymns, Prayers and Bible Reading
7.30 to 8.30	Main Subject of the Class
9.0 to 10.0	Practical Application of the Subject
1.0 p.m. to 2.0 p.m.	Music and Mathematics
2.30 to 3.30	History
4.0 to 5.0	Language Exercises

For the younger children the proposal is that class lessons should not exceed four hour periods per day, two in the morning and two in the afternoon, with the remaining hours spent 'profitably in domestic work (especially among the poor) or in some form of relaxation'. Again there is emphasis on regularity with the morning 'devoted to the exercise of the intellect and memory and the afternoon to that of the hand and voice'.[89] In the *Pampaedia* Comenius favours more emphasis on practical work and recognizes that 'the ability for movement must be trained' so that it develops the 'powers of observation, attention and differentiation'.[90] At every stage the purpose of education is the same – 'that every single individual shall rise out of darkness and barbarism'[91] and learn everything 'good for him as a man' so that 'he shall later 'encounter nothing which is absolutely new to him'. Comenius concludes: 'So much is bound in this that we may say that our whole hope of restoring the world to better ends hangs upon the instruction of the young before they are corrupted'.[92]

Comenius was not able to put to the test his ideas about the

Vernacular School. Other people took advantage of them, of whom may be mentioned Andreas Reyher who in 1642 put forward proposals for the education of all children in the State of Gotha.[93] The influence of Comenius may be traced in the later educational efforts of the Moravian Church particularly in North Carolina and Pennsylvania.[94] But his *Brief Proposal* for the 'glorious renewal of Bohemia' was abortive and he was never able to see the 'hundreds of men, learned in the art of languages . . . and perfectly trained in all branches of science' who would have provided the 'capable administrators at all levels'.[95]

The Sketch of the Vernacular School begins with strong disagreement against Alsted's suggestion that it should be reserved for those 'destined for manual labour'. The argument is the social one that class distinctions are undesirable and that it is wrong 'to give some children the opportunity of considering their own lot with satisfaction and that of others with scorn'.[96] The curriculum suggested emphasizes fluency in skills of communication which should be with 'accuracy, speed and confidence'. Comenius retains his faith in the value of learning by heart such things as well-known melodies, psalms and hymns apart from the Catechism and portions of the Bible. In mathematics the importance of practical work is stressed – 'to measure with skill and count for practical purposes'. Social studies are all to be studied with reference to the child's own time and environment. Finally 'they should learn the most important principles of the mechanical arts, both that they may not be ignorant of what goes on in the world around them, and that any special inclination may assert itself later on'.[97] The learning of modern foreign languages should be between the Vernacular School and the Latin School by spending a period in the country concerned.

The Grammar School of Přerov, at which Comenius received his grounding in Latin, was one of the foremost educational establishments of the Unity of Brethren and it used the methods advocated by Johannes Sturm. Comenius taught there for a short time and, finding its approach unenlightened, he tried his hand at an easier method of teaching grammar.[99] At Leszno, where he went in 1628, he found the tradition of Melanchthon and Trotzendorf in the Grammar School which had been given the status of a gymnasium a few years earlier. He 'suffered himself to be employed in scholastic duties'[100] under the Rectorship of an historian named Ondrzej Wegierski. The school was a somewhat polyglot community with German, Polish and Czech students but it enjoyed the patronage of Count Raphael V. Leszczyński.[101] His reforming zeal found an outlet in the preparation of text-books which he hoped would revolutionize the teaching of Latin and he prepared a Report on this for the Count. He received encouragement from the Governors of the school to publish his work and immediately achieved fame all over Europe. His books were adopted by the Gymnasium of Breslau whose Council immediately wrote to him for guidance and he sent them a dissertation on method.[102] In 1638 the rulers of Sweden invited him to reorganize their schools and as he was now Rector of the Leszno School there was a challenge to implement his schemes there. There were numerous reasons for his failure to undertake either task. His patron, Count Raphael, had died in 1636 and the successor, Count Bohuslav, became a Catholic. He had reason to fear jealous opposition from schoolmasters and co-religionists. He was fully occupied with his work as Bishop and Secretary of his Church. But the chief reason was the chance to make his ideas universal by association with Samuel Hartlib and his associates. After his long preoccupation with general pansophic works another opportunity to apply them came in 1647 when Count Opaliński of Poznań invited him to prepare special editions of the text-books for a new school which he projected under the Rectorship of Jan Misalski. The books were printed at Leszno in 1651 and the Inaugural Address of Jan Misalski bears enthusiastic evidence of the influence of Comenius in this scheme. During the short history of the school (1650-1655) three classes were established in which the pupils learnt subjects recommended by Comenius but through the medium of Latin. The subjects were arithmetic, geometry, music, history, geography, law and ethics with special attention to rhetoric in the highest class since Opaliński wished to secure students for political office. This was a deliberate and promising attempt to realize the Comenian programme and the school had its own library, printing press and theatre; unfortunately the ravages of war brought it to an untimely end.

In 1650 a request came to the Synod of the Unity from Prince Sigismund Rákóczi of Transylvania and his mother, the Countess Susanna Lorantfy, that Comenius should reorganize the school of Saros Patak along pansophic lines. There were grounds for both fear and hope in the proposition. Comenius had but recently married his third wife; his presence in Leszno was highly desirable to revive the flagging spirits of his Church; reports about educational facilities in Hungary were not encouraging. On the other hand the Rákóczi family were staunch supporters of the Protestant cause, might even be the instrument under God of defeating the Hapsburgs, and favoured the Calvinist point of view. In addition Hungary had become a place of refuge for a number of religious exiles – Alsted had died there in 1638 while Nicholas Drabík was beginning to put forward prophecies that revived sagging confidence. The school at Saros Patak was an ancient one; it had been remodelled on Calvinist lines by George II Rákóczi in 1608; the Rector was John Tolnai who had been to England in 1633 and taken part in the discussions of the Hartlib group.[104] Above all Sigismund Rákóczi undertook to provide buildings large enough to house the seven classes Comenius had in mind together with all the amenities necessary for the experiment and there were in the neighbourhood enough 'patrons of the Church' to ensure local support. The picture in the Budapest Royal Museum gives evidence that the school was a substantial establishment not inadequate for the great experiment Comenius had in mind.[105]

The first nine months of his stay in Saros Patak were spent by Comenius in writing and lecturing in order to prepare the minds of teachers and supporters and, in particular, he gave an *Outline of a Pansophic School*.[106] The first class was opened in February 1651 with a panegyric delivered by Comenius; the students were all boarders with a mixture of commoners and nobles and numbering in all about one hundred.[107] There was great rejoicing when, in the summer, Comenius gave his blessing to the wedding of his young patron to Henrietta, daughter of the man on whom so many hopes had centred – Frederick of the Palatinate.

From that point all went wrong. Within months Sigismund and Henrietta was dead. The printing-press turned out to be inadequate for the text-books desperately needed. The pupils lacked the ground-work necessary for the programme he had in mind. The Rector became jealous. The 'patrons of the Church' were narrow-minded bigots. All these difficulties, however, might have been surmounted if Comenius could have gained the support of the teachers whom he tried desperately to arouse.[108] Unfortunately he failed. The teachers lacked the deep sense of vocation which alone would have enabled them to accept the discipline necessary and they were inclined to regard the class-room as a place of temporary employment rather than of permanent life-service.[109] Comenius made Herculean efforts, for so much was at stake. The school of Saros Patak continued and celebrated its tercentenary in 1950 not, indeed, in the form he would have liked but as a significant contribution to educational history. W. S. Monroe says, 'The Saros Patak plan became a model for educators in many lands, and the progenitor of a long line of graded schemes of instruction'.[110] Comenius interpreted his relative failure as a demonstration of the futility of educational reform in isolation from social reform.[111] In any case the approach of war in Poland made it necessary for him to hasten back to Leszno.

The *Outline of the Pansophic School* gives the most mature exposition of the practical side of pansophy. In some ways it is even more ambitious than Milton's *Tractate* and it is more carefully thought out than the Sketch which Comenius gave in Chapter XXX of the *Great Didactic*. In the Sketch he proposes that 'the pupils should learn four languages and acquire an encyclopaedic knowledge of the arts' and he envisages that the work of each year should be given its own slant but admits, 'it is open to argument whether the mathematical class should or should not precede the Natural Philosophy class' and concedes, 'if others suggest a different order, and justify their preference by theoretical or practical reasons, I have no wish to gainsay them'.[112] He does, indeed, state very clearly the principle of realism in education – 'Thought and speech have no meaning apart from things' and therefore, 'it is absolutely necessary to give our pupils a thorough preliminary training in real studies'. Nevertheless he concludes, 'Of this we can speak more fully elsewhere; that is to say, if it be necessary, since the details will work themselves out in practice'.[113]

In the *Outline of the Pansophic School* he goes into more detail concerning the manner of concentrating the work of each year on a particular aspect. There are three ways of doing this – first, dealing with the 'essence' of the subject, second, applying the subject to 'good living' (here he mentions history as an example), third, dealing with things that by themselves do not promote wisdom but maintaining the freshness of the body and the nimbleness of the mind.[114] To understand the essence of a subject it must be experienced from many different angles – through the senses, through hand-work, through the emotions and through verbalizing. Comenius even recommends that one hour per week should be given to reading 'the newspapers of the merchants'.

Instead of the six classes suggested in the *Great Didactic* the Pansophic School has seven as follows:

1. The Vestibule Class – here the beginner covers the whole range of knowledge at an elementary level but in Latin –the 'main matters on which the universe hangs'.

2. The Gateway Class – here the student learns the external structure of things and their differences and, in particular, plane figures in Geometry.

3. The Courtyard Class – here he learns to converse fluently in Latin and pays attention to the adornments of speech and musical harmony. In Mathematics he studies Solid figures.

4. The Class of Philosophy – in which the student works in the laboratory and dissecting room and wherever he can observe the natural world. In Mathematics he learns proportion, trigonometry and statics. In music he becomes skilled in musical instruments which 'would be specially an adornment to the nobility'. A beginning is made with Greek which should be learnt easily since Comenius does not envisage a deep knowledge.

5. The Class of Logic – here the purpose is to study the progress of the human mind through arts and inventions and through logic. Among the 'delightful' studies for the afternoons Comenius suggests the measurement of distances, heights, and

surfaces, and such subjects as Geography and Optics.

6. The Class of Politics – the student covers here society and economics and continues with Greek.

7. The Class of Theology – a beginning is made of Hebrew and there is a grounding in Christian belief and practice.

Although for each year there is a central theme certain interests and activities continue throughout. Thus reading, writing, acting and speaking should be given significance by being associated with real things. Public dramatic displays have advantages at all stages as a means of 'laying aside rural bashfulness'.[115] Above all Comenius recommends the study of history in all classes. It 'attracts the mind, kindles the imagination, enriches the language and sharpens the judgment'. In the *Great Didactic* he speaks of history as the 'most important element in a man's education and, as it were, the eye of his whole life' though he takes a wider view of its scope than the traditional one. Thus in the Fifth Class he recommends the history of mechanics 'treating of the attractiveness of man's ingenuity'.[116] There is a suggestion that once a week ('say Wednesday at noon immediately after dinner') the Franco-Dutch *Mercury* should be read aloud about 'noteworthy events which have occurred anywhere in the world during the preceding six months'.[117]

Comenius hopes that work in the Pansophic School will be 'like a walk through a pleasant garden' even though 'every year, month, day and even every single hour shall have their task . . . lest time be spent to no avail'. Thus he does not advocate long oral lessons – 'it is not possible for children to absorb more material than the teacher can present and explain in a quarter of an hour'.[118] He believes that play has a higher purpose than amusement and that, since the continuous motion of body and mind are essential for education, careful provision should be made for outdoor and indoor games.

Confident of eventual success, Comenius foresees 'great crowds of students' for whom poverty must be no bar and wherever necessary there should be a complete remission of fees. His answer to the charge of an over-burdened curriculum is the amount of honey the bees can produce from 'the sweetest drops from little flowers in smallest quantities' and therefore the course of pansophic study is 'a task for average intellects'. The greatest reward any student can gain is the ability to continue his own subsequent education, 'wise in sense experience, prudent in behaviour, and eloquent in speech'. The objective is not erudition but 'so to secure the business of life within the bounds of prudence that all things are secure'. Thus Comenius sees no reason why, with right methods, children should not learn one or two languages of neighbouring nations as well as the classical ones if they are 'cultivated in order that intercourse with other people may be reasonable, nice and enjoyable'.[120] On the other hand he is very certain that 'daring gluttony, exaggeration in dress and unbridled licence' are always the enemies of true education.[121]

For universities Comenius had mixed feelings. He himself gained very much from his years at Herborn and Heidelberg but in general he found the men of learning to lack 'inward freshness of mind'.[122] The method of teaching by which he hoped to transform schools was not 'really concerned with University studies', but the same principles of universality applied at every stage of learning. Though specialization is necessary for the majority, a university would not fulfil its proper function unless some of 'quite exceptional ability' devoted themselves to an encyclopaedic view of knowledge. For research Comenius maintains that co-operation is essential so that 'through associated labour the foundations of all sciences may be established'[123] and this co-ordination of effort demands that there should be some central institution which should bear 'the same relation to other colleges that the belly bears to the other members of the body'.[124] In the *Pampaedia* Comenius gives the three main aims of higher education as, first, to establish the harmony of wisdom, second, continuous experimentation, and third, 'the examination of libraries'. He realizes the opposition between 'the quietness essential for harmonizing knowledge' and the 'whirling of disciplines in the centre of a city' which is required for experimental work. Foreign travel he regards as best deferred until it really serves to increase wisdom and not simply to see the 'sights' and in the same way he deprecates too early vocational specialization.[125]

It is significant that in the *Pampaedia* Comenius uses the word

academy rather than university because he realized the conservatism of the older centres of learning and looked rather to
the voluntary societies of scholars which were springing up in
Europe. As Harnack says, 'The Universities of Europe . . . corresponded to the medieval view of transmitting a body of knowledge in fixed terms. The academies of the seventeenth century
were expressions of the new spirit'.[126] The ideal of Comenius was
of a kind of Solomon's House, supported by the state but enjoying academic freedom and devoting itself to 'such parts of
knowledge as have not hitherto been laboured'. It came nearest
to fulfilment in England and Holland and Comenius prayed that
mankind should not for ever be 'mocked by a philosophy empty,
superficial and uselessly subtle'. There was at one time a real
hope that the group of Baconians at Oxford, with the outlook
of Lord Herbert of Cherbury, would establish institutions of
learning as 'workshops of the education of the human race' and
like the Royal Society 'devoted to the investigation of the
mysteries of nature'.[127]

COMMUNITY SCHOOLS

The starting point of Comenian reform was that the deplorable
state of society could only be alleviated by a universal awakening to the necessity for educational provision for every person
This was the 'morning glow of the newly-arising age' and the
'noble counsel' of Luther which had unfortunately been
ignored.[128] He asks for something more than literacy which could
lead to nothing but a 'spurious veneer of morality, a fastidious
and exotic clothing of culture'. There is the danger that mass
education divorced from the practice of virtue will produce more
evils than it cures. It could yield 'fiery wild asses and restive
mules' smarting under the sense of educational failure and regarding equality of opportunity as a bitter mockery. The
Comenian concept of universal education was fundamentally
radical because it was directed to the needs of the average and
below average – 'If any ask, 'What will be the result if artisans,
rustics, porters and even women become lettered?' I answer, 'If
this universal instruction of youth by the proper means be
brought about all will . . . regale themselves, even in the midst

of their work and toil, by meditation on the works of God' . . .
'Does not such a condition represent to us the only paradise that
it is possible to realize on this earth?'[129] Comenius believed that
the education of the follower was just as important as that of
the leader and therefore every member of society must be concerned with the provision of education since 'the salvation of
the human race is at stake'.

The proposals of Comenius were designed to take the sting
out of selection. If all men were taught 'what belongs to
humanity' they would not all need to 'devote themselves heart
and soul to books'[130] It is 'no obstacle that some seem to be
naturally dull and stupid for this renders more imperative
universal culture'.[131] It is clear that Comenius regards the first
twenty-four years of life as being primarily for education for the
'entire youth of a nation' since this is the natural time for all
who are to become men. The restrictions in the *Great Didactic*
of the Latin School to those 'who aspire higher than the workshop' and of the university for 'teachers and leaders' are not
repeated in the *Pampaedia* where, after describing the three
public schools Comenius says, 'When I say that the young
people (of the whole village, town or province) should be exercised together I mean . . . that they should all come to school
together and be loved and trained with the same care . . . and
that they should learn all things together'.[132] Nor should there be
any distinctions whatsoever. 'Admission (to the Latin School)
should not be reserved for the sons of the rich . . . the wind
blows where it will, and does not always begin to blow at the
same time'.[133] If the children of noble and common birth go to
school together the 'glorious prophecy will be fulfilled of the
lion eating straw like the ox'. Comenius is completely in favour
of the common education of boys and girls though there should
be some separation 'for the sake of decency' and girls should be
educated in 'all those things that enable a woman to promote
the welfare of her husband and family'.

Schools are to be 'the image of civic life where all will learn
how to be governed and to govern, if fate should lay upon them
the necessity of ruling others'. The vocational education is not
for particular forms of employment but as a 'prelude to church
and government' and so that there may be 'a harvest of well-

bred men everywhere'.[134] In the pansophic school there is a recommendation that different forms of government should be tried out – the first two classes in a democratic way, the second two in an aristocratic way the last in a monarchic way'.[135] Yet in some ways the school should be, not an imitation of, but an example to the wider community. Thus Comenius hopes that the children will be in school for the whole of the day so that they do not continually return to 'bad habits, feeling disgust at anything better. They should not be allowed to see anything but what is wise, honourable and pious'.

Education is, in the opinion of Comenius, the highest civic priority in which every individual is concerned. Although he favours the dual control of Church and State the primary responsibility belongs to the civil power. It is the 'governors of nations' who should promote and maintain educational institutions 'from the highest to the lowest'. In the reconstruction of Bohemia Comenius anticipates that the incomes of Jesuits and monastic orders ('having in any case been originally dedicated to pious uses') will be a great help.[136] In addition he puts a special responsibility on rich men to undertake the education of poor children so that 'there will not need to be so many maintained at public expense'.[137] Finally he seems to advocate a kind of general rate for each community 'to hire a shepherd for their flocks' or in other words to pay the teacher's salary.

The civic responsibility to provide the means of education is no greater than to see that the money is well spent and this presupposes a rigid system of supervision. For the School of Infancy both parents and godparents are subordinate to the Elders of the Church. Inspection of the Vernacular School is shared between the Church Administrator and the civil authority, of the Latin School between the Dean of the region and a body of wardens, and of the University between the Bishop and a Council elected from the higher estates.[138] The powers of the local administrators or curators are 'to take charge of matters concerning schools and refuse no outlay required'.[139]

In order to give equality of standards in all places Comenius proposes an extra-territorial authority in the form of a College of Light. The members were to be taken 'indifferently' from laymen or ecclesiastics and to form 'an alliance of a great number of men'. These men will 'pay earnest attention that schools are opened among all nations and communities and to ensure this inspectors should come at certain times, 'preserving all things in good condition and reforming any errors that have crept in'.[140] They will have power 'to remove from office those who cannot be reformed' and will 'tolerate nothing but what is clear, ardent and pleasant'.

NOTES

1. *Great Didactic* VII.2-3.
2. *Great Didactic* XIX.16.
3. *Informatorium* VI.
4. *Great Didactic* VIII.9.
5. Samuel Harmer: *Vox Populi* or *Glostershere's Desire* (1642).
6. *Pampaedia* II.4.
7. *Pampaedia* II.7.
8. *Great Didactic* IX.3.
9. *Pampaedia* III.21.
10. *Pampaedia* II.30.
11. *Via Lucis* VI.2.
12. Karl Mannheim: *Ideology and Utopia* p. 193.
13. cf. *Great Didactic* XIV.6.
(a) *Schools of Life*
14. *Via Lucis* XVII.3.
15. *Via Lucis* XV.3.
16. *Pampaedia* V.15. *Via Lucis* I.1.
17. *Pampaedia* V.1.
18. *Pampaedia* V.2.7.
19. Seifferth: *Church Constitution* p. 146.
20. *Pampaedia* VIII.1.12.
21. Anna Heyberger: *Comenius* p. 173.
22. cf. Plato: *Laws* 643.
23. *Pampaedia* XIII.
24. cf. Pestalozzi: *Letters on Early Education*.
25. *Great Didactic* XXVIII.25.
26. *Informatorium* VIII.
27. *Informatorium* VIII.
28. *Great Didactic* XXVIII.9.
29. *Informatorium* VIII.
30. *Great Didactic* XXVIII.13.
31. *Great Didactic* XXVIII.12.
32. *Informatorium* XI.
33. *Informatorium* V.
34. *Informatorium* VI.
35. *Pampaedia* IX.

36. *Informatorium* II.
37. *Informatorium* III.
38. *Informatorium* IX.
39. *Great Didactic* XXIV.11.
40. *Labyrinth* VIII.
41. *Pampaedia* IX.
42. cf. Anna Kolářová: *Žena v Jednoté Bratrské* (1942).
43. *Analytical Didactic* 138.
44. *Pampaedia* X.
45. *Pampaedia* XI.
46. *Pampaedia* III.7.
47. *Spicilegium Didacticum* Pt. 1.
48. *Pampaedia* XI.
49. *Pampaedia* XII.
50. *Pampaedia* XIII.
51. *Pampaedia* XIV.
52. cf. Carl Jung: *Development of Personality* p. 193.
(b) *Schools for Youth*
53. *Pampaedia* V.9.
54. *Pampaedia* IX.
55. *Pampaedia* V.28.
56. *Great Didactic* VIII.2.
57. *Pampaedia* V.8.
58. *Outline of Pansophic School*, 3.
59. *Methodus* XXV.
60. *Panorthosia* XVI.7.
61. *Informatorium* III.
62. *Outline of Pansophic School* VIII.
63. *Via Lucis* XVII.3.
64. *Outline of Pansophic School* 8.
65. J. Adamson: *Pioneers of Modern Education* p. 155-6.
66. *Panorthosia* XXII.
67. *Panorthosia* XVI.7.
68. *Great Didactic* XIII.16.
69. *Panorthosia* XXII.24.
70. *Great Didactic* XXXII.20.
71. *Great Didactic* XI.13.
72. *Pampaedia* V.26.
73. *Outline of Pansophic School*: Add. Deliberation.
74. *Panorthosia* XXII.21.
75. *Pampaedia* V.13.
76. *Great Didactic* XXXII.4.
77. *Great Didactic* XIX.16.
78. *Great Didactic* XXVIII.23.
79. *Analytical Didactic* 141.
80. *Pampaedia* IV.8.
81. *Pampaedia* I.8.
82. *Outline of Pansophic School* 50.
83. *Outline of Pansophic School* 55.
84. *Great Didactic* XXVII.1.
85. *Outline of Pansophic School* 51.
86. *Great Didactic* XIX.29.

87. *Analytical Didactic* 158.
88. *Pampaedia* V.27.
89. *Great Didactic* XXIX.17.
90. *Pampaedia* X.
91. *Via Lucis* XVII.5.
92. *Via Lucis* XVII.3.
93. J. Adamson: *Pioneers of Modern Education*, p. 95-96.
94. Adelaide L. Fries: *Records of Moravians in N. Carolina* (1922-54).
95. *Brief Proposal* 4.
96. *Great Didactic* XXIX.1-2.
97. *Great Didactic* XXIX.6.
98. *Great Didactic* XI.14.
99. *Grammaticae Facilioris Praecepta* (1616) Not extant.
100. *Continuatio* 39.
101. Stanislaw Tync: *Szkola w Lesznie* (1957).
102. *Didactica Dissertatio* (1638).
103. L. Kurdybacha: 'The First Comenian School in Poland' (*Acta Comeniana* 1959.2) p. 117-131.
104. Endre Kovács: *Selections from Saros Patak* (1962) Introduction.
105. A. Turek: *Comenian System of Education* (1951).
106. 'De Cultura Ingeniorum Oratio' (ODO. III.72).
107. 'Methodi Verae Encomia' (ODO. III.739-744).
108. *Fortius Redivivus* (1652) *Leges Scholae Bene Ordinate* (1653).
109. 'Methodi Verae Encomia: Preface' (ODO. III.736). Leges Praeceptorum (ODO. III.796).
110. W. J. Monroe: *Comenius* p. 68.
111. *Gentis Felicitas* (1654).
112. *Great Didactic*: XXX.7.8.
113. *Great Didactic*: XXX.5.15.
114. *Outline of Pansophic School* 58.
115. *Outline of Pansophic School* 87.
116. *Outline of Pansophic School* 70.
117. *Outline of Pansophic School* 76.
118. *Brief Proposal* 11.
119. *Pampaedia* I.12.
120. *Pampaedia* XI.
121. *Panorthosia* XXII.21.
122. *Labyrinth* X.9.
123. *Great Didactic* XXXI.15.
124. *Great Didactic* XXXI.15.
125. *Pampaedia* XII.
126. A. Harnack: *Geschichte der Königlich Preussischen Akademie* (1910) I.5.
127. cf. W. H. G. Armytage: *400 Years of English Education* (1964) p. 22. *Via Lucis*: Dedication.
(c) *Community Schools*
128. *Great Didactic* XI.4.
129. *Great Didactic* IX.8.
130. *Via Lucis* XXIV.16.
131. *Great Didactic* IX.4.
132. *Pampaedia* V.15.
133. *Great Didactic* XXIX.2.

SCHOOLS

134. *Pampaedia* V.9-10.
135. *Pampaedia* XI.
136. *Brief Proposal* 16.
137. *Via Lucis* XVII.7.
138. *Brief Proposal* 16.
139. *Panorthosia* XVI.5.
140. *Panorthosia* XVI.5.

CHAPTER 11

TEACHERS

MOST of the evidence points to the fact that in the seventeenth century the conditions of teaching were unsatisfactory. In his book for children (the *Orbis Pictus*) Comenius gives a picture of the typical classroom in these words: 'The master sitteth in a chair. Some of the boys stand and rehearse things committed to memory. Some talk together . . . and are chastised with a ferula and rod'.[1] The scene is not a disorderly one but the instruments of punishment are shown prominently and the method of teaching through learning by heart and reciting individually must always have put a heavy strain on the powers of concentration of those supposed to be learning. Other illustrations of classrooms from the sixteenth to the eighteenth century give a much worse impression of overcrowded conditions, utter boredom and invariable violence.[2] Martin Luther was voicing the opinion of most enlightened men when he attacked teachers as 'tyrants and jailers who made schools nothing but so many dungeons and hells'[3] and Comenius adds his testimony that the pupils 'must have skins of tin to endure the process of education'.[4]

Of course, there were exceptions. There were Humanist teachers whose practice was that applied by one of the best of them, Vittorino da Feltre, who 'refused after fair trial made, to force learning upon unwilling scholars, holding that nature had not endowed all with taste or capacity for study'.[5] There were Protestant teachers like the French Hugenuot of the sixteenth century, Mathurin Cordier, who proved that even the traditional methods could be redeemed by sympathy for children and love of learning.[6] The system of individual recitation could be made very effective if it were preceded by explanation and followed up by interpretation as may be seen from Roger Ascham's description of the 'Schoolmaster' of which Dr Johnson said many years later: 'It contains perhaps the best advice ever given for the

3. Title-page of The Collected Works
   (Opera didactica omnia)

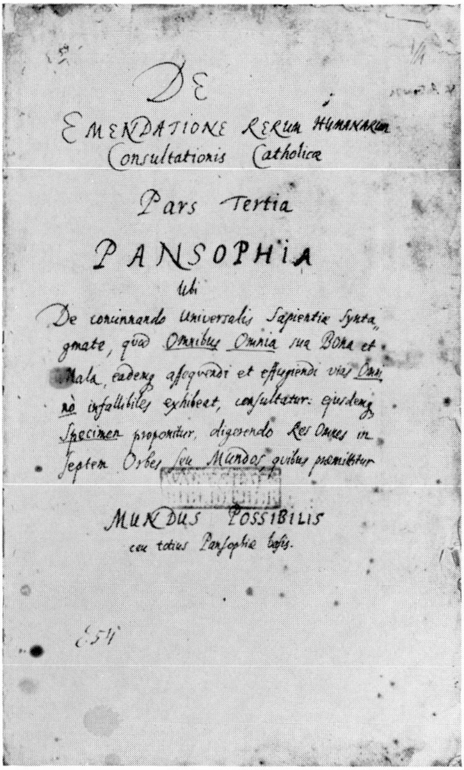
De
Emendatione Rerum Humanarum
Consultationis Catholicæ
Pars Tertia
PANSOPHIA
ubi
De concinnando Universalis Sapientiæ Synta-
gmate, quâ Omnibus Omnia sua Bona et
Mala, eademque assequendi et effugiendi vias Omni-
nò infallibiles exhibeat, consultatur: ejusdemque
Specimen proponitur, digerendo Res Omnes in
Septem Orbes seu Mundos quibus præmittitur
MUNDUS POSSIBILIS
seu totius Pansophiæ basis.

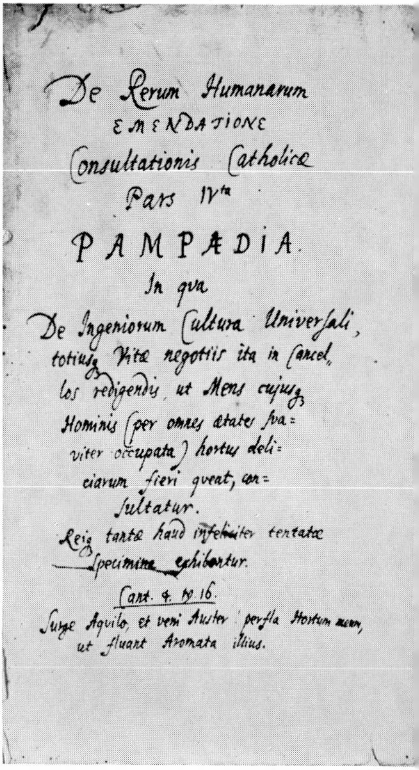
De Rerum Humanarum
EMENDATIONE
Consultationis Catholicæ
Pars IVta
PAMPÆDIA.
In qua
De Ingeniorum Cultura Universali,
totiusque Vitæ negotiis ita in Cancel-
los redigendis, ut Mens cujusque
Hominis (per omnes ætates sua-
viter occupata) hortus deli-
ciarum fieri queat, con-
sultatur.
Reique tantæ haud infeliciter tentatæ
Specimina exhibentur.
Cant. 4. v. 16.
Surge Aquilo, et veni Auster: perfla Hortum meum,
ut fluant Aromata illius.

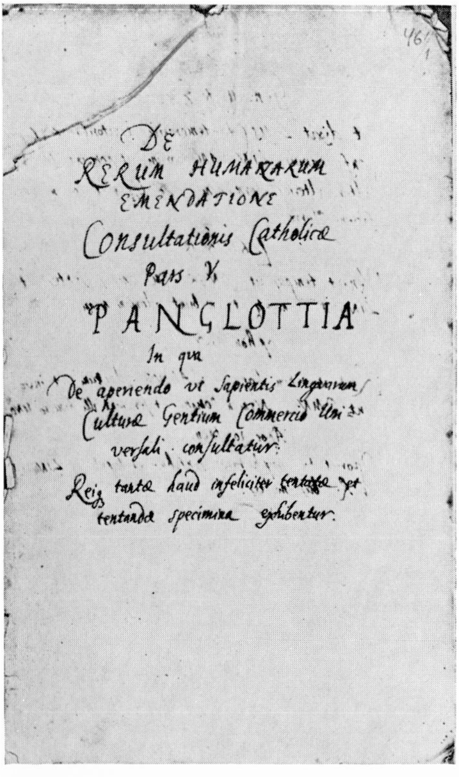
De
Rerum Humanarum
Emendatione
Consultationis Catholicæ
Pars V.
PANGLOTTIA
In qua
De aperiendo ut Sapientis Linguarum
Culturæ Gentium Commercio Uni-
versali consultatur.
Reique tantæ haud infeliciter tentatæ et
tentandæ specimina exhibentur.

4. *Manuscripts of Consultation*

study of languages'.[7] However, the best teachers were, without doubt, the Jesuits. Their methods were formal indeed but they were selected and trained for the work. Their Plan of Studies (*Ratio Studiorum*) said: 'It would be most profitable if those who are to be Preceptors were privately taken in hand by some one of great skill, and for two months or more were trained by him in the method of reading, teaching, writing, correcting and managing a class'.[8] The Plan of Studies also demanded careful preparation of the lecture (prelection) in these words: 'It will help much if the master does not speak on the spur of the moment without preparation, but reads carefully what he has thoughtfully prepared at home'.[9]

Nevertheless Comenius was not being presumptuous in giving to the eleventh chapter of the *Great Didactic* the heading, 'Hitherto there have been no perfect schools'. The harshness of teachers was a reflection of social opinion that evil was innate in the child and had to be exorcised. The grammar schools were seriously handicapped by the absence of good teaching at the primary level since teachers of young children were so poorly paid that they often had to combine some other trade with their schoolmastering in order to live.[10] Erasmus feared that 'this matter of profit lay at the root of the whole matter'[11] and William Petty bewailed the fact that teaching attracted only 'the worst and unworthiest of men'.[12] There were some very good grammar schools and some outstanding teachers but generally the schools were inefficient and the teachers uninspiring. Montaigne's criticism of their teaching as a 'certain method of high-flight and obsolete language quite different from the ordinary way of speaking'[13] is probably a fair comment on the normal teacher and Charles Robbins in his book, *Teachers in Germany in the 16th Century* confirms the general low standard of the schools. It was small wonder that, in the words of Roger Ascham, boys usually left school 'great lubbers, always learning and little profiting'.[14]

Comenius realized that this lack of good teachers was the biggest obstacle in his plans for reform – 'the task of fashioning men . . . could not be expected from those who only intended to remain in the profession for one year and meant to leave it as soon as they could find more lucrative employment',[15] He complains of the 'windy and parrot-like loquacity' of teachers whose learning he describes as 'husks without kernels'.[16] He condemns them above all because they hardly ever 'raise the question of virtuous living' and therefore do nothing to remedy the 'dissolute morals of all classes'.[17] For Comenius it was a matter of deep concern that 'schools were being set up all through Europe with a zeal hardly ever equalled in any age . . . but have multiplied vain indolence and punishments but not pleasantness'[18] and it seemed to him that no improvement was possible while the instructors of the young were, in the words of his friend and mentor, J. V. Andreae, the 'dregs of society'.[19]

Consequently one of the most important tasks of universal education was to improve the status, training and competence of teachers.

THE TEACHER'S IMAGE

An American educational sociologist, William Waller, describes school discipline as 'morale under institutionalized leadership' which depends upon 'formality setting the stage for social interactions, upon social distance which keeps primary group attitudes from eating away at formal relations, upon the reinforcement of respect for superiors by the respect of superiors for each other'.[20] It was because the Jesuits brought orderliness into their prelections and disputations, so that the teacher presided 'in such a way that he seemed to take part on both sides'[21] that they had fewer disciplinary troubles than other schools of their time. Later in the century De la Salle was able to demonstrate that the same methods could be used in dealing with the poorest children. The Christian Brothers came to their work with deep humility but also with deep sense of vocation and they were supported by their Order in combining a certain aloofness with constant impact upon the attention of their charges – 'The master shall not speak to the pupils as if he were preaching, but he shall interrogate them almost continuously, putting question upon question'.[22] Protestant educational reformers of the Hartlib group realized that they must do something to provide an alternative to the Catholic religious orders if they wanted to achieve 'morale under institutionalized leadership' and Hartlib himself in his Introduction to John Dury's *Reformed School* said, 'The schoolmaster in a well-ordered Commonwealth is no less considerable than either the minister or the magistrate, because neither the one nor the other will prosper or subsist long without him'.[23] John Dury proposed a 'Christian Association only of free persons' who should live together 'for the joint exercise of daily worship and for the furtherance of profitable employment by mutual concurrence'.[24] Another suggestion from the Protestant side was that of J. V. Andreae that the teachers of Christianopolis should be 'well-advanced in years' as well as 'specially remarkable for integrity, activity and generosity'.[25]

Comenius was well aware of the need for improving the public image of teaching. He found the lack of good teachers the chief obstacle to the carrying out of his plans and realized that in such a 'grave matter' as education it was not enough to have 'any man from the crowd'.[26]

To start with, the teacher must have a measure of independence both financial and psychological. His salary must be 'adequate' and such as would 'prevent a man of excellent gifts having reason to desert his appointment' and headmasters, in particular, deserve enough 'for their beautiful work'.[27] The teacher should be paid an assured sum by the state or local community though Comenius saw nothing objectionable in providing extra stimulus through fees from parents.[28] If there had to be any differentiation the 'teachers of the youngest children should receive the greater fee since they should be the wisest'.[29] A nice balance must be kept between stimulus and avarice and the ideal would be, in the words of Vives, that it should be 'just as much as a good man would desire but such as a bad man would despise'.[30] Financial sufficiency meant 'not to be in want and therefore not to covet the goods of others'[31] but to 'run to and fro, toil and scrape silver together from all directions and yet never have enough'[32] would be to lose psychological independence. The teacher should be able to enjoy a station of life without worry but without ostentation.

In return for social security the teacher must be a person of great industry. 'Idleness' in the opinion of Comenius was 'the sepulchre of a living man' and a teacher, more than anyone, should be a person to whom 'indolence and distaste are unknown'.[33] It was the nonchalance of the teachers at Saros Patak that upset him so much. Only the habit of industry could make the teacher 'never ashamed on account of his mission and never break down easily under burden of work'.[34] Comenius constantly invokes his analogy of the gardener or farmer in this respect – 'It is more profitable to sow less and to plough more' he quotes from Pliny[35] and the great principle which he discovers in the operations of nature is that of Thoroughness.[36]

With reasonable independence and zeal Comenius sees no reason why a teacher should not enjoy a high social status and, in fact, this is necessary for Waller's 'institutionalized morale'. He must be 'without blemish in the eyes of men so that he may never be ashamed'. Comenius speaks several times of the necessity that the 'matrons' also should be 'most respected' and wherever there are men or women 'outstanding among their fellows for their age, their knowledge and their skill there can be no lack of teachers'. They should be the 'élite endued with no less wisdom and practical ability than the shepherds of the churches and the superiors of communities'. 'Indeed,' adds Comenius, 'they should be even more so endued, for they are to lay the foundations for both Church and State'.[37] He is not above a little public relations in the form of dramatic displays which will demonstrate 'the care which the teachers devote to their charges' and encourage the parents 'not to spare expense'.[38]

The essence of education is that 'children should be in the company of wise, honourable and industrious men' and Comenius would have none of the easy familiarity which makes of the teacher a benevolent elder brother. Perhaps some measure of aloofness with the teacher 'on an elevated platform' . . . 'like the sun that supplies each creature with light and warmth' was the only possible condition for the huge classes described in the *Great Didactic* but Comenius felt it would also enhance the dignity of the teacher who would be 'like a miner who trembles with excitement when he discovers a rich vein of ore'.[39] In the *Outline of the Pansophic School* he gives other reasons for the 'elevated place from which he (the teacher) can turn on all his pupils the same rays of learning' since, if he is turned towards the light and should (for sake of better demonstration) draw something on the blackboard, all the pupils might clearly and properly see it'.[40] But a good teaching situation demands that 'a teacher whose learning merits esteem should possess such authority and command such respect that a pupil would think it sinful to offend him'.[41]

Comenius was concerned that the teachers of Saros Patak were not only indolent; they would 'rather be feared than loved'. The good teacher must gain the love as well as the respect of his pupils and only a 'sweet and mild carriage' could make authority and dignity bearable and the school a 'retreat of ease and mental delight'.[42] Especially was it necessary that mothers should build up in the minds of little children a favourable attitude towards the teacher while the teacher must constantly remember the need for humility. He must remember that it is 'nature who teaches and he is only the servant of nature' and Comenius would remind him that 'schools can learn a great deal from the nurse who teaches a child step by step'.[43] Anna Heyberger distinguishes a strong element of tenderness in the character of Comenius. She speaks of him 'bending over the cradle in which he has gently laid the little sovereign of human kind'[44] and the rather charming letter from his son-in-law, Peter Figulus, describing family life at Leszno, gives him news of his little daughter, Suzanna, who had just learned to read and write.[45] For the older children the teacher shows his pedagogic skill 'by forestalling the need for discipline and penalties' and Comenius asks, 'Who would ever resort to rancour, gall, or blows in a game? . . . This is not appropriate even in the apprenticeship of a craft; and should the status of teaching be worse?'[46] It was this aspect of the teacher image put forward by Comenius that caused Krause to draw the attention of Froebel to his work. The teacher's dignity is not inconsistent with his geniality. If he draws strength from his status as the representative of society he draws humbleness from his responsibility as a custodian of the 'vessels of the spirit of God'.[47] The teacher's function 'in loco parentis' is indicated very clearly – he 'should never be morose in the discharge of his duties but should perform all of them with paternal kindness'.[48] Comenius is aware that an intelligent person will often have a conflict in stooping to the level of the pupil and therefore he recommends that for backward pupils the teacher should not be 'excessively talented' or he must be 'schooled in patience' and in any case he needs the greater skill to stimulate the dull child with 'vivid examples' and 'fresh and diverting manner'.[49]

Only a high sense of vocation can realize the teacher ideal as envisaged by Comenius and in a sense he recognized that to lead mankind out of the cave of darkness into the light was a task for God alone. As Schaller puts it, 'God is the only true leader of man, his true teacher'[50] and Comenius was not without a fear that in proposing the ladder of pansophy he might be 'transforming the work of converting men which appertains to God'.[51] It could only be feasible in the hands of men 'wholly devoted to God, in order that they might have God as a partner'.[52] A universal teacher, therefore, is one who 'is capable of educating all people in all things that lead human nature to perfection'. Comenius goes on to say that the Apostles were 'instituted by Christ' for this purpose but 'the time of the apostles having passed, we must see to it that those who take over the education of men should be capable of becoming such teachers'.[53]

THE TEACHER'S TRAINING

Such an image of the teacher surely pre-supposes training and Comenius did not shrink from the role of being a 'teacher of teachers'. 'My Saviour knows,' he says, 'that my mind is simple so that I am indifferent whether to learn or to teach, whether to be a teacher of teachers (if I dare give myself this title) or a pupil of pupils, if in this way I can be of use.'[54] It was, in fact, largely due to his influence that the idea of teacher training came to be accepted. The 1963 *Year Book of Education* speaks of his significant contribution to training as a 'pleasant irony' since he seemed to propose a pedagogic method that would 'virtually make the teacher's ignorance a matter of indifference'.[55] Even though the English Civil War 'confounded all plans' and forced Comenius to turn elsewhere, his ideas continued to stimulate speculation about teacher training and universal education. As Samuel Hartlib put it, 'the readiest way to reform both Church and Commonwealth . . . was to send forth reformed schoolmasters'. Thus in 1645 John Dury wrote a *Description of a Transmarine School* in which the master displayed his skill for all to see and thus instructed beginners. This was evidently borrowed from the Jesuit Schools which, in Bacon's words, excelled in 'point of usefulness' in their methods of training.[56] In 1649 a Dr Bathurst put forward a proposal for a state-supported institution 'for the making and training up of schoolmasters' but nothing came of it.[57] Dr Bathurst was a member of the Oxford Philosophical Society and it was at this time that Hartlib proposed an 'Office of Public Address' with headquarters in Oxford to help to perfect Comenius' educational reforms.[58] The training of 'ushers' was an important part of Dury's Reformed School in which the master-teacher or Governor took responsibility for a group of them and 'so prepared, methodized and ordered' the day that 'nothing could be tedious to the children'.[59] There was to be a similar system for the 'Associated Women'. William Petty's 'Advice' of 1648 was that craftsmen should join a collegiate body for the educating of children and inform them 'of all things and actions' before they were introduced to books.[60] Nevertheless J. W. Adamson says, 'At the very moment when Comenius' theories failed to gain the public ear of London, scholastic reforms of an epoch-making kind were putting those theories to the test in Central Germany'.[61] Here he is referring to the work of Duke Ernest of Saxe-Gotha and his adviser, Andreas Reyher, from 1641 to 1674 and it is significant that when the good Duke died he recommended in his will the institution of a teachers' training college. Later in the century the pioneer work of Hermann Francke in teacher training derived its inspiration from Comenius and since this led to the development of the Prussian state system of pedagogical training the influence of Comenius is considerable, if indirect.

To the problem of the training of teachers Comenius had a number of answers though none of them were fully worked out. At the beginning it is necessary to say that the preparation of a teacher must have its roots in childhood and that 'training' in the narrow sense can only be effective if the right foundations have been laid and the right attitudes established. The teacher is the servant of nature but he himself must have developed to the maturity of nature if he is to be capable of helping others. Carl Jung puts the dilemma of teacher-training in these words: 'Our whole problem suffers from a one-sided approach to the child who is to be educated and an equally one-sided lack of emphasis on the uneducatedness of the educator'.[62] Herbert Spencer makes the same point though in different terms: 'Bad teachers will fail even with the best methods . . . True education is practicable only by a true philosopher . . . Judge then what chance a philosophical method has of being carried out'.[63] Therefore the pansophical or universal teacher begins his development in the cradle and it must be admitted that 'the entire hope for the coming of better times is exclusively concentrated in the right up-bringing of the young',[64] while, on the other hand, 'what is completely corrupted is not worth repairing'. Whatever later 'training' he may be given the teacher will tend to reproduce the relationships which he experienced in the family and the didactic approach by which he himself was taught in the school. The ideal of teacher training is that every educative agency to which the child is submitted should have a unity of aim and method – the family instruction by parents, the teaching in the Church, the didactic approach of the different schools, the agencies of mass communication in adult life. In such a situation it could be assumed that every person might be in some sense both student and teacher and that there would be an unlimited field from which to choose those who by inclination and aptitude were specially fitted for the profession of teaching. With such a social background many people would share Comenius' own judgment of a 'fashion of life which contains least of cares and violence and most of peace and cheerfulness'.[65]

Hence the answer of Comenius to the problem of teacher supply and selection was that the pansophic school would produce its own teachers. He accepted that 'only a man with pansophic knowledge could teach pansophy',[66] but then such teachers would 'continually improve their erudition by teaching others'. It must be 'men who will keep learning from day to day' who must be 'sought and prevailed upon to come and allured with any entreaties or rewards'.[67] Even if, at first, they were not 'wise and eloquent, conversant with mathematics and metaphysics' the very nature of their work would eventually make them 'leaders and directing forces'.[68] The essential qualifications of the universal teacher were:

1. 'That he should possess the qualities he is to develop in others;
2. That he should know how to form others accordingly; and
3. That he should be eager in his work'.[69]

Preparation could not begin too early and this gives point to the emphasis in the *Analytical Didactic* on the Axiom 'Every pupil should acquire the habit of also acting as teacher'.

However, until such time as a self-perpetuating system of teacher production could be established Comenius must needs look for models of training methods in other fields and the one to which he would naturally be drawn was that for ministers of the Unity of Brethren. In fact this parallel between priest and teacher was normal in his day,[70] and Comenius says that only a 'pedant would think the reform of schools has nothing to do with the vocation of a Theologian'.[71] He himself took an active part in the training of ordinands at Fulnek and directed their practical work in the school. For some years as Secretary of the Unity he had responsibility for the studies of theological students both in Leszno and abroad and thus he was very familiar with all the problems.

The Rule of Discipline of the Brethren put every Pastor under obligation to board some young men in his house and 'to take care for their instruction'. Comenius adds that this was often at 'the urgent request of the parents', and since there was at Fulnek a commodious manse he doubtless had a number of acoluths or deacons. These students performed many of the duties concerned with divine worship such as ringing the bell and lighting the candles. They read the Bible at Family Prayers and taught the Catechism in the school. The time-table was a full one beginning at an early hour with devotions and then dividing the day between study, manual work and singing in the evenings. The over-riding condition was obedience to rule and they were required to submit to the judgment of the Pastor in all things. The ordination of an acoluth, the lowest order in the ministry, took place before the whole Synod and the young aspirant was required to make a solemn promise before his acceptance. He then became a deacon and took a more active part in the work of the Church including the teaching of religion to young people and participation in the sacraments. When the bishop came on his periodic visit to the Church he would subject the young man to a searching examination concerning his sense of vocation and might transfer him to his own house or send him to study at a foreign centre – Comenius himself was sent in this way to Herborn by Bishop Lanecký. A deacon could not be ordained until he was twenty-four years old and until he reached that age he would work with a minister, or, as Comenius did, teach in a school. The Rule of Discipline says, 'Ministers among us do not rush into the administration of the sacred office' and they made the final ordination service a very solemn affair – seldom heard 'without tears' as Comenius admits. Even then, new ministers usually remained for a few years as assistants before being called to a pastorate and Comenius probably stayed with his Bishop at Přerov before being inducted at Fulnek. The young minister was not allowed to marry without the agreement of the bishop and in Comenius' case he was definitely advised to take a wife so that he might better fulfil his duties. Teaching was an essential part of pastoral work since all members were presumed to be able to read and write.

During this somewhat arduous training the pastor had a personal responsibility for the practical work of the student. Thus on Saturday he would require each acoluth in turn to speak on the text appointed for the Sunday service and during the week he supervised the teaching in the school. The close connection between theologue and teacher, which Schaller calls the 'primary factor in Comenian education',[72] was later realized in the Halle schools by Francke who made teaching a part of the training of pastors for two hours daily under the supervision of head teachers.[73] Comenius required that both the headmaster and his deputy in the Pansophic School should be theologians and he proposed that some of the pupils should stay on after the seventh grade as boarders in the headmaster's house. They might spend part of their time teaching the younger children, especially of nobles, and part in studying, amongst other things, the theory of teaching. The very serious attitude which he took towards the personal guidance of students is shown by the 'Rules of Life' which he wrote for a student ('on the day on which you depart from me') bidding him to let his theories 'be inseparable companions with practice' and to do whatever he knew to be good'.[74] As a minister of the Brethren Comenius saw nothing incongruous in requiring a student teacher to occupy part of his time in manual work. It had a moral value in helping him to realize the truth that 'none may eat the bread of idleness' but it also had didactic value in emphasizing the importance of practical work – 'Mechanics do not begin by drumming rules into their apprentices. They take them into the workshop and bid them to look at the work that has been produced, and then, when they wish them to imitate this, they place tools in their hands and show them how they should be used'.[75] It may have been his own experience as a lad at Uhersky Brod that made him say, 'In these matters artisans are indeed far-sighted. None of them lectures his apprentice on the abstract rules of his craft; instead, he sets to work, with the apprentice looking on'.[76] It is evident that Comenius saw much in a kind of pupil-teacher system of training as a basis for the preparation of the teacher provided, of course, that sufficient master-craftsmen could be found to demonstrate their art. He puts practical teaching under supervision high in any training programme since 'as no man becomes a smith except by hammering so pupils must be framed to be men by handling human beings'.[77] Thus the school should be an association of children with adults at varying levels of competence and maturity somewhat after the pattern of the congregations of the Brethren in which there were the Beginners, the Proficient and the Perfect. The Perfect were those so established in the faith that they could guide and 'see to the good conversation of the rest' and similarly in the Pansophic School there might be a similar division, all devoted to 'improving their own erudition by teaching' but the most senior using the school as an educational laboratory for constantly raising standards.

The kind of in-service training that most appealed to Comenius was that which went on in the school and for this purpose he envisaged 'an alliance of a great number of men' who would maintain standards and disseminate ideas throughout the world. The members of the College of Light or Universal College were to be 'the executants who will carry the schemes which have been excellently thought out to the desired completion',[78] and their place was to be, not in some academic ivory tower, but in the schools 'instructing those who were ignorant of their art'.[79] Partly this constant surveillance was because of the human tendency to be satisfied with the *status quo* – 'Men tend to break down under the pressure of work and are, like Proteus, all too ready to change into monsters of various shapes unless they are seized and bound with the bonds of order'.[80] Even headmasters, whose duty it is 'to make the round of the class-rooms' may be tempted to relax[81] and the history of education proves that an efficient system of inspection can be a positive force for good by ensuring efficiency without curbing initiative.[82]

The necessity for a theoretical basis for activity as well as the supervised practice of it became apparent to the Church of the Brethren as soon as conditions became more stable. As early as 1531 a Synod recommended a more thorough intellectual training of the ministers and Jan Blahoslav found for his part 'no fear that learned men will ever ruin the Church'. Comenius agreed that piety, though indispensable, was not enough by itself – it could be used 'as an excuse for neglecting other adornments of the rational life'. At the same time experience showed the dangers of the university as it existed then. R. F. Young gives an account of the university studies and subsequent career of a young man named Jan Bernart. After attending school at Přerov, he was sent to Wittemberg in 1574 but soon transferred to Heidelberg. After three years there he went to Oxford where he stayed for three years, finally coming back to Bohemia in 1585. This was exceptional but the results were not encouraging since he died in 1600 having 'ruined his health by much drinking'.[83] This was unfortunate and gives some justification for Comenius' complaints about luxury and revelling at universities that 'speak out too loud'.[84] Nevertheless both he and his Church were willing to run the risk and Young says, 'In no sphere was the liberalizing influence of the Transalpine Renaissance so noticeable as in the arrangements made by the Brethren for the education of their ministers from 1543 onwards'. However, the chief complaint of Comenius against the universities as a means of preparing teachers was that they failed to show the wholeness of knowledge. They made truth 'estranged because of the tearing of science into pieces'. Thus Prague University, although founded by Emperor Charles IV in 1348 so that 'the nation might find the fruits of learning set out on its own table', was closed to students of the Unity because of sectarian bias. In most of the other universities of the time the teaching was in Comenius' words 'not enough accommodated to the uses of life'.[85] The universities generally concentrated on the higher and professional branches of learning and disregarded universal education. Comenius asked that they should 'bear in mind both the general aim of the entire education of man as well as the particular and proper aim of his profession'.[86] A university should have universal aims. It should not confine wisdom 'to the Latin tongue or imprison it in schools'.[87] It is clear that, when he came to design the Temple of Wisdom of his dreams, Comenius relied very much on the medieval synthesis of the Liberal Arts dominated by theology but nevertheless he gave a reasonable outline of universal knowledge – 'the common notions of man's understanding, the whole of the Visible World, all the works of man effected by art and wit, and the spiritual experience of man'. Thus he united the two worlds of science and the arts whose division is so much deplored by Sir Charles Snow. He provided a basis for the study of education in philosophy, psychology and sociology. And by his theological assumption he provided, not a rigid framework setting the boundaries of human thinking but a foundation from which man could 'without ceasing discover the infinity of his own desires and of his capacity'. E. T. Campagnac says, in his 'Introduction' to the Via Lucis,

'He (Comenius) was satisfied that we can make experiments and progress, only if we accept our place in a scheme or system which he calls 'universal' and of which the basic hypothesis is God . . . and this is an hypothesis which makes room for new things and for new interpretations of old things'.[88]

Hence arises the necessity that the teacher should have an ideology which is more than a set of slogans. It must have its roots in childhood. It must have a 'slow and calm' development over the years gradually bringing into its view every aspect of reality. It must have a dynamic power sufficient to 'remove the countless difficulties, huge as the rocks of Sisyphus, with which mankind has been beset'.[89] Finally it must provide a stimulus for research on a co-ordinated front and not as a host of unrelated specialisms.

THE TEACHER'S FUNCTION

When he was writing the *Great Didactic* Comenius seemed to put methodology above the personality of the teacher and to assert that a valid method would make the teacher's ignorance a matter of indifference. Method appeared to offer an 'efficacious remedy' for the vicious circle in which mankind found itself and he compares it with Columbus' discovery of America or Faust's invention of printing. If adopted, it would make 'the perplexities of one age afford amusement to the next'.[90] Consequently his appeal was to practising teachers that they should become the instruments of the principle of order 'which holds together the fabric of the world, down to its smallest detail'. Their function was, therefore, to bring the art of teaching to perfection 'though the difficulties may be somewhat alarming at first'.[91]

His preoccupation with pansophy did not, as Jelínek suggests, maim his ideas since he tried to recast his method in a more firmly based logical form. Jelínek agrees that the *Analytical Didactic* is a 'true didactic or rationale of pedagogic method whereas the *Great Didactic* and its Czech counterpart are merely guides to methodical practice'.[92] In it Comenius states his purpose as follows:

'We shall explore the paths of the art of teaching and examine all the general and particular activities that meet in the act of teaching, learning and knowing, to the end that we may determine what their nature is, what they consist of, and how they develop, for in that way we may determine how we can and ought to treat them'.[93]

The teacher's function in the *Great Didactic* was a mechanical one 'to facilitate the multiplation of learned men in precisely the same way that the discovery of printing has facilitated the multiplication of books'.[94]

In the later works there is still an emphasis on imitation and orderly progression but there is also a recognition of the pupil's unique contribution to his own learning. Thus the three basic principles of learning laid down in the *Great Didactic* are:

1. Facility.
2. Thoroughness.
3. Conciseness.

In each case the argument is that success comes from exact imitation of nature and that any deviations must be rectified immediately. The individual must converge in his thinking and behaviour towards a model already determined. To some extent the same approach is taken in the *Analytical Didactic*. Axiom XXXIX states categorically: 'Without examples, precepts, and exercises, nothing is taught or learned unless it be incorrectly' and the corollary is simply: 'Therefore, if you want a student to learn something, reduce it to an example, explain the underlying idea, and then bid him to strive to approximate the example.' Yet when Comenius comes to define his basic principles he gives attention to the spontaneous reaction of the student. The principles are:

1. Rapidity.
2. Agreeableness.
3. Thoroughness.

and in discussing the second of these he comes much closer to accepting some divergence from the norm. Thus he says, 'To deal with aptitudes as their nature demands is the basis of progress! . . . because human nature is free, loves spontaneity, and abhors compulsion. Consequently it wishes to be guided on its course; it does not wish to be pulled, pushed or driven'. Later on he puts the case for creative activity thus: 'Human nature, being the ordained mistress of things, is always forming, transforming, or building something to exercise mastery over things' . . . 'Children find no pleasure in merely listening while someone else talks; they like to interrupt and make themselves heard'. In the *Pampaedia* there is again an understanding of the dual nature of the didactic process. In chapter VII the three objectives or principles of the universal teacher are given as

1. 'Universality, so that all might be taught all things.
2. Simplicity, so that they might be taught reliably.
3. Voluntariness, so that they might learn . . . as if they were at play.'

But the conclusion of the matter is, 'One might call the entire process of human education: "School as Pastime".'

Thus the function of the teacher to restore man to the image of God must be understood as a balancing of opposite forces. On the one side is order, perfection and convergence. On the other side is creativity, infinite variety and divergence from pattern. Comenius believed that he had found a means of integrating them in the master principle of universality. To say that the universal teacher is one who teaches all things does not mean that he has or wishes to transmit encyclopaedic knowledge of all facts but rather that he sees the relevance of every new fact of which he becomes aware to the total body of knowledge. It is not necessary that he should know facts as isolated verbal descriptions but that he should know what is required for full humanity and be able to turn his knowledge to advantage – 'so to enclose the business of this life in the bounds of prudence that all things here are secure' and 'to let his senses be directed to everything material, his reason to everything spiritual, his faith to all that is revealed'.[95]

In this very delicate process of making men the teacher has both negative and positive functions. On the negative side he must stand in the way of corrupting influences and eradicate evil wherever it has found entrance. Comenius cannot 'refrain from severely reprimanding the shallow-brained mockery of affection of those who permit children to grow up without correction',[96] and without some degree of discipline, he finds a school to be like 'a mill without water'.[97] In a social situation, such as home or school, it is not possible to leave natural consequences as an automatic corrective for bad habits and the adult cannot abdicate

5. J. A. Comenius by Vaclav Brožík

JOH. AMOS COMENI
PORTAEL der
SAECKEN
en Spraecken
VESTIBULUM
RERUM.
et Lingvarum

Amsterdam
M.DC.LVIII.

Crispyn de pas delin.

Title Page of Vestibulum

his responsibilities because of the risk that he will give an excess of control. However, as he grew older Comenius came to emphasize the positive role more and he moved away from the external pressure of eternal vigilance so strongly marked in the *Great Didactic*. Instead of the teacher being 'always present in the room to scold the idlers and praise the hard-working',[98] he finds a guiding role in so arranging the situation that the 'workroom becomes a playground'.[99] The teacher does not cease from making the 'simultaneous training of mind, tongue and hand' an activity in which there is play without triviality and work without drudgery. In chapter XXV of the *Methodus* there is an analysis of the integration of the negative and positive functions of teaching which achieves the following results:

1. It gives full scope to intellectual and physical activity through spontaneous effort.
2. It promotes co-operative effort consistent with well-regulated competition.
3. It overcomes boredom by constant variety of sense experience and practical occupations.
4. Nourishes honest rivalry.
5. Insists upon well-regulated competition and fair play.
6. Requires constant practice with a minimum of theory.
7. Lays stress upon sense experience and observation.
8. Is sufficiently varied to prevent boredom.

Comenius believed firmly in the principle of auto-education. But he did not go to the extreme of thinking that the teacher was no more than a sympathetic director of didactic apparatus. Nor was his interpretation of progressive education that the teacher's task was simply 'to understand what needs to be favoured' and 'to focus all his efforts on providing the most favouring conditions' as a modern writer, Nathan Isaacs, defines it.[100] The teacher himself is part of the educative environment and his example or the model which he provides will 'accustom' the pupil to produce perfect work. The skill of the teacher is in selecting the most appropriate example for the occasion. He must lead the pupil 'through the theatres of God'[101] and 'in distinguishing well he teaches well'. In so far as he has also to instruct his pupil he can pursue a number of techniques of varying value. Thus he can adopt one of the following methods or combine them together:

1. Analysis which means 'the breaking up of the whole into its parts'.
2. Synthesis which 'consists of reassembling of parts into the appropriate whole'.
3. Syncrisis which 'denotes an appropriate comparison of parts with wholes and wholes with wholes'.[102]

In the Analytical Didactic Comenius says of this, 'Very true is the saying – "Parallelism makes for greater clarity".'

The ideal technique is a combination of techniques. The teacher may guide his pupils to 'read many authors or books' or to make 'diverse experiments', but the hardest method of all is to help him to understand the 'notion' or inner meaning of things and this gives knowledge of the kind possessed by God. But the 'safest' method is to 'combine these three roads, though gradually'.[103]

Complementary to the didactic function of making 'men in the image of God 'was that of making society fit for the Millenium. Comenius was under no illusion that the task of cleansing the Augean stables was immense but he was no iconoclast, he had a high regard for the past, for tradition, for European civilization, and, above all, for the culture of his own land, and these things it was the function of education to preserve and transmit. It must be admitted that he was inclined to equate the Unity of Brethren with Czech Protestantism and the burgher class with Czech democracy. The rich were 'hogs stuffed with bran' and the poor, 'paltry little asses laden with burdens'.[104] It must be admitted, also, that Comenius had little awareness of the social changes of his day tending towards an industrial and capitalistic organization of society nor of the cultural riches of the non-Christian world. Nevertheless he was firmly rooted in his native soil. From early youth he was, as he says, 'led by the desire to render a service' to his mother tongue and 'only the conditions of his life compelled him to write in Latin'.[105]

Thus an important function of the teacher was to act as

guardian of the heritage of the past and preserver of all that was good in the present. The transforming of society need not involve bloody revolution if education became its major preoccupation. Comenius believed that 'the future of every state lies in its youth and care for the schools means assuring the future of the state'. His thought has a parallel with Matthew Arnold's dictum: 'The state's proper business is popular education' but he put it even more personally in these words: 'The attitude of those who would limit education to themselves and their children is that of people betraying the common good'.[106] Thus the teacher has a positive social function apart from the conservative one. First he must consider the average pupil. The average and below average are more than 'half the future'. They constitute 'a very important point of the whole fabric of the school'.[107] Comenius is definitely on the side of the broad highway concept of education rather than the ladder of opportunity one, and therefore the teacher must accept the social function of compensating by his skill and diligence for 'lack of aptitude and discernment'.[108] Second the teacher must accept the principle of collective teaching. The school is a 'kind of public assembly' to which all should 'be invited and led by the hand to the true knowledge of wealth'.[109] Within the school the basic unit of instruction is the class – 'a gathering into one entity of those pupils who are joined by the same standards of proficiency'. Each class must have its own master, 'who is in charge of it', its own basic text-book and its own room separated from all external distractions and equipped to show its particular slant. Comenius did not favour a specialist time-table and his curriculum was not subject-orientated. The master was a shepherd of the flock who knew his pupils intimately and each class was 'a wrestling school for the small candidates of wisdom'.[110] Thirdly the teacher must accept mass media as a means of instruction. The only form of mass media with which Comenius was familiar was the book – that 'marvellous device' the benefit of which to mankind 'can scarcely be told',[111] and it is quite clear that he regarded it as an instrument of science. The teacher was the artist constantly adjusting himself to the needs of the situation but he could use an instrument consciously based on science. The attempt to elaborate such a scientific foundation for the function of teaching is, in the opinion of Jean Piaget, the 'main claim to glory' of Comenius.[112] Krause wrote to Froebel along the same lines – 'Comenius proposes an entirely new basis of education. He attempts to find a method consciously based on science, whereby teachers will teach less and learners will learn more'.[113] But this scientific approach was only possible by the use of mass media and still left scope for the intuitive approach of the teacher himself and the 'Gellianic exercises' in which pupils meet in groups and exchange their knowledge 'as merchants exchange their wares'.[114] Finally the teacher had a social function in convincing the adult world of the potential of education. He must cultivate public relations. In his description of Humanity in the *Orbis Pictus* (Ch. CXV) Comenius emphasizes the pacific motif. To be 'human' is to be 'like the turtle-loves, harmonious, gentle and benevolent on all sides'. To be 'angry, cruel and implacable' is not to be like men but 'rather like wolves and lions'. Only teachers can draw men back to this proper view of their nature and help them to change their inmost attitudes. Comenius takes his illustration from the Old Testament story of the Samaritans who hastened to tell the king's household of the disappearance of the Syrian army and adjures teachers, 'the ushers of human kind to wisdom' that they should 'do away for good and all with the three foes of the happiness of all mankind – barbarous conduct, wicked ways and war'.[115] A 'normal' school should not simply be a demonstration of good teaching method. It should also be a demonstration of reformed humanity.

NOTES

1. *Orbis Pictus* Ch. C.
2. e.g. P. Monroe: *History of Education* p. 434. J. S. Brubacher: *History of Problems of Education* p. 194.
3. M. Luther quoted by Eby: *Early Protestant Educators* p. 32.
4. *Labyrinth*: X.2.
5. W. H. Woodward: *Vittorino da Feltre* p. 34.
6. W. H. Woodward: *Education in the Age of the Renaissance* p. 160.
7. P. Monroe: *History of Education* p. 385.
8. T. Hughes: *Loyola and the Educational System of the Jesuits* p. 160.
9. E. A. Fitzpatrick: *St Ignatius and the Ratio Studiorum* p. 201.
10. J. S. Brubacher: *History of the Problems of Education* p. 501.

11. Erasmus: *De Pueris Instituendis* Quoted by W. H. Woodward: *Erasmus* p. 209.
12. W. Petty: Advice of W. P. to Samuel Hartlib.
13. L. E. Rector: *Montaigne – The Educator of Children* p. 89.
14. Roger Ascham: *Schoolmaster* Bk. II.
15. Leges Scholae bene Ordinatae (ODO. III.784-803).
16. *Great Didactic* XI.10.
17. *Great Didactic* XI.8.
18. *Panorthosia* XXII.
19. J. V. Andreae: *Christianopolis* LII.

The Teacher's Image

20. W. Waller: *The Sociology of Teaching* (New York, Wiley, 1932).
21. E. A. Fitzpatrick: *Op. cit.* p. 154.
22. De la Salle: *Conduct of Schools* quoted by J. W. Adamson: *Pioneers of Modern Education*, p. 232.
23. S. Hartlib: *Introduction to Dury's Reformed School* (Ed. H. M. Knox) p. 20.
24. J. Dury: *Reformed School* p. 23.
25. J. V. Andreae: *Christianopolis* LII.
26. *Great Didactic* XXXIII.4.
27. *Outline of Pansophic School*: Deliberation.
28. *Panorthosia*: XXII.28.
29. *Pampaedia* X.
30. L. Vives: *De Tradendis Disciplinis*.
31. *Pampaedia* III.22.
32. *Labyrinth* Ch. 46.
33. *Analytical Didactic* 14.
34. *Pampaedia* VII.4.
35. *Analytical Didactic* 152.
36. *Great Didactic* XVIII.
37. *Pampaedia* VII.7.
38. *Outline of Pansophic School* XX.87.
39. *Great Didactic* XIX.16.
40. *Outline of Pansophic School* 52.
41. *Analytical Didactic* 38.
42. *Informatorium* III.
43. *Methodus* VII.
44. Anna Heyberger: *J. A. Comenius* p. 174.
45. Patera: *Korres.* p. 171-2 Quoted by Heyberger p. 85.
46. *Pampaedia* VII.3.
47. A. Heyberger: *Op. cit.* p. 13.
48. *Analytical Didactic* 140.
49. *Analytical Didactic* 116-117.
50. K. Schaller: *Die Pädagogik des J.A.C.* p. 345.
51. *Diatyposis* p. 64.
52. *Pampaedia* VII.4.
53. *Pampaedia* VII.2.

The Teacher's Training

54. *Great Didactic*: Greeting 21.
55. *Education Year Book* (1963) Article by John C. Osgood: 'Contribution of Comenius to Teacher Training' p. 60-64.

56. T. Corcoran: *Studies in the History of Classical Teaching* p. 231-237. cf. H. M. Knox: *Introduction to Dury's Reformed School* p. 8.

57. G. H. Turnbull: *Hartlib, Dury and Comenius* p. 64.

58. H. M. Knox: *Introduction to Reformed School* p. 9.

59. J. Dury: *Reformed School* p. 28 (Ed. H. M. Knox).

60. W. Petty: 'Advice of W. P. to Samuel Hartlib'.

61. J. W. Adamson: *Op. cit.* p. 93.

62. C. Jung: *Development of Personality* p. 169.

63. Herbert Spencer: *Essays* p. 56. (Everyman Ed. 1916).

64. *Panorthosia XXII.*

65. *Labyrinth I.*

66. *Outline of Pansophic School*: Deliberation.

67. *Outline of Pansophic School*: 100.

68. *Outline of Pansophic School*: Deliberation.

69. *Outline of Pansophic School*: 3.

70. C. Robbins: *Teachers in Germany in 16th Century* p. 41.

71. *Great Didactic*: Greeting 19.

72. K. Schaller: *Die Pädagogik des J.A.C.* p. 163.

73. J. W. Adamson: *Op. cit.* p. 245.

74. *Regulae Vitae* (1645) Tr. Edw. Synge (1736).

75. *Great Didactic XXI.7.*

76. *Analytical Didactic* 28.

77. *Reformation of Schools (Praeludia)* 33

78. *Via Lucis XXI.7.*

79. *Panorthosia XVI.6.*

80. *Pampaedia VII.4.*

81. *Panorthosia XXII.* cf. Outline.

82. cf. W. H. G. Armytage: *400 Years of English Education* p. 150-151.

83. R. F. Young: *Jan Bernart of Přeřov* 1553-1600.

84. *Reformation of Schools* 15.

85. *Reformation of Schools* 12.

86. *Pampaedia VII.7.*

87. *Reformation of Schools* 101.

88. E. T. Campagnac: Introduction to *Via Lucis* VI and IX.

89. *Via Lucis XXI.15.*

The Teacher's Function

90. *Great Didactic* XII and XIII.

91. *Great Didactic XXXII.2.*

92. V. Jelínek: *Analytical Didactic* p. 18.

93. *Analytical Didactic* 5.

94. *Great Didactic XXXII.27.*

95. *Pampaedia I.12* and VII.13.

96. *Informatorium* IX.

97. *Great Didactic XXVI.1.*

98. *Great Didactic XXVI.5.*

99. *Pampaedia VII.29.*

100. Nathan Isaacs: *Piaget and Progressive Education.* (Froebel Foundation 1955).

101. *Pampaedia VII.27.*

102. *Pampaedia VII.16.*

103. *Pampaedia VII.28.*

104. *Great Didactic. VI.8.*

TEACHERS

CHAPTER 12

BOOKS

IN his attempt to universalize education Comenius frequently used particular words in a universal sense. Thus he speaks of the world as the School of God's wisdom, and calls upon men 'to imitate the School of Paradise'. He proposes to make 'the whole of life a school' divided into seven stages 'for the gradual perfection of man'. The word 'man' is almost always used in a universal sense to cover 'all peoples, conditions, families, persons, never omitting anybody' and all made in the image of God. But since the Creator has put man into the school of life He has also equipped this school 'richly with books' so that the education of man might be 'a leveller road for spreading the light of Pansophy'. Thus the word 'book' is also used in a universal sense as meaning 'a copy of the eternal nature of God'. The 'first and greatest book of God is the visible world'. The second is Man himself that is to say 'the reasoning mind which is the measure of all things'. But God has given into man's hands a third book 'to serve as a commentary upon the external world and a guide to the inner world' namely the book of revelation.[1]

In a slightly narrower sense books might be defined as 'instruments of representation' of ideas which must originally emanate from God. The doctrine of the 'logos' as expounded by St John was an attempt to personalize in God the pure form, pure act, pure thought of Greek philosophy but from an educational point of view it still left the problem of interpreting the 'Word' into intelligible terms. God Himself has shown the way by creating a universe of 'things' each of them presenting some facet or another of the original idea and at times Comenius takes the realist view that all knowledge comes through sense experience of tangible objects. To some extent this was part of the reaction against the scholastic theory that 'words have a closer relation to causing knowledge than have the mere perceivable

things outside the mind, inasmuch as words are symbols of intelligible content'.[2] Comenius puts 'the description of things
given by speech which we call books' as subordinate instruments
to 'things presented directly to the senses' or 'pictures of things
prepared by the painter or modeller'.[3] Nevertheless he realized
that 'things' by themselves have no message for the mind until
they are transformed into 'images' and that learning is a process
of identifying objects and assigning them their proper classifica-
tions. Books, therefore, are not simply descriptions. They are,
also, by their very arrangement and structure interpretative and
as such he quite rightly considered them 'the foremost instruments in the reformation of the world'.[4]

Comenius spent the best part of his life writing books which
he hoped would be instruments of universal education but he
always kept an awareness of the limitations of what he was
doing. He feared that he was promising more than could be
accomplished by such means and that he 'had a mind to cheat
the world'.[5] He was conscious of his own weaknesses as 'a man
of little ability and almost without literary training'.[6] The project which he set for himself of a series of books covering the
whole of human knowledge, every stage of human development
in this world and the next, and every condition of life was one
for which 'no single man and no single generation was
sufficient'.[7] He constantly regretted that he was so 'distraught
with divers affairs' that he could not give undivided attention
to his main task. He even complained to his friend, Samuel
Hartlib, of being dragged into the limelight of popularity to the
detriment of his aim: 'If there is one man who hath brought
hindrance to the pansophic study, thou art he, friend, in that
thou has not allowed me to do what I had to do in peace'. To
which Hartlib replied, not without justification, 'Whither
rushest, mortal that thou art, and darest things too small for thy
powers'.[8] Perhaps his most trying period was the five years at
Elbing (1642-47) when he tried in vain to get collaborators.
Partly, as G. H. Turnbull suggests, it was his own fault[9] but he
certainly did have some bad fortune. One of his helpers, George
Vechner, could not leave Leszno to join him. Another man,
Johannes Rave, who entered into the partnership of Comenius
with Dury and Hartlib, proved to be 'given to loytering' until

Dury said of him, 'I feare we shall not have much good of him, and what he will doe will come from him by flashes'.[10] George Ritschel worked with him for two years at Elbing and wrote a book which shows a pansophic slant but he was too much 'living in want' to be of much service.[11] Finally there was Cyprian Kinner concerning whom Turnbull says, 'It was probably impossible for them to continue in collaboration for any length of time, whatever the conditions'.[12] At Saros Patak there was a similar race against time which Comenius says, 'rightly worries me because it seems an immense task to write all these books in exact harmony with their intention. It is beyond one who is broken by age and already has death at his side'.[13] He was frank in his self criticism of a literary output, which can fairly be described as enormous, in a book entitled *The Fanner of Wisdom*, or the Art of Retracting one's own opinions.[14]

Concerning books in general Comenius never ceased to be suspicious of the pretensions of scholars. His main charges were of fraudulence and prolixity. Writers were 'pasters of quotations'; they 'highly spiced what another had already cooked'; they distorted the truth 'according to the fashion in which their glasses were put on' and wrote obscurely and not 'in the manner of mathematics'.[15] The men of learning 'grieved him to tears' because they put so much emphasis on controversy. Argument was fruitless and words fallacious when all they produced was a 'rage for disputation'.[16] It is not so certain that Comenius realized the danger of using books as authoritarian instruments since he constantly sought for a book which would supersede the vast volumes 'of every matter which would take millions of years to peruse'.[17] Books are constantly in danger, as Plato pointed out, of being used inflexibly, as if the written word had some inherent superiority over the spoken word,[18] and Comenius was not altogether free from the faults which he condemned so strongly in others. He criticized the tendency to publish too quickly, to overload with references that 'disgust the reader', to confuse things that can be said briefly.[19] He condemned the impudent 'Searchalls' who 'wandered through the world, peeping into corners and spying out everything that is secret'.[20]

As Bishop and Secretary (písař) of the Unity of Brethren Comenius had a special concern that libraries should be for use and not for storage. According to the Book of Church Government he was bound 'to care for a library and increase it with useful books'.[21] Even the best libraries of his day were badly indexed and catalogued and bore resemblance to his description of 'a hall so large that I could not see its ending, and on all sides so full of shelves, compartments and receptacles that a hundred thousand carts could not have removed them'.[22]

As Comenius saw the problem there was no great advantage in accumulating volumes while the outstanding need was for the mass circulation of a comparatively few good books. Hence his enormous admiration for the art of printing. This was 'the marvellous device for multiplying the number of books with amazing speed infinitely'.[23] Comenius himself showed considerable knowledge of the art of printing, which he likens to education,[24] and he took a personal interest in the Kralice Press which was taken to Leszno and also in the press provided for him at Saros Patak. He had a high opinion of printers generally, writing to Peter Montanus as a trusted friend, and acknowledging his indebtedness to Michael Endter of Nuremberg for his edition of the Orbis Pictus as 'entirely new in your profession'. He argued that printers should be attached to universities and 'not allowed to exist clandestinely'. They should be devout men and 'associate with the learned' and be appointed by the College of Light. They should maintain the highest standards of accuracy.[25]

TEXT-BOOKS

It is perhaps ironical that Comenius, having determined to write in his mother tongue, achieved international fame through a Latin translation of his text-book, the Janua, in 1631, and that the collection of all his works, also in Latin, published in 1657 was largely ignored by his own and succeeding generations while two of his text-books, the Janua and the Orbis Pictus, came close to being 'universal' books for two centuries.

The Janua or Gateway of Language Unlocked, the result of 'the leisure hours of nearly three years', achieved a success 'favourable beyond expectations'. In the University of Prague Library Handbook eighty editions are listed during the author's life-time and twenty-six subsequently, the last being a French edition of 1898. According to Keatinge it was familiar in every class-room, and Hesenthaler, historiographer to the Duke of Wurtemberg, records its use in more than 250 German grammar schools.[26] Though Milton speaks of it rather slightingly others take it for granted as essential in grammar schools as, for instance, in Evelyn's *Diary* (Jan. 27, 1658) or John Dury's *Reformed School*.[27] Even his critic, Pierre Bayle, said, 'Had Comenius written no other book than this he would have rendered himself immortal'.[28] During his journey from England to Sweden in 1642 Comenius was overwhelmed by evidence of the popularity of his book. At Leyden Golius told him of its translation into Oriental languages and remarked, 'You see, Comenius, how happily your *Janua* opens a gate to the Gentiles'. To which he replied suitably enough, 'Not unto us, O Lord, but to Thy name be the honour'.[29] Throughout Germany he found himself accepted as an educationalist and when he came to meet the Royal Princess Christina of Sweden it was to find that she was learning Latin by his method.

His other best-seller was the *Orbis Pictus* or the Picture of the World. He began work on this in 1653 at Saros Patak and some eight pages were printed under the title of *Lucidarium* but it was not completed because there was no one able to make the wood-cuts.[30] Eventually it was sent from Leszno to Nuremberg and printed in 1658 and almost immediately an English translation was made in 1659 by Charles Hoole commending the 'well-deserved author'.[31] Hoole was a teacher in a private grammar school at Lothbury in London and he had already written a book entitled A *New Discovery of the Art of Teaching School*. The popularity of the *Orbis Pictus* was even greater than that of the *Janua* with twenty-one editions in the seventeenth century, forty-three in the eighteenth, thirty-three in the nineteenth and no less than nine in the twentieth.[32] The last English edition was in 1887 by C. W. Bardeen who introduced it as an excellent means for preparing 'flickering wits for study'. Although it may not be quite correct that the *Orbis Pictus* was, as F. P. Graves says, the 'first illustrated reading book on record',[33] since Schaller mentions among others the '*New Latin Grammar in Pictures*' of Johannes Bunos (1651),[34] It is certain that Goethe's evidence proves its uniqueness in educational history – 'No other book like the *Orbis Pictus* ever came into our hands'.

The *Vestibulum*[35] which was the introductory book to the *Janua* did not achieve quite the same success although it ran to thirty-eight editions, with one in Hungarian as late as 1876. Comenius wrote a number of other books for children with varying success. For the Vernacular School he wrote a series of books for each of the six classes but none of them survived – popular demand for vernacular education was not strong. Comenius describes them as parts of a garden – Bed of Violets (with most pleasant flowerets of instruction), Bed of Roses (with nosegays of knowledge), the Garden of Letters and Wisdom (with everything necessary to be known in heaven and earth), the Labyrinth of Wisdom (with an encyclopaedic quiz), the Balsam Bed (describing sciences and arts) and finally the Paradise of the Soul (with Bible History, Psalms and Hymns).[36] In the *Great Didactic* he gives a few more details making it clear that the books 'should comprise the names of all the objects that children of this age can understand' as well as a selection of the 'most common phrases in use'.[37] For the Latin School he projected a series of books each of which was to be in three parts so that the student would have in front of him first a text which names things, second, on his left, a lexicon, and third, on his right, a grammar. Between 1643 and 1649 he recast the original versions to bring them more into line, as he thought, with his pansophic theories but later he tended to favour the earlier plan.

The series as envisaged was as follows:

1. The *Vestibulum* or Porchway of 1633 contained 1,000 words arranged in 427 sentences. The new version was not arranged in sentences but had 5,000 words classified according to basic concepts in order to give 'a logical and pansophic view of the world'.

2. The *Janua* or Gateway of 1631 contained 1,000 sentences arranged into 100 chapters and taking in 8,000 words in all. The sentences are at first simple but becoming more complex in order to illustrate grammatical constructions. The new version retained this plan but the text was fuller and there were added sections on jurisprudence and theology. The grammar stressed

'only essentials sufficient to enable anyone to read, speak and write the language on the basis of logical rules'.

3. The *Atrium* or Courtyard was projected to teach rhetorical ornament which 'makes truth attractive despite frequent misuse'. By this is meant figures of speech and proverbial sayings but there is still the same emphasis on things as in the *Janua*. The only edition is contained in the *Collected Works* of 1657.

4. The *Thesaurus* or Treasury was to be the culminating point of the series consisting of a collection of extracts from classical writers dealing with the subjects of the *Janua* but it was never completed.

This series was virtually the assignment which he undertook for De Geer at Elbing and he did send a considerable part of them to Sweden in 1647 and arranged for their printing at Leszno. When this proved impossible the books were sent to Amsterdam in 1650 but not received by the Swedes with much enthusiasm. Laurence de Geer wrote that it would not be right for Comenius to go to Hungary as was suggested until he had brought the matter to a satisfactory conclusion.[38] However, he did go to Saros Patak and included some specimens of the new texts in his *Collected Works* of 1657 but still failed to achieve the goal of a 'proper supply of comprehensive and methodical class-books'.[39] In the Fanner of Wisdom (*Ventilabrum*) he recognizes that the Elbing books were too complex and recommended the simpler version of 1652.[40]

Amongst other books written for children three may be mentioned. In 1661 he published a revised edition of the Czech Catechism known as *Children's Questions* which was eminently practical and non-theological.[41] Also in Amsterdam in 1658 he published his Czech *Manualnik* which was an abbreviated version of the Bible originally written in 1623[42] and in the following year a Hymnal which contained 743 Hymns and Psalms. Many of them are still in use today and there was an edition in Prague in 1952.

Finally there was the book of plays written at Saros Patak, the *Schola Ludus*, and the eight parts into which it was divided were intended as a scenic representation of the facts learnt in the *Janua*, each with its prologue and epilogue.[43] There is no plot in any of them since they are designed rather as didactic exercises to express the facts of the universe. They deal with the various sciences of nature and the physical and psychological characteristics of man; a number of scenes deal with the stages of education and the duties of family and civic life and there is a dramatic representation of the issues of peace and war. S. S. Laurie speaks of the *Schola Ludus* as 'dreary'[44] but Comenius asserts in the Dedicatory Epistle that it was popular with the boys and the spectators. It had the merit of using a large cast of up to fifty-two actors.

It may be that the manuscripts discovered at Leningrad in 1931 by S. Souček were intended as text-books. Four Sections were published in the Acta Coheniana for 1963 and the remaining Sections in Latin on metaphysics and profane history appeared in the 1965 Volume 45. The sections on geometry and geodesy are presented in mathematical form with definitions, theorems, axioms and diagrams while those on cosmography, though medieval in outlook, are precise in form. There are two Czech treatises which have already been edited – the one on poetry by A. Škarka and that on astronomy by K. Cupr.[46]

Comenius constructed his text-books as a complete series from infancy to manhood so that the pupil or student would continually revise the same ideas though at different levels of complexity. His basic principle was to build up an integrated apperception-mass. If all studies were based on parallel lines so that each new fact fitted into an existing pattern it could be that even the five thousand single-word schema of the *New Vestibulum* would not have been such a 'pedagogic nightmare' as Jelínek suggests,[47] although Comenius did abandon this particular idea. But he wanted the same disciplines to be taught 'in the school of adolescence as in the school of infancy'[48] with no energy dissipated on irrelevances and a continual insistence on the universality of knowledge. Thus he maintains that 'each class-book should embrace all the subjects but at different levels' though 'if your allotted time is strictly limited, you should perform nothing except that for which there is utmost need'.[49][50] Thus every text-book should have a universal aim and should be constructed according to the same epistemological, logical and psychological principles. Even though his scheme was never completed and considerable parts have been lost it is still possible to appreciate the concept.

Comenius speaks of text-books as funnels 'through which the wisdom of the three books of God's wisdom will be poured into the minds of attentive readers'.[51] Though the figure seems to over-emphasize the receptive aspect of learning it also contains the idea of adapting the flow of new experience to the capacity of the learner and it presupposes that the teacher knows the end result of the operation. Both of these ideas are essential to programmed learning and it is not enough to prepare particular areas of learning in isolation. Comenius had in mind a simple but comprehensive twenty-four year curriculum leading to an 'accurate anatomie of the universe, dissecting the veins and limbs of everything' and he tried to arrange his programme accordingly, as rungs of a ladder or concentric circles. His method may be illustrated by his treatment of the concept of a kingdom at different levels of complexity:

1. *Orbis Pictus* (CXXXVI) – 'Many cities and villages form a Region and a Kingdom. The King or Prince lives in the Capital.

2. *New Janua* (ODO III.XCI.576) – 'A Kingdom is the union of a number of cities and lands under a ruler, so constituted that the moral force thus established may be sufficiently powerful to resist the evil which men might be able to provoke'.

3. *Atrium* (ODO III.695) – The passage is of some length and ascribes sovereign power to the necessity of providing favourable conditions of life with just laws. There is a comparison with the animal world and an argument for the single ruler.

4. *Schola Ludus* (ODO III.1001-3) – The discussion is between Solon and his courtiers, before Publius addresses the representatives of the people on the conditions for establishing a just state.

The second principle which Comenius had in mind in constructing his text-books was the principle of realism. His aim was 'an education in the objects that surround us' but ultimately that 'to the knowledge of actual facts may be added by degrees that of the causes which underlie those facts'.[52] Thus the 'bare naming of things' was essential but it was only a preliminary to the revelation of their inner meaning. The simile of Plato's cave did not mean that man could be converted from the 'twilight of error' without first being thoroughly acquainted with the world of things, of men and of God. Thus the text-book must deal with mundane things as well as with abstractions – with 'flying vermin', 'bread-making' and the 'besieging of a city' as well as with moral virtues and the structure of the Heavens.

In bringing reality into the text-book Comenius early became convinced of the importance of visual methods as suggested to him by the Didactic of Lubinus.[53] He mentions it particularly for young children as accustoming them 'to the idea that pleasure is to be derived from books'[54] and proposed to introduce pictures into the *Janua* and *Vestibulum* in 1637.[55] When he came to write the new *Janua* he expressed the same intention, particularly for such things as could not easily be shown directly,[56] and in the *Analytical Didactic* he puts the case for pictures as a substitute for reality.[57] Soon after he reached Saros Patak he began work on a picture book, the *Lucidarium*, but he found the same difficulty which had prevented him so far – the technical one of making the pictures. It has been suggested that he tried to prepare them himself and only gave this up when a skilled engraver was found by Michael Endter at Nuremberg.[58]

In making his pictures Comenius had a number of considerations in mind. First of all they must give pleasure by their vividness since 'children (almost from their infancy) are fond of pictures and delight over them' and they make learning 'a kind of light amusement'.[59] Here he recognizes the limitations of the printer's art since 'certain things, such as colour and odour, cannot be demonstrated by printer's ink'.[60] Secondly the pictures must be accurate so that 'everything is open, distinct and articulate like the fingers of the hand', and here Comenius recognized his own limitations and always hoped for collaborators with more specialized knowledge. Later in the century William Penn, the Quaker, called for 'books by some curious and careful naturalists, and also Mechanics',[61] and so indicated the need for teachers to join forces with the men of practice. Thirdly Comenius realized that neither an object nor a representation of it is complete as a mental 'notion' until it has been supplemented by language. Mass communication can be facilitated by visual methods but cannot dispense with the verbal approach because the image brought to the mind by sensation is always a vague reproduction which must be assimilated. And this process of assimilation is really a form of instruction which Herbart calls 'the chief means of positive education'.[62] Thus although Comenius asserts, 'We should observe everything with as many senses as possible' he goes on

'To understand anything is largely a matter of perceiving why and how that thing in any one of its parts is related to something else and how and to what extent it differs from other things that are similar to it. Indeed to teach means scarcely anything more than to show how things differ from one another in their different purposes, forms and origins'.[63]

Consequently the pictures of the Orbis Pictus are more than a source of visual pleasure to make the text more palatable; they are directly linked with the text by nomenclatures (titles) and descriptions which 'explain the individual parts of the picture (identified by suitable names) in such a way that a number, appended to each such part as well as to its corresponding name, always shows their correlation'.[64]

It was inevitable, though regrettable, that Comenius gave so much of his attention to text-books for the study of Latin rather than for the study of things through the vernacular. He did, indeed, hope that everyone would become bi-lingual and for a long time thought of Latin as the obvious second language. Then he says, 'The entrance into the Latin tongue we called a Gate, but in this matter of Pansophy a Gateway seems to drive more nearly to our intention. For, one by one enters a gate but whole troops through a gateway'.[65] Thus his main purpose was not to teach Latin but to 'frame such a book wherein a true Anatomy of the Universe may be given so that all things are reduced to their general kinds and species'.[66] Thus his aim was fundamentally different from that of the great humanist teachers and of the Jesuits. Comenius followed Lubinus in seeking a 'natural method' of teaching Latin through daily conversation about every-day things but he went further by providing a foundation

of the same facts in the vernacular. He insists that Latin should
be taught through the vernacular and condemns 'the absurd
practice of forcing children to struggle simultaneously with the
words of a rule, the meaning of a rule, and the genius of an
alien speech'.[67] On the other hand he rejects the 'direct method'
advocated by Lubinus because it would only be possible for a
minority of children and imposed an impossible handicap on
even the best teachers of a ban on the vernacular.[68]

However, Comenius did try to treat Latin as if it were potentially a living language and as Johannes Caselius remarks, 'this
will produce a new and half-barbarous language, not Latin'.[69]
T. Corcoran puts the case for the 'settled principle of post-
Renaissance teaching, that the study of Latin must begin with
authors' even though the passages must be carefully chosen to
accord with the interests of the pupils.[70] Thus the Plan of Studies
of the Jesuits recommends that pupils start immediately with
Cicero, though adjusted to the standard of the class, and the aim
is a higher one than a mere knowledge of things. It is 'to train
to a finished power of expression'. Johannes Sturm (whose
edition of Cicero Comenius had himself studied) put the argument thus: 'Style must be our aim from the beginning . . . ex-
tempore speech cannot be ventured on except after long and
arduous practice in written expression'. It was a noble ideal but,
as Monroe says, 'a mad race for eloquence'[71] from which
Comenius turned away.

The basic idea of the *Janua* which Comenius took from the
Didactic of Bodinus[72] was to select a number of words (8,000)
which would give a comprehensive knowledge of the language
and also cover every aspect of reality and then arrange them in
sentences (991) covering 100 topics that seemed to him of importance. The book of the Irish Jesuits in Spain, William and
John Bateus and Stephen White, was brought to him while he
was working on his own *Janua* and he took from it the idea of
using each word once only but came later to abandon it as a
'false superstition'. The Irish *Janua* took moral training as its
prime objective and this is obvious 'in every line'[73] and caused its
vocabulary to be somewhat limited but on the other hand the
Comenian *Janua* in its endeavour to cover every field of
knowledge contained many words of doubtful practical value.

Text, grammar and lexicon were combined to 'contain the whole task assigned to a class'.[74] The text consisted of simple sentences (a) 'to uncover a fuller chain of things in their primary aspects, (b) 'to produce the whole vocabulary of Latin with the original meaning of each word, and (c) all inflexions'.[75] The grammar was a compromise between Luther's contempt for detail and Melanchthon's veneration of it while the lexicon was a glossary for the *Janua*, not so much for ready reference as for etymological study. The real problem according to Comenius lay in the inconsistencies and irregularities of language itself and he finds 'wealth of inflexion' a serious impediment. Grammar is not a 'a peculiarity of Latin' and he joins with the 'great master Vossius' in blaming teachers for the mass of rules and exceptions.[76] The ideal grammar should be 'complete, accurate, easy and pleasing' and Comenius is convinced that if the same material could be used as basic vocabulary Latin could be learnt in three years, Greek in two and Hebrew in one.[77]

Comenius soon became aware that there were difficulties in his method and he gave much thought to the technique of using the text-books properly. Thus the *Didactica Dissertatio* of 1637 gave detailed suggestions to the Gymnasium of Breslau – pupils must be able to read and write fluently in the vernacular before beginning Latin, they must learn the vernacular version first by reading and re-reading and writing out. Then the Latin version must be gone over ten times until the pupils understood it thoroughly. He frequently emphasizes the need for pupil activity. Pupils should be 'charged with excerpting . . . pearls and jewels of sentences'. They should make collections of synonyms and figures of speech and keep note-books with questions and answers. In the *Outline of the Pansophic School* he speaks of a 'booklet made up of blank sheets of paper' which he calls 'Priscian's Whip' in which a pupil should record any error he had made, and there is also a general note-book in which 'anything of interest that might turn up' should be recorded.[78] Diaries were always a favourite form of exercise for Comenius in which the child 'can create his own world of imagination'. On the other hand he several times condemns the 'pernicious habit' of dictated notes.

Although the *Janua* and the *Orbis Pictus* became the common text-books of Europe they were often used wrongly by people who did not understand the principles on which they were constructed. Thus a certain Henry Appelius, Rector of a Latin School at Purmerent, wrote to Hartlib in 1648 complaining that pupils who had done the *Vestibulum* must fatigue their memory with the same words set out in a different way in the *Janua*.[79] As for the Vernacular School the text-books were unfortunately lost but it is possible to see how Comenius would have expected them to be used from the account in the *Great Didactic* (Ch. XXIX) – 'In the morning the master shall read over the lesson several times, while the class attends, and shall explain . . . He shall then bid the boys read it in turn . . . at last even the stupid ones will try to repeat it by heart . . . In the afternoon the lessons done in the morning should be transcribed . . . and they will see who is most proficient in writing, in singing, and in counting'. It must be added that in his later works he showed far more appreciation of a more varied response through mind, tongue and hand.

GUIDE BOOKS

It was a cardinal point of theory with Comenius that everyone at every stage of life was both pupil and teacher and in fact the more frequently the roles were interchanged the better. Therefore it followed that there should be a text-book for every stage of learning and a guide-book for every teaching situation. Thus the production of guide-books was a task of greatest importance which should ideally be undertaken by the College of Light. The style should be 'as if written by the rays of the sun', and they should be revised annually so that there might be 'a harvest of light' and shortcomings and complaints should be examined by the College of Light. This work is 'the most substantial thing of the whole universal reform'.[80]

Some idea of the range of books of this kind which he contemplated can be gained from the list of projects which Comenius drew up in October 1641 as suitable for the proposed Pansophic College:

J. A. COMENIUS

1. A Message to Civic Authorities describing the need for School Reform.
2. A Book for Parents.
3. First Reading Book for Children.
4. Children's Encyclopaedia.
5. Epitome of Scripture.
6. Book of Ethics for Youth.
7. Book of Christian Faith and Practice.
8. Book on Speech Structure.
9. Vernacular School Methods.
10, 11 and 12. Revision of Comenius' own books – *Vestibulum, Janua* and *Atrium*.
13. Teacher's Handbook for Latin School.
14. Universal History of Things.
15. Account of Controversial Issues.
16. Book of Wise Sayings.[81]

Many of these suggestions were, in fact, carried out by Comenius himself though none of them gained the same success as the Latin School text-books. The *Brief Proposal for the Renewal of Schools* was written in 1632 and outlined a democratic and unified system of school education. The *Informatorium* or 'Guide to the Education of Infants' was written between 1628 and 1631 and the Latin translation was published in the *Collected Works* of 1657[82] but the Czech manuscript was not discovered until 1858 by A. Gindely. In the same year David Benham made an English translation which he calls 'a work of inestimable value to the Christian mother'.[83] Its great importance is in the fact that Comenius made the years of infancy an integral part of the education system and not simply a period of waiting before school begins. It deals with the same subjects as the formal school and ascribes as much importance to the mother as to the professional teacher. The *Great Didactic* itself may be regarded as a Teacher's Guide-Book but unfortunately it was never widely known or used because Hübner's criticism of the Latin version made Comenius hesitate to publish and eventually it got lost in the voluminous bulk of the *Collected Works*. The *Didactica Dissertatio* of 1637 was written primarily for Professor Kurzmann for the Gymnasium of Breslau but Turek asserts that 'it deserves to be counted among the great didactic works'.[84] The *Pampaedia* is, however, the most comprehensive guide-book of all because it gives advice for every stage of life and death.

IDEOLOGICAL BOOKS

It may seem a narrow interpretation of 'universal books' to limit them to text-books for learning and guide-books for teaching and it must be admitted that Comenius had little appreciation of literature as such. Poetry he calls 'the wine of devils' (quoting Jerome) 'which intoxicates the incautious'.[85] He really suspected anything which seemed likely to draw men away from universal reform. The Muses are, therefore, 'sirens lulling to sleep un-heedful men by the false sweetness of their song' and books may come to be used as 'a litter for comfortable dozing'.[86] The danger in mass literacy and mass communication is that men may be content 'to wander through the Elysian fields in prefer-ence to the gardens of Paradise' and he exclaims with prophetic insight, 'Perverse is the heart that finds its pleasure in the names of gods and goddesses . . . where all is romance'.[87]

Therefore his advice to young men (and perhaps even more to young women with 'their tendency to curiosity') is 'to use not many but useful books' and gradually to 'break off the habit'[88] since too much reading does not help the mind 'but swamps it'.[89] The fear is not without some justification that culture for the masses may prove to be no culture at all but a form of drug addiction in which men 'turn over dead paper rather than the living book of the world'.[90]

One answer to this problem is censorship and Comenius shows himself not unaware of the dangers of this unless public opinion is sufficiently educated to make it virtually unnecessary. Thus he concludes his attack on pagan books by saying, 'Let there be no misunderstanding. We do not absolutely prohibit Christians from reading heathen writings . . . but great caution should be used'.[91]

For each stage of life selection in reading is necessary. For the adolescent 'exceptional reading' should be allowed of certain historians and poets.[92] For young manhood a selection of contemporary writers can be regarded as 'brooklets from Divine sources'.[93] Then the adult can safely enjoy variety and abundance and contemporary history is to be preferred to ancient and still he should 'imitate the bees who take honey from flowers and not poison'.[94] Comenius agrees that evil must be known if it is to be avoided though 'it is certainly safer not to know it'[95] or, at least, to know it as something to be condemned as it is shown in the Bible. Normally a right education should provide its own safeguards against what is bad so that 'we avert our eyes, shut our ears and hasten away' and enable us in Bacon's words, 'to smell out the fopperies of books'.

There are some things, however, so harmful that they should not be tolerated at all in a good society and it is no restraint of individual freedom to be denied the opportunity of contact with 'evil books and scandalous pictures' which should be destroyed.[96] Comenius realized that all forms of censorship are difficult – 'easy enough to command; would that it were so easy to observe'[97] – but he could not accept that they were also either tyrannous or futile nor that even the College of Light might become what Milton called 'the impertinent yoke of prelatry, under whose inquisitious duncery no free and splendid wit can flourish'.[98] Certain things can be said in extenuation. Comenius was far less of a censor than most of his contemporaries. He had experienced a fairly rigid control in his own church without any sense of oppression and with much experience of good. He wanted the control to be in the hands of scholars and not of politicians and to have nothing to do with the suppression of heresy. Finally it must be noted that the seventeenth century produced many great books despite a very rigid control of printing while the twentieth consumes whole forests to provide fodder for its uncontrolled printing presses but throws up more trash than treasure.

The real answer to the problem of worthless reading matter must be to produce something better and to educate people to have a palate for it. Ultimately, Comenius realized, there is no way of distinguishing between good and bad and the task of education is to eliminate those books that are like 'sterile virgins whose contribution is mere speculation',[99] by providing ideological books that either contained 'the very marrow of eternal truth' or that 'unfolded all the variety of particular things' or that 'reviewed theories or opinions which have been held'.[100]

Comenius spent many years of his life trying to write books that might fairly be called ideological. Even as a student at Herborn he began that survey of the 'Universal Theatre of Things' (*Theatrum Universitatis Rerum*) which he later described to his printer friend, Peter Montanus, as his greatest work (*Opus Principale*) and spoke of his bitterness when the labour of many years was destroyed in a few minutes at Leszno.[101] Since then fragments have been discovered – in 1893 at Holešov and in 1919,[102] – from which the plan of the whole has been revealed. It was to cover (it is not possible to say how much was completed) the origin of life and of the universe, an outline of Christian theology, a description of all human activities, the physical and political geography of the world, the history of mankind up to the present and finally the end of the world according to Revelation. Without doubt (as we can tell from the *Physica* or Natural Philosophy of 1632) a great deal of it would have been medieval in outlook but as Herbert Butterfield says, 'Modern Science springs from men whom we can only call "philosophers"'[103] and Comenius had a certain breadth of vision and height of imagination that made him a prophet and seer, Also as a student he began to write that 'Treasury of the Bohemian Language' by which he intended to refine his mother tongue. This also was lost at Leszno. Comenius says of it: 'Only with my last breath will I cease to deplore this loss'.[104] There was even another Treasury of Language (*Sylva Pansophica . . . Thesaurus*) on which he had worked for twenty years.[105]

Above all ideological books Comenius desired that the Bible should be available to everyone and he made this task the 'primary care' of the College of Light[106] while the Universal Consistory of the Church should provide 'accurate translations from the original languages, commentaries (especially of those places that seem to be contradictory') and indexes.[107] Comenius had in the Kralice Bible an excellent example of popularity combined with accuracy. It was written in a simple yet dignified style, was supplied with an index of quotations, and above all was printed on such thin paper that it was only an inch and a quarter thick and therefore very easy to use.[108] Comenius was greatly concerned for the propagation of the Gospel to 'the many who do not even know that such a book exists'[109] and he took special interest in translations of his own *Janua*, for instance into Moslem languages, which might 'promote the study of the Bible'.[110]

As for other books of an ideological character Comenius gave much attention to the problem of popularizing great books through summaries. These 'epitomes' were to contain 'the whole author only somewhat reduced in bulk' and to be for the use of those 'not in a position to read the complete work'.[111] They should be 'small in extent, not numerous, but significant' – in fact a prevision of the modern 'paper-back'. This was the 'broad field in which the members of the College of Light could employ their wisdom',[112] and the possibilities of mass production seemed to open up if only the 'funnels of light' could be made in an international language 'ready to express all concepts and things'.[113] There was just one point he remembered, small but important – 'a book without an index is like a house without windows'.[114]

Of a somewhat similar character were books popular in Europe at the time, using 'emblems' or symbolical illustrations of texts or proverbs, such as the work of Francis Quarles in England. Comenius recommends them 'for an easier, truer and better understanding of Scripture . . . because the Bible speaks of the abstruse and invisible in words designating the obvious and the visible'.[115] He suggests that 'it would be good to have a book with 100 Emblems to explain the whole of pansophy' but he would like it to be 'a little book which would serve as a library for everyone, a *"Vademecum"'* so that they 'would know how to speak as in proverbs and parables'.[116] It is with some hesitation that Comenius recommends a collection of quotations from 'significant men of all nations' but if 'composed in a right way' he feels confident that it might unify 'truth which is splintered all over the world'.[117] As a minister he was naturally concerned that suitable devotional books should be produced on a universal scale and he himself made a Czech translation of the German version of a well-known book by the Englishman, Lewis Bayly – *The Practice of Piety*.

It is an irony of history that a man who dreamt so much of taking part in the production of books on a universal scale to

BOOKS

elevate the minds of all mankind should have been the means of keeping alive the faith and love of freedom of a small and oppressed nation. But so it was, and during the Age of Darkness that succeeded the Thirty Years War the voice of the 'Sad Shepherd' was chiefly heard in the homes of poor Bohemian peasants where the sign of the Secret Seed – the Juniper tree – stood outside.[118]

NOTES

1. *Via Lucis* I. *Pampaedia* I.11.
2. Thomas Aquinas: *De Magistro* p. 15. Quoted by M. H. Mayer: *Philosophy of Teaching of St Thomas Aquinas.*
3. *Pampaedia* VI.1.
4. *Panorthosia* XVI.10.
5. *Diatyposis* (Tr. J. Collier) p. 172.
6. *Great Didactic*: Greeting 20.
7. *Great Didactic* XXXI.15.
8. *Continuatio* 58 cf. Virgil, Aeneid, X.811 gives 'maiorague'.
9. G. H. Turnbull: *Hartlib, Dury and Comenius* p. 382-413.
10. G. H. Turnbull: *Hartlib, Dury and Comenius* p. 364.
11. R. F. Young: *George Ritschel of Deutschkahn, A Bohemian Philosopher at Oxford in the Seventeenth Century* (1926) p. 13. cf. G. H. Turnbull: *Op. cit.* p. 372.
12. G. H. Turnbull: *Op. cit.* p. 413.
13. *Outline of Pansophic School*: Deliberation.
14. ODO IV.41-64.
15. *Labyrinth* X.
16. *Panorthosia* VIII.
17. *Reformation of Schools* (Tr. S. Hartlib) p. 5.
18. K. Freeman: *Schools of Hellas* p. 204-7.
19. *Pampaedia* VI.18.
20. *Labyrinth* II.3.
21. Seifferth: *Church Constitution of Moravian Brethren* p. 114.
22. *Labyrinth* X.6 cf. R. F. Young. *Comenius in England* p. 2.
23. *Via Lucis* XIII.7.
24. *Great Didactic* XXXII.
25. *Panorthosia* XVI.9.
Text-Books
26. Kvačala: *Korres* I.355 Quoted by Heyberger: *J.A.C.* p. 12.
27. J. Dury: *Reformed School* p. 53.
28. Pierre Bayle: *Dictionnaire Historique et Critique* (Rotterdam 1697) I.882.
29. *Continuatio* 58.
30. G. H. Turnbull: 'An Incomplete Orbis Pictus' (*Acta Comeniana* 1957.1) p. 38.
31. Charles Hoole: *The Visible World* (Tr. of *Orbis Pictus* 1659) Intro.
32. *Soupis Děl* J.A.K. (Státní Pedagogické Nakladatelství 1959).

J. A. COMENIUS

33. F. P. Graves: *Students' History of Education* (New York, 1936).
34. K. Schaller: *Die Pädagogik des J.A.C.* p. 432.
35. ODO II.293-298.
36. ODO I.248-249.
37. *Great Didactic* XXIX.
38. G. H. Turnbull: *Hartlib, Dury and Comenius* p. 373.
39. *Great Didactic* XXXIII.8. For Bibliographical details cf. Heyberger: *J.A.C.* p. 251 Jelínek: *Analytical Didactic* p. 217-219 and Novák-Hendrich: *J.A.K. Jeho Život a Spisy Index.*
40. ODO III. 213-592.
41. J. E. Hutton: *History of Moravian Church* p. 80-81.
42. *Methodus* XXIII.
43. ODO III.831-1062.
44. S. S. Laurie: *J.A.C.* p. 194.
45. *Acta Comeniana* (1963) p. 191-222 (1965) p. 81-121.
46. J. Patocka: *Present State of Comenian Studies* (*Historica* 1959) p. 199-201.
47. Jelínek: *Op. cit.* p. 46.
48. *Pampaedia* XI.
49. *Analytical Didactic* 132.137.
50. *Great Didactic* XXIX.9.
51. *Pampaedia* VI.15.
52. *Great Didactic* XXIX.5.
53. *Methodus* VIII.
54. *Great Didactic* XXVIII 25-26.
55. ODO I.370 (*Didactica Dissertatio* 1638).
56. G. H. Turnbull: *An Incomplete Orbis Pictus*. Letter to Wolzogen 1647.
57. *Analytical Didactic* 54.
58. G. H. Turnbull: *An Incomplete Orbis Pictus*. quoting W. Toischer: *Zur Entstehungsgeschichte des 'Orbis Pictus'* p. 38.
59. *Orbis Pictus*: Preface.
60. *Orbis Pictus*: Preface.
61. W. Penn: *Some Fruits of Solitude* (1693) Sec. 15-17.
62. H. Herbart: *Aphorisms* XXI.
63. *Analytical Didactic* 55.58.
64. *Orbis Pictus*: Preface.
65. *Reformation of Schools*: 102.
66. *Reformation of Schools*: 17.
67. *Methodus* VII.
68. cf. W. H. Woodward: *Education during the Renaissance* p. 158 quoting Cordier.
69. *Methodus* VIII.
70. T. Corcoran: *Studies in the History of Classical Teaching* p. 136.
71. W. S. Monroe: *Comenius* p. 7.
72. Elias Bodinus: *Bericht von der Natur* (Hamburg 1621).
73. T. Corcoran: *Op. cit.* p. XIII.
74. *Outline of Pansophic School* 26.
75. *Methodus* XII.
76. *Methodus* VII.
77. *Pampaedia* XI.16.
78. *Outline of Pansophic School* 78.84.
79. G. H. Turnbull: *Hartlib, Dury, and Comenius*, p. 441.
Guide Books

BOOKS

80. *Pampaedia* VI.
81. G. H. Turnbull: *Op. cit.* p. 360.
82. *ODO.* I.198-249.
83. D. Benham: *Apology.*
84. A. Turek: *The Comenian System of Education* II. p. 129.
Ideological Books
85. *Great Didactic* XXV.14.
86. *Panorthosia* IX. *Pampaedia* VII.1.
87. *Great Didactic* XXV.20.
88. *Pampaedia* XII.
89. *Pampaedia* IV.21.
90. *Physica*: Preface.
91. *Great Didactic* XXV.22.
92. *Outline of Pansophic School* 82.
93. *Pampaedia* XII.14.
94. *Pampaedia* XIII.10.
95. *Pampaedia* III.30.
96. *Pampaedia* III.48.
97. *Pampaedia* IV.15.
98. J. Milton: *Areopagitica.*
99. *Panorthosia* IX.15.
100. *Via Lucis* XVI.4.
101. Patera: *Korres.* CCX.2. Reprinted in *Communio Viatorum* 1962/4 p. 298.
102. VSJAK Vol. I(5) 1897 *Časopis Matice Moravske* XLIX (1925).
103. H. Butterfield: Article in *Observer* (1964).
104. Patera: *Korres. Op. cit.* p. 206.
105. Kvačala. *Korres.* I p. 206.
106. *Panorthosia* XVI.9.
107. *Panorthosia* XVIII.11. *Pampaedia* VI.22.
108. J. E. Hutton: *History of Moravian Church* p. 128.
109. *Pampaedia* II.17.
110. *Methodus* XVII.
111. *Great Didactic* XXXI.8.9.10.
112. *Panorthosia* XVI.8.
113. *Via Lucis* XIX.6.21.
114. *Pampaedia* VI.18.
115. *Methodus* XXIII.
116. *Pampaedia* XII.12.
117. *Pampaedia* VI.17.18.
118. cf. Lützow: *Introduction to Labyrinth.*

CHAPTER 13

CONCLUSION

JEAN PIAGET begins his Introduction to the UNESCO book of Selections from Comenius with these words: 'Nothing is easier, or more dangerous, than to treat an author of three hundred years ago as modern and claim to find in him the origins of contemporary or recent trends of thought'. This warning must be kept in mind, also, when he is criticized for faults and limitations which properly belong to his age and profession. He was a child of his time. In some respects he was even behind the more advanced thinking of his time and he was not able to emancipate himself altogether from the traditions which he inherited.

It is, therefore, possible to criticize Comenius quite frankly without belittling him. He was prolix – sometimes to the point of tediousness – and lacked what Keatinge calls 'the instinct of limitation'. To some extent this was because he was often at such pains to emphasize the importance of the obvious. He was so determined to refer everything to universal principles that he sometimes reduced them to triviality. His prolixity was a part of his passion for systematization. Every point had to be divided and sub-divided and then reiterated because he was determined to make abundantly clear an idea which seemed so simple and obvious and yet which was so generally overlooked and ignored. But this enthusiasm tended to over-reach itself and reduce the sublime to the ridiculous. There comes a point where the Messianic message becomes banal and Comenius could not always pull himself up in time to avoid it.

His belief in the principle of parallelism coloured his whole approach and with great advantage but also with some risk. Comenius used analogies in the same way that Jesus did with the parables, not simply as illustrations from nature, but as transpositions of truth from one field to another. His use of imagery was not simply for literary embellishment but with deliberate intention to convey a concept. Frequently this gives a certain vividness of conviction to his words and lights up with flashes of inspiration passages which tend to weariness. But, of course, he is not always so successful because he frequently sees parallels where there is no parallel and the result is to obscure his meaning or even to contradict it.

He was always searching for a foolproof method of exposition by which an argument could be made completely valid. He wanted truth to be so expressed that no man could reasonably doubt or deny it. Consequently he had no fears that reason could over-topple revelation or that a pragmatic approach could undermine faith. Yet he often spoke in favour of censorship and his readiness to accept prophecies which fathered his wishes led him into quagmires of credulity which antagonized even his co-religionists. His under-estimation of the irrational element both in himself and in mankind generally tended to detract from the completeness of his argument and in distinguishing between black and white he was inclined to ignore the many intermediate shades of grey. He wanted all his patterns to be symmetrical because of his conviction that the universe was harmonical but this involved him in distortions of fact which verged on the naïve.

He could never overcome his astonishment that men could not see what seemed to him so self-evident and that was why he constantly called for a reawakening. It was in his view such a simple matter for men to turn away from the shadows which deluded them to the possibilities to which he beckoned them. But if, indeed, they were so steeped in their present unhappy situation that they could not break away from it then Comenius looked confidently to a new generation to redress the failings of the old. He saw the universal dawning as a problem of education and brushed aside the 'monstrosity handed down from one to another by the law of heredity'. Though he certainly did not deny 'the difficulty facing such great desires' he generally concluded his discussion of them with the admonition: 'let no man talk of impossibility'. This was wonderful optimism but sometimes too much of a leap to retain contact with the ground.

There were certain aspects of life to which Comenius was, if not blind, at least antipathetic. It would be impossible to say how far his attitude to sex was determined by the ascetic traditions of his Church and by his responsibilities as a Minister. He was three times married and was tender in his dealings with women but, at least in his writings, he showed little appreciation of the mystical significance of physical love. Erotic pleasure was a temptation of the devil and men should procreate 'piously and holily as sons and daughters of God'. But in his anxiety to ennoble sex Comenius ran some risk of emasculating it. Somewhat similar criticism can be made concerning his aesthetic sense. He had an appreciation of beauty, but only in a religious setting, and dismissed classical literature as 'junk' and Renaissance art as of very dubious value. Any other attitude would have been impossible for the Bishop of such a body as the Unity of Brethren.

The claim of Comenius to greatness rests upon his power to transcend his situation and circumstances. Many men in the first half of the seventeenth century felt that they lived in an age 'with all coherence gone' as the English poet, John Donne, expressed it, but Comenius, in von Raumer's words, 'gave unfailing inspiration and lifted up in a large part of Europe many good men prostrated by the terrors of the times and inspired them with hope that by pious and wise systems of education there might be raised up a race of men more pleasing to God. His capacity for heroism is nowhere more clear than in his relationship to his Church. When in 1650 it seemed inevitable that the Unity would be dispersed Comenius wrote his *Bequest of a dying Mother*, the Unity of Brethren, by which, ceasing to exist in her own nation and her separate individuality, she distributes among her sons, daughters and heirs the Treasures which God has entrusted to her'. When, however, the remnants survived Comenius devoted himself to preserving the slender thread of continuity until, years afterwards, they revived under Count Zinzendorf and, as the Moravian Church, became a significant power for good in the world. Hardly less was his devotion to his own people, the Czechs, though he spent over half his life in exile but his spirit kept alive in Bohemia and Moravia the flickering flame of national self-respect through many dark days until it was fanned into brightness by Palacký. On all the countries in which Comenius found refuge he left some mark for good. Even his brief visit to England made a significant contribution through those whom he influenced upon the radical thinking that went on before the Restoration in religion, politics and education. Nevertheless the highest loyalty of Comenius was not to any particular group but to the whole of mankind. The yearning for universal reform was the daemon that made his life dynamic and that tipped the scales in favour of the extraordinary in one who might otherwise have been 'a simple, good man' as Campagnac describes him. The history of reform is the comparison of fact with an idea and this constant comparison requires a prophetic urgency which Comenius possessed in a very high degree. At times it was a source of acute pain to him – 'O, that it had pleased God to instil these intellectual desires in another mind' – but he was not unfaithful to the message he had received though 'his life went down in sorrows, and his years in lamentations'. This heroic yearning must be, at the personal level, his claim to greatness.

Many writers on education before and since Comenius have discussed the concept of universal education but none has taken so many aspects into consideration or integrated it so completely to a philosophy of life. Erasmus had an ideal of cosmopolitan culture allied with practical Christianity but his educational ambition was to translate the New Learning into terms acceptable to the intellectual life of Northern Europe. Francis Bacon took all knowledge as his province but he had curiously little to say about the process of education. John Locke put forward many ideas which are inherent in the concept of universal education – the primacy of sense experience, the value of natural progression in learning, the necessity for freedom of the reason – but his view of the curriculum was much narrower than that of Comenius and his educational aims were class-conscious – 'That which every gentleman desires for his son, beside the estate he leaves him, is contained in these four things, virtue, wisdom, breeding, and learning'. (*Some Thoughts concerning Education*, p. 134). Of all those who have tried to universalize the process of education from a narrow bookish orientation none have had more influence than Jean Jacques Rousseau and there are many similarities in his works to Comenius but in truth his view of nature as the universal basis is altogether narrower than that of Comenius. The education of Émile, though soundly based upon a consideration of child nature, was quite impossible to adapt to a system of universal schooling. Pestalozzi had many illuminating things to say about the education of the common man so that he could live with dignity in any station of life. He gave due emphasis to the influence of the mother as nature's own teacher and through his insistence on insight or *Anschauung* as a basis for pedagogic method he pointed the way to a true science of education. He comes nearest, probably, to Comenius but in one respect, at least, his point of view was less universal. He had no theory of knowledge and therefore the knowledge which he imparted through his object lessons was fragmentary and unsystematized. Froebel was indebted to Comenius for his ideas but even more so to Pestalozzi and in *The Education of Man* he put forward views essentially universal and suitable for the education of all human beings. He, also, very consciously tried to integrate school education with a mystical and cosmic philosophy. But circumstances forced him to exert his greatest influence in the education of young children and his contribution to universal education is chiefly in his recognition of the educative value of inherent forces in the child for which the teacher must encourage spontaneous expression. Froebel did, perhaps, show more insight than Comenius into the concept of freedom in education and, possibly, he had more success in translating his principles into concrete schoolroom procedures. Nevertheless it is significant that the Froebelian movement has been largely confined to the education of young children and has resulted in a somewhat artificial distinction between 'Infant Method' and 'Formal Teaching'. Heinrich Herbart is another writer who touches many of the problems of universal education with which Comenius wrestled. He also searched for the essence of reality behind its superficial appearance, he believed that the whole task of education was to produce 'good' men, and he accepted the positive contribution of instruction and method in the educative process. But, despite his theory of the apperception-mass as a psychological basis for pedagogic method, Herbart failed to unify knowledge and life and in other hands the Formal Steps of Learning became artificial and disconnected. Herbart himself saw this possibility when he says, 'Only too frequently do masses of ideas remain isolated despite the fact that the objects corresponding to them are most intimately and necessarily interconnected'. (*Outlines of Pedagogical Lectures*, p. 211.) Comenius saw most clearly the need for the curriculum to be seen as a whole and for each successive step to have its place in a scheme going from early infancy to mature manhood. There is a link between Comenius and Maria Montessori in the emphasis which they put upon 'didactic apparatus' as an automatic and universal means of self-education. It is true that for Comenius the apparatus consisted largely of text-books whereas Montessori was more concerned with sense stimulation but the chief difference from the point of view of universal education is the much wider scope of Comenius. He tried to include in his scheme the whole of society, the whole of life, and a complete system of philosophy. The movement from a 'child-centred' education to a 'life-centred' education is most clearly seen in the teaching of John Dewey. Dewey's educational philosophy is based on universal principles of evolution and growth and his criticism of contemporary educational practice is aimed at the fragmentation of knowledge into 'subject' compartments which have no reality in child experience. Nevertheless it must be admitted that the Project Method, by which Dewey hoped to make a continual reconstruction from the child's present experience into the organized body of human knowledge, has not been free from artificiality and this is partly, at least, because the pragmatic philosophy has no unifying principle such as Comenius conceived essential for a system of universal education.

It is not suggested that Comenius put forward a concept of universal education which is more adequate in any one aspect than that of those who followed him nor is there any need to attempt to prove a direct link between him and others. His contribution lies more in the fact that he tried to integrate all the aspects and that he suggests the inter-relatedness of the aim that education should be 'of all men, about all things, and in all ways'. It is demonstrably true that this is still very far from being achieved despite notable advances in particular respects.

The twentieth century is far better placed than was the seventeenth for the education of the whole human race but despite mass media and mechanical techniques we are far from complete achievement. It is difficult to find accurate criteria but on the basis of school enrolment or adult literacy the UNESCO World Survey of Education for 1950-1954 (p. 15) puts forward statistics to show that little over half the world's population are receiving school education. Even this half is very unevenly distributed and leaves the Comenian ideal of universal education without discrimination of sex, race, religion, social status or place of domicile far from realized. Even where such a principle is enshrined in law, as it is in England, the fact is that the education of the 'Average and Below Average Child' is 'pitifully inadequate'. (Newsom Report 1963, p. 26.)

Nor has the second condition of universal education – that it should be 'about all things' – been realized. Here we have a problem greater than Comenius could have envisaged in that the body of human knowledge has expanded beyond the wildest dreams of the seventeenth century and as new subjects have been added and old ones transformed the problem of curriculum reform has become next to impossible. The consequence has been socially serious in that schools are continually out of step with modern knowledge, that education has become a means of social division rather than integration, and that cultural barriers have been erected between different departments of knowledge or skill.

The third condition of universal education – that it should be 'in all ways' – is difficult to define and difficult to assess but in the mind of Comenius it raised such fundamental problems as the relation between school education and education outside school and beyond the years of schooling, the relation between the education of the individual as an end in himself and his education as a member of society, and the function of education in reducing such social evils as inter-group tension and prejudice.

An analysis of the principles which Comenius believed must be included in a concept of universal education together with the spheres in which they must operate will indicate the contribution which he could make to contemporary problems.

A principle which he regarded as fundamental was that of panharmony by which he meant the unifying element underlying the infinite variety of the universe. The following passage from the *Pampaedia* will serve to illustrate this approach to education: 'That all things should be taken as a whole and not piecemeal and partially, now this, now that, is shown by this very true thought, and the experience with which it is linked: that if the force of human nature is directed entirely towards one sole point, and not to the whole theatre of things, it cannot preserve a harmonious balance but oversteps the limits to a harmful degree, to the certain prejudice of itself, things, and other men'. (IV.4.) To the objection that the universe is evidence of contrariety and opposition even more than of parallelism and unity the answer of Comenius is that man shares with God the creative task of continually bringing order out of chaos and of combining disparities into a new synthesis. Thus panharmony is a dynamic, not a static, principle which must be closely linked with the syncritical method. The syncritical method is, in the mind of Comenius, a means by which the reciprocal relations of different strata of reality can be made to establish the panharmony which is there potentially all the time.

Closely linked with the principle of panharmony is that of perfectibility. This was essential to the concept of universal education and Comenius gave much attention to the obvious arguments that could be brought against it. To be 'wholly educated' can mean nothing less than to be educated 'in all things which perfect human nature' and anything less would bring 'ignominy to God's glory'. In fact, Comenius finds justification for what some would call unwarranted optimism in 'our constant impulses and longings for better things' which would be a sad mockery of God's love and power if there were not the possibility of their being satisfied. Nevertheless the principle is of perfectibility, not of perfection. Perfection is something given; perfectibility is something to be achieved. One is a datum, the other is a quest. Comenius believed that there could be perfectibility at many levels and he gives several definitions which indicate this. Thus in the Dedication to the *Via Lucis* he says: 'This would be the most perfect restoration of human nature to the likeness of God, if no man were bidden to desire anything against his will, to feel without lively and individual sensation, to act under compulsion – that is, to desire, to feel, to act in vain, and to the destruction within himself of the image of God'.

Consequently perfectibility means simply 'that no man should degenerate into not being a man' and this is possible at every age or level of development. This may be illustrated by reference to material standards of living. Modern societies, backed by industrial organization, have at their disposal standards of living far beyond the expectations of kings and queens in former ages, but without contentment, and against that can be set the Comenian ideal that men should 'delight in all things but need little'. (*Pampaedia,* 1.9.) As to knowledge and understanding perfectibility does not mean that man should be omniscient but that he should 'stand beyond the precipices of error'. Thus perfectibility is the capacity for rejection as well as the capacity for achievement – the rejection of 'superficial knowledge', 'garrulous loquacity, however witty' – in fact all the 'empty smoke of vanity' (*Pampaedia,* IV.2) and for this each man has his own criteria of measurement and his own powers of renewal.

The refusal to accept external standards to measure success or happiness arises from a third principle of the autonomy of nature. The ultimate ends of education are indicated by nature itself and Comenius maintains that the 'one root of transgression' is that men 'take no care for the ends, particularly the ultimate ends, to which all should tend in everything'. (*Pampaedia,* 11.9.) This concern with the process of nature as a whole enabled Comenius to include in his concept a number of different meanings – nature in its external and physical manifestations, nature as a law of causation, nature as a genetic principle of growth, nature as a creative principle of uniqueness and individuality, and finally nature as an expression of the mind of a Creator in whom all the endless varieties are transcended. Comenius found in his belief in nature good grounds for optimism that all men must be 'endowed with everything that can educate them for humanity'. Since nature 'being active, pours itself out completely wherever it turns' it must be 'very suitable for education' (*Pampaedia,* 11.16) and the teacher can be confident that man is made so that 'he can hold all things if he is offered them'.

Granted these principles of universal education Comenius proceeded to examine all the spheres in which the concept could be worked out in practice. The first sphere is the whole of life and here Comenius shows clearly that he regards schooling as only a part of education. In fact, he would go further and say that life itself is only a part of a process which extends beyond each individual's earthly existence or each generation's span of experience. It was certainly not the case that he rejected this life or regarded it as a vale of tears to be hurried through as quickly as possible to something better. He was an unregenerate materialist who condemned materialism. His whole attitude was that man needed all the years of his earthly span in order to learn the lessons required for happiness and to this end he must conserve health by 'fleeing that which injures health', he must learn 'the art of being rich', he must learn 'to live in honour and not to suffer ignomiy'. (*Pampaedia* III, 22, 24, 37.)

But though Comenius took this wide view of the sphere of universal education he also regarded the organized learning which took place in schools as essential to the higher perspective. The fundamental reason for this is not because of the expediency of organizing instruction for large numbers but rather because of the social nature of the educative process. The attitude towards education which falls short of a universal aim is that life educates but that for certain specific vocational purposes something extra, which might be called schooling, is required. This is particularly necessary for those who are destined to teach, lead and rule others – that is for the intelligentsia or whatever term may be in current use – but that, for the masses, it is, if not a work of supererogation, little more than a safeguard against social disorder or a means of industrial efficiency. This is a not uncommon, if unconscious, point of view and against it Comenius says: 'If we weigh the matter on just scales, we see that precisely for this reason (that wisdom is necessary for the leaders of society) education is necessary for all men. For not only should every man be in the first place teacher, leader and ruler of himself, but he should be them for others too'. (*Pampaedia*, 11.29.) It is for this reason that school – a public assembly of young people – is a fundamental sphere of universal education and it has, or should have, two essential characteristics to fulfil its function. The first is that it should be progressive with each successive stage fitting in to a total scheme from early childhood to maturity and the second is that each stage should be self-contained in that it is concentric to all the other stages having the same approach, the same subject matter and the same methods but at different levels of complexity. Though Comenius advocated a division of schooling into stages – infancy, childhood, adolescence and young manhood – he would not accept that informal methods at one stage must give way to more formal ones later on nor would he agree that the instruments of instruction need to be changed.

In thus calling attention to universal schools as essential for universal education Comenius does not overlook that each individual is a sphere of education in himself. The individual is a microcosm of the universe and therefore universal education must provide those conditions in which personality can develop. This has become almost a cliché of modern education but little progress has been made towards the ideal stated by Sir Percy Nunn as being that each should 'make his original contribution to the variegated whole of human life as full and as truly characteristic as his nature permits'. (*Education: Its Data and First Principles*: Preface.) The contribution of Comenius to this is to suggest that human personality can only develop within a wider ideological sphere which transcends it. Personality must be rescued from its ego-centric imprisonment and to this end Comenius saw universal education as a movement towards universal peace. The panharmonic principle that could lead man to wisdom could also lead him to reconciliation and mutual understanding. Human perfectibility must operate in a sphere of social collaboration and tolerance and the concept of universal education must envisage a process of barrier-breaking between individuals, groups and nations. Comenius concludes his vision of the Way of Light with the prayer: 'May Thy will be done even now in the whole earth as it is in the whole heaven! Through the whole of Europe, of Asia, of Africa, of America, through the land of the Magallanes, and through all the islands of the sea, may Thy kingdom come!'

Thus the concept was perhaps more of a vision or a prayer than a scientific definition. It finds more of an echo in saints and prophets than in pedagogues and philosophers (though Comenius comes in both groups) and the closest parallel might be with one, contemporary with Comenius, though never acquainted with him – the English Quaker, George Fox. There is the same Millenialist passion, the same confidence in 'that of God' in every man, the same unflinching desire for peace. The dying words of George Fox aptly describe the religious basis for the educational ideas of John Comenius: 'I am glad I was here. Now I am clear, I am fully clear . . . All is well; the Seed of God reigns over all and over death itself. And though I am weak in body, yet the power of God is over all, and the Seed reigns over all disorderly spirits'. (*Journal*.)

BIBLIOGRAPHY

A. Works by Comenius

(a) Collected Works
Opera Didactica Omnia. Edition of the Czechoslovak Academy of Sciences, Prague, 1957.

Veškeré Spisy J.A.K. Brno, 1910-1929.

Korrespondence J.A.K. Ed. A. Patera. Prague, 1892. Ed. J. Kvačala. Prague, 1897 and 1901. Analecta Comeniana. Jurjcv, 1907.

(b) Lists of Individual Works
Anna Heyberger: J.A.C. Sa Vie et son oeuvre d'éducateur. (Paris, 1928) p. 243-265.

G. H. Turnbull: Hartlib, Dury and Comenius (Liverpool, 1947) p. 440-449.

J. Brambora: Knižní dílo J.A.K. Prague, 1954. 1957.

Soupis Děl J.A.K. (Prague, Státní Pedagogické Nakladatelství).

(c) Recent Editions
Ed. J. Hendrich: Vševýchova (Prague, 1948).

Ed. J. Hendrich: Všnýprava (Prague, 1950).

Ed. D. Čyževskij: Pampaedia (Heidelberg, 1958).

Ed. D. Čyževskij: Nejnovější Metoda Jazků (Prague, 1964).

Ed. J. Červenka, V. T. Miškovská: De Rerum Humanarum Emendatione Consultatio Catholica. (CSAV – Prague, 1966).

(d) English Translations
1. Selections

J.A.C. Selections (Paris UNESCO, 1957).

A Perfect Reformation (A. Molnár. Prague, 1957).

J.A.C. Selections from his Works (Prepared by J. Kyrašek. Prague, 1964).

A. Turek: The Comenian System of Education (M. Ed Thesis Durham, 1951).

J. C. Halliday: The Pampaedia (from the German) (Ed. B. Thesis St Andrews Univ., 1963).

2. Individual Works

The Angel of Peace: Tr. W. A. Morison (1944).

A Reformation of Schools (Prodromus and Dilucidatio) Tr. S. Hartlib (1642).

A Patterne of Universall Knowledge (Diatyposis) Tr. J. Collier (1651).

An Exhortation to the Church of England (De Bono Unitatis) 1661.

B. Seifferth: Church Constitution of the Bohemian and Moravian Brethren (1886).

The Great Didactic: Tr. M. Keatinge (1896).

Janua (The Gate of Tongues Unlocked) Tr. J. Achoran (1633).

Janua (from the Czech Version of K. H. Tham 1805). Tr. A. Turek (1951).

BIBLIOGRAPHY

The School of Infancy: Tr. D. Benham (London, 1858). W. S. Monroe (N. Yk., 1893). E. M. Eller (N. Carolina, 1956).
The Bequest of the Unity of Brethren: Tr. M. Spinka (Chicago, 1940).
The Labyrinth of the World and the Paradise of the Heart: Tr. Count Lützow (1st Ed. London, 1900). Tr. National Union of Czechoslovak Protestants (Chicago, 1942).
Methodus Linguarum Novissima: Short Version by A. Turek (Durham Univ., 1951).
Analytical Didactic: Tr. V. Jelínek (Chicago, 1953).
Orbis Pictus (The Visible World) Tr. C. Hoole (1659).
Natural Philosophy (Physicae ad Lumen Synopsis) (London, 1651).
Rules for the Conduct of Life (Regulae Vitae) Tr. E. Synge (1736).
Prophecies of C. Kotter and others (Lux e Tenebris) Tr. R. Codrington (1664).
Vestibulum (Porch of the Latin Tongue) Tr. J. Brookbank (1647).
The Way of Light (Via Lucis) Tr. E. T. Campagnac (Liverpool, 1938).
History of the Bohemian Persecution (1650).

B. Books concerning Comenius
Alt. R.: *Der Fortschrittliche Charakter der Pädagogik Komenskys* (Berlin 1954).
Bovet P.: J.A.C. *Un Patriote Cosmopolite* (Geneva 1943).
Butler N. Murray: *The Place of Comenius in the History of Education* (New York, 1892).
Gindely A.: *Über des J.A.C. Leben und Wirksamkeit* (1855).
Geissler H.: *Comenius und die Sprache* (Heidelberg, 1958).
Halliday J. C.: *The Pampaedia of J.A.C.* (Ed. B. Thesis St Andrews, 1963).
Heyberger A.: J.A.C. *Sa vie et son oeuvre d'éducateur* (Paris, 1928).
Jakubek J.: J.A.C. (Prague, 1928).
Jelínek V.: *The Analytical Didactic of J.A.C.* (Chicago, 1953).
Kvačala J.: J.A.C. (Berlin, 1914).
Keatinge M.: *The Great Didactic* (London, 1896).
Krasnovskij A. A.: J.A.C. (Moscow, 1953).
Laurie S. S.: J.A.C. *His Life and Work* (London, 1899).
Lordkipanidze D. O.: *Didaktika J.A.C.* (Moscow).
Monroe W. S. *Comenius and the Beginnings of Educational Reform*, London, 1900).
Möhrke M.: J.A.C. *and J. V. Andreae* (Leipzig, 1904).
Needham J.: *The Teacher of Nations* (Cambridge, 1942).
Novák J. V. and Hendrich J.: J.A.K. *Jeho Život a spisy* (Prague, 1932).
Piobetta J. B.: *La Grande Didactique* (Paris, 1952).
Pope J. D.: *The Educational Writings of J.A.C. and their Relevance in a changing culture* (Florida, 1962).
Popelová J.: J.A.K. *Cesta Komenského k Všenápravé* (Prague, 1958).
Quick R. H.: *Educational Reformers* Ch. X (New York, 1868).
Schaller K.: *Pan* (Mouton, 1958).
Schaller K.: *Die Pampaedia des J.A.C.* (Heidelberg, 1958).
Schaller K.: *Die Pädagogik des J.A.C.* (Heidelberg, 1962).
Seiler K.: *Comenius und die Erziehung von Heute* (Nuremberg, 1957).

J. A. COMENIUS

Spinka M.: *That Incomparable Moravian* (Chicago, 1934).
Turnbull G. H.: *Hartlib and his relations with Comenius* (Oxford, 1920). *Hartlib, Dury and Comenius* (Liverpool, 1947). *Two Pansophical Works* (Prague, 1951).
Wright C. J.: *Comenius and the Church Universal* (1941).
Young R. F.: *Comenius in England* (Oxford, 1932).

Monographs, Journals, Films and Illustrations
    Kyrášek J.: *Synkritiká metoda v díle J.A.K.* (Prague, 1964).
    R. F. Young: *Comenius and the Indians of New England* (London, 1929).

Journals
Monatshefte der Comenius-Gesellschaft (Berlin, 1892-1900).
Archiv pro Bádání (Brno, 1910-1936).
Pedagogika (Prague, 1957 and 1963).
Communio Viatorium (Prague Quarterly).
Český Jazyk (Prague, 1955-1956).
Acta Comeniana (Prague, 1957-1963).
Časopis Českeho Musea
Listy Filologicke
Slavonic Review (London Bi-annual)
Harvard Slavic Studies
Encounter, Feb. 1960. Vol. XIV.
Osiris. Vol. 9. 1949 (Mid 17th Century Science).
Adult Education. Apr. 1935. Vol. VII.

Illustrations
Čapkova D. and Kyrášek J.: Život a Dílo J.A.K. v Dokumentech (Prague, 1963).
Orbis Pictus (Selections in 6 Languages (Prague, 1958).
Pavlašek-Novák: J.A.C. Life and Work in Pictures (Prague, 1958).
Diafilm – J.A.C. (UNESCO, 1958).
Film – J.A.C. (Director, V. Količ, Prague, 1957).

C. *Background Sources*
    1. *Contemporaries of Comenius*
        Barnett Pamela R.: *Theodore Haak* (Mouton, 1962).
        Batten J. M.: *John Dury, Advocate of Christian Reunion* (1944).
        Cole P. R.: *Alsted, a Neglected Educator* (Sydney, 1910).
        Dalgarno G.: *Ars Signorum* (Oxford, 1661).
        Dircks H.: *Biographical Memoir of Samuel Hartlib* (London, 1865).
        Dury J.: *The Reformed School* (Ed. H. M. Knox. Liverpool, 1958).
        Farrington B.: *Francis Bacon* (1951).
        Held F. E. *Andreae: Christianopolis* (New York, 1916).
        Hartlib S.: *Description of the Famous Kingdom of Macaria* (London, 1641).
        Hoole C.: *New Discovery of the Old Art of Teaching* (1660).
        Kinner C.: *Diatyposis* (Tr. S. Hartlib 1648).
        Milton J.: *Of Education* (1644).
        Petty W.: *Advice of W.P. to S.H.* (1648).

BIBLIOGRAPHY

Seiler K.: *Das Päedagogische System W. Ratkes* (Erlangen, 1931).
Wolfe D. M.: *Milton and the Puritans* (Appendix on Comenius) Nelson, 1941).
Young R. F.: *George Ritschel*, a Bohemian Philosopher (1926).
Translations of the Works of Bacon, Descartes, Spinoza, Galileo, Gilbert and Harvey in Great Books of the Western World. (Ed. R. M. Hutchins 1952).

2. *Religious Background*
Barbour H.: *Quakers in Puritan England* (Yale, 1964).
Brock P.: *Political and Social Doctrines of the Unity of Brethren* (1957).
Fitzpatrick E. A.: *St Ignatius and the Ratio Studiorum* (New York, 1933).
Hughes T. G.: *Loyola and the Jesuits* (1892).
Hutton J. E.: *History of the Moravian Church* (London, 1909).
Říčan R. and others: *Jednota Bratrská* (1457-1957) (Prague, 1956).
Jones Rufus: *Spiritual Reformers of the 16th and 17th Centuries* (1928).
Jones Rufus: *Studies in Mystical Religion* (London, 1923).
Kinloch T. F.: *Pioneers of Religious Education* (Oxford, 1939).
McNeil J. T.: *Unitive Protestantism* (1930).
Schweinitz E. de: *History of Unitas Fratrum* (Bethlehem Pa., 1885).
Stickelburger E.: *Calvin* (J. Clarke 1959).

3. *Historical Background*
Armytage W. H. G., *Heavens Below* (Kegan Paul, 1961).
Armytage, W. H. G., *The Rise of the Technocrats* (Kegan Paul, 1965).
Bronfenbrenner, Martha, *The Role of Scientific Societies in the 17th Century* (Chicago, 1928).
Clark G. N.: *The Seventeenth Century* (1950).
Collingwood R. G.: *The Idea of Nature* (Clarendon 1945).
Copleston F.: *History of Philosophy* (1953).
Denis E.: *La Bohême depuis le Montagne Blanc* (Paris, 1903).
Denis E.: *Fin de L'Indépendence de Bohême* (Paris, 1890).
Hill Christopher: *Century of Revolution* (Nelson 1961).
Hill Christopher: *Intellectual Origins of English Revolution* (Oxford, 1965).
Morton A. L.: *The English Utopia* (London, 1952).
Mumford L.: *The Story of Utopia* (London, 1922).
Rice E.: *The Renaissance Idea of Wisdom* (Harvard, 1958).
Seton-Watson R. W.: *History of Czechs and Slovaks* (1943).
Spratt T.: *History of Royal Society* (1667).
Wedgwood V. C.: *Thirty Years War* (Pelican).
Willey B.: *Seventeenth Century Background* (Chatto & Windus 1953).

4. *Educational Background*
J. W. Adamson: *Pioneers of Modern Education* (C.U.P. 1905).
Boyd W.: *History of Western Education* (A. & C. Black, 1947).
Brubacher J. S.: *History of the Problems of Education* (McGraw, 1947).
Castle E. B.: *Moral Education in Christian Times* (London, 1958).
Corcoran T.: *Studies in the History of Classical Education* (Dublin, 1911).
Cubberley E.: *History of Education* (Mass. 1920).
Dilthey W.: *Pädagogik: Geschichte und Grund Linien des Systems* (1934).
Eby F.: *Early Protestant Educators* (1931).

J. A. COMENIUS

Raumer K. von: *Geschichte der Pädagogik* (1843).
Robbins C.: *Teachers in the 16th Century* (New York, 1912).
Smith Ashley J. W. *The Birth of Modern Education* (1954).
Vincent W. A. C.: *The State and School Education 1640-60* (SPCK., 1950).
Watson Foster: *Vives on Education* (C.U.P., 1913).
Weimer H.: *Concise History of Education* (Owen, 1962).
Woodward W. H.: *Humanist Educators* (C.U.P., 1897).
Woodward W. H.: *Education during the Renaissance* (C.U.P., 1906).

APPENDIX

Biographical Notes on some of the Contemporaries of Comenius

ALSTED, JOHN HENRY (1588-1638) was one of the teachers of
Comenius at Herborn, though only four years his senior, and one of
the most important influences on him despite some differences of
opinion. (e.g. *Great Didactic* XXIX.1.) It was from Alsted's
Triumphus Biblicus that Comenius drew support for his faith in the
validity of Scriptural prophetic truth and therefore accepted the
doctrine of the Millenium. Alsted was convinced that man himself
had an important part to play through education in bringing the
purposes of God to fruition and he devoted his attention to the
problem of a universal system for the reform of mankind. (Section
on Education in the *Encyclopaedia*.) He was a man of immense industry (cf. his anagram 'Sedulitas') who occupied much of his life in
systematizing all human knowledge. He wrote an *Encyclopaedia of
Philosophy* when he was only twenty but his major work, the
Encyclopaedia Omnium Scientarium, was published at Herborn in
1630. This contained a lengthy section on Education in which Alsted
outlined his views on the organization of schools and pedagogic
method. Like Comenius, Alsted was a war refugee but he found
shelter in Hungary and worked with Bisterfeld at Weissenburg. They
were both interested in the possibility of an ideal short encyclopaedia
which would include all things necessary for complete wisdom. (cf.
Comenius' ideas on this problem in *Continuatio* 45) and Bisterfeld's
correspondence with Hartlib. (R. F. Young, *Comenius in England*,
p. 32.) Although he died eighteen years before Comenius went to
Saros Patak, Alsted prepared the way for the Pansophic School there.
> (P. R. Cole, *J. H. Alsted, A Neglected Educator* 1910)
> (P. Bayle, *Dictionnaire historique et critique*)

ALTING, HENRY (1583-1644) was a student at Herborn but when
Comenius went to Heidelberg he was already a teacher there. In
addition he was attached to the court of the Elector Palatinate and
accompanied him to England for the marriage negotiations with the
Princess Elizabeth. He took an active part in establishing the reputation of the University of Heidelberg as a centre of tolerance as well

as learning and in 1616 he was put in charge of the College of Wisdom there. His influence on Comenius was towards a simple and undogmatic theology and, with David Pareus, he inspired him with the ideal of the unity of all Christians. The work of Alting was cut short by the fall of Heidelberg to Tilly in 1622 and he escaped to the Hague where he joined his unlucky master, the Elector, whose son he took as pupil. In 1627 he became Professor of Theology at Groningen but his latter years were saddened by Protestant intolerance.

(P. Bayle, *Dictionnaire*)

ANDREAE, JOHN VALENTINE (1586-1654) was one of the most powerful influences on Comenius (cf. *Methodus* XXIX and *Prodromus*, Preface). He was born at Herrenberg and received a wide education at Tübingen and during seven years' travelling in various countries. He settled down to the pastoral life of a Diakonus at Vailingen and became deeply interested in the Order of the Rosicrucians, a somewhat shadowy fellowship of mystical reformers. Between 1614 and 1619 Andreae wrote a number of books dealing with the origin of this Order the most famous of which was the *Fama Fraternitatis* (1614) which purported to give the life of the founder, Christian Rosenkreutz, who lived from 1378 to 1484. How authentic this account was cannot be proved but Andreae aroused great hopes in the Rosicrucian programme. Comenius devotes a chapter to it in the *Labyrinth* (Ch. XIII) showing the alternation of excitement and disillusion with which it was greeted. Andreae founded a society, the Fruchtbringende Gesellschaft, in 1616, which was designed as a lodge of the Rosicrucian Order and the mixture of alchemy, mysticism and social reform is shown in another book, the *Chymical Marriage*, published in the same year. Then in 1619 he published his most important work, the *Reipublicae Christianopolitanae Descriptio* – which made a deep impression on Comenius. In several ways it was an advance on previous Utopian literature particularly in relation to education. It combined the best elements in Baconian philosophy with the Rosicrucian ideals. In 1620 Andreae went to Calw and devoted himself to the task of enlisting the co-operation of all sections of the community in building up a good social order and of establishing in the Fruchtbringende Gesellschaft a nucleus for universal brotherhood and the diffusion of scientific knowledge. The Thirty Years War brought such plans to an end and Andreae found his way to Nuremberg where in 1628 he founded a Christian Union with three friends which probably provided the stimulus for similar efforts by Hartlib. (G. Turnbull, *Hartlib, Drury and Comenius*, p. 74.) In 1639 Andreae became Lutheran Court preacher at Stuttgart and published a book, *Evangelische Kirchenharmonie*, in 1646. In the Preface he seemed to blame Comenius for irreverence towards Martin Luther and this brought from Comenius a strong protest against such a charge. (Kvačala, Korres. No. 102).

(F. E. Held, *Andreae, Christianopolis* 1916)
(Max Möhrke, *J. A. Comenius u. J. V. Andreae* 1904)

BOEHME, JACOB (1575-1624) died a year before Comenius visited his home town, Görlitz, but there is good evidence of influence in the *Labyrinth* and in the *Centrum Securitatis* (1625) and the works of Boehme were widely circulated in Europe. The central thought of Boehme was derived from Paracelsus and was concerned with the manifestation of God first in the structure of the physical universe but ultimately in the human soul and this became the key concept of Pansophy.

Boehme was born at Alt-Seidenberg near to Görlitz. Though his formal education was very limited he acquired an intimate knowledge of the Bible and was well versed in the mystical works of Schwenckfeld and Weigel. He had a vivid imagination and from an early age showed a capacity for intense psychic experience in visions. He received these 'illuminations' with ecstatic joy and believed that he had seen into the inmost secrets of nature. He revolted against conventional religion and sought alone for the 'Divine Light' through prayer and meditation. In 1600 he had a 'sabbatic' experience and though only a humble wandering cobbler he was impelled to write an account of what he had seen. This became known as the *Daybreak* (Aurora) and it was circulated over a wide area. It exposed him to the malice of the local Lutheran pastor, Gregorius Richter, because it implied the uselessness of sectarianism. His enemies tried to silence him but in 1623 his visions were collected into a volume known as the *Way to Christ*. Boehme's faith in the 'principle of light' was always an inspiration to Comenius – indeed to many others even in England.

(Rufus M. Jones, *Spiritual Reformers in Sixteenth and Seventeenth Centuries*)
(Franz Hartmann, *Life and Doctrine of Jacob Boehme*)

BOURIGNON, ANTOINETTE (1616-1680) was a mystic with whom Comenius corresponded in his latter years and who lived in Amsterdam for the last two years of his life.

Antoinette Bourignon was born at Lille with a physical deformity from which she gradually recovered. As a young woman she resisted the attempts of her parents to get her married and following a succession of visions she tried to escape to live as a hermit. She was able to form a small community of like-minded women but was often afflicted with delusions of diabolical possession of herself or her associates. In 1653 she administered a hospital for the poor and invalid but gave herself up to the attainment of peace of mind through meditation and prayer. Believing herself to be the spouse of the Holy Ghost she had frequent apocalyptic visions but continued her obsession with devil possession which caused her to be brought before the magistrates and accused of sorcery. She fled to Amsterdam where her book, *The Light of the World* was published in 1668, the same year in which Comenius wrote *The One Thing Necessary* which expressed in a similar way the anticipation of union with God. In 1671 Antoinette Bourignon went to Germany and finished her earthly life in good works and renunciation of liturgical exercises. She suffered persecution at the hands of Protestants as she had done previously from Catholics.

(P. Bayle, *Dictionnaire*)

DRABIK, NICHOLAS (1588-1671) was strangely linked with Comenius to whom he was in some sense an evil genius.

Drabík was born at Strážnice to which town Comenius came in 1606, following the death of his parents, so that it may be assumed they were fellow pupils for a short time. Certainly they were inducted into the ministry together in 1616 and became pastors soon after. While Comenius found refuge at Leszno Drabik fled to Lednitz in Hungary and for a time the connection ceased. Indeed, Drabik, finding the ministerial calling impossible, became a cloth merchant and so scandalized the Brethren by his way of life that a Synod suspended him. He came to repentance and in 1638 had the first of many visions in which he foresaw the complete overthrow of the Hapsburg power and the restoration of Protestantism. His associates found no difficulty and much joy in accepting these prophecies and eventually they came to the notice of Comenius who was eagerly awaiting the conclusion of peace negotiations at Osnabrück. The only thing that remained in some doubt was the instrument by which this judgment of God should be effected and Drabik revealed the name of George I Rákóczi, Prince of Transylvania. The Prince repudiated the honour and, in any case, died soon after but Drabik quickly transferred his prophecy to the new Prince, Sigismund. This seemed more auspicious since Sigismund was betrothed to Henrietta, daughter of Elizabeth of Bohemia and Comenius came to celebrate the marriage in an excess of joyful anticipation. This is surely understandable. Even more so his despair when the young couple both died soon after. Drabík's prophetic powers survived even this blow and he not only named George II Rákóczi as the new saviour but invoked the help of all people, including Turks and Tartars. In 1657 Comenius collected the prophecies of Drabik, Kotter and Christina Poniatowska into a book, Lux in Tenebris, for circulation to friends and supporters. It seemed that no set-back could destroy his faith and he continued in affectionate correspondence until the end with this strange visionary. Within eight months of Comenius' death Drabik retracted his prophecies and embraced Catholicism which, however, did not save him from the vengeance of the Emperor by whose order his tongue was cut out and he was executed.

Nicholas Drabik brought ruin to his friends and disillusion to his Church but it is possible to see in him an example of psychopathological religious experience rather than of blatant hypocrisy.

FLUDD, ROBERT (1574-1637) was a leader of the Rosicrucians in England in the early seventeenth century for whom he wrote an Apologia in 1616. It was from him that Comenius derived ideas concerning the physical structure of the universe (cf. Great Didactic, XX.11).

Robert Fludd was born at Milgate in Kent and spent six years on the Continent studying medicine before he established himself as a physician in London. According to Fuller he practised a form of faith-healing and he believed that all science was rooted in revelation. He combined mysticism with alchemy and there is evidence of his interest in Baconian experimental methods (G. Turnbull, Hartlib, Dury and Comenius, p. 128). He was a voluminous writer who made mystical anticipations of empirical discoveries, for instance, of Harvey's theory of the Circulation of the Blood (Journal of the History of Medicine 1961, 16, pp. 374-393. Alan G. Debus).

It is in Fludd's theory of the Universe as Macrocosm and Microcosm that may be found the source of one of Comenius' main principles, namely, that 'all things have been harmoniously arranged that the higher can be represented by the lower' (Great Didactic XX.11). For Fludd physics must begin with an alchemical interpretation of the Creation and he assumes three basic principles – Light and Darkness and Water as an intermediary between them. Belief in a 'vital spirit' of the air is found almost everywhere in alchemical literature (cf. *Isis*, March 1964, p. 59. Alan G. Debus, *The Paracelsian Aerial Niter*) and therefore it is impossible to say how much Comenius was indebted to Fludd and in the *Physica* it is to Paracelsus that he particularly refers.

(J. B. Craven, *Dr Robert Fludd*, 1902)

JONSTON, JOHN (1603-1675) is of interest because, although a native of Leszno, he was well acquainted with England and negotiated connections between Comenius and members of the Hartlib group. (cf. Turnbull, *Hartlib, Dury and Comenius*, p. 342.) Comenius himself names Jonston as a possible collaborator in his pansophic schemes. (R. F. Young, *Comenius in England*, p. 36.)

John Jonston was born near Leszno though he came from an old Scottish family and was sent for his education to St Andrew's University. He studied in various German Universities and in 1630 wrote a book called *Thaumatographia* which was a compilation of natural curiosities. Soon after, he conducted two young lords in their travels to England, Holland, France and Italy. On his return to Poland he settled down at Lignitz in Silesia and devoted himself to scientific studies.

He wrote a considerable number of books on medicine, botany and zoology, some of which were well known. For instance the *Natural History of Animals*, 1649, served as a standard work until Linnaeus and contained interesting illustrations. Shortly before, in 1648, he published a book on medicine, *Idea Universae Medicinae Practicae*, which shows his concern for an encyclopedic approach to science. Two other books show by their titles how closely he shared the approach to knowledge of Comenius – *Sceleton historiae civilis et ecclesiasticae* published at Leyden in 1639 and *Theatrum Universale historiae naturalis* published at Frankfort-on-Main 1650-54. He differed from Comenius in that he seems to have found it possible to pursue his studies in peace.

JUNGIUS, JOACHIM (1587-1657) was one of the foremost of the German professors having connections with Comenius, Dury and Hartlib. Thus when arrangements were being made for Comenius' visit to England it was suggested that he should go via Hamburg and discuss his pansophy with Jungius and Tassius. (G. Turnbull, *Hartlib, Dury and Comenius*, p. 345.) Then when Comenius had left England for Sweden it would seem that he tried to make some arrangements for Jungius to meet Chancellor Oxenstiern. (Turnbull, op. cit. p. 367.)

APPENDIX

Jungius was born at Lubeck but was left an orphan at the age of two. He learnt with incredible rapidity at school and at Rostock University pursued the study of Mathematics with great ardour. In 1609 he became Professor of Mathematics at Giessen. In 1615 he returned to Rostock where he studied medicine and in 1618 visited Italy and took a degree in Medicine at Padua. For a time he then settled at Rostock dividing his attention between Maths and Medicine but seeking to establish a society for scientific research – the Societas Ereunetica. The inspiration for this came from Andreae but the Baconian approach is indicated by the motto *Per inductionem et experimentia omnia*. His purpose was 'to free all arts and sciences from sophistry' (Martha Bronfenbrenner, *The Role of Scientific Societies in the Seventeenth Century*, p. 168) and to show that they could be taught 'more comfortably, perfectly and explicitly in German than in Latin'.

The Societas Ereunetica was short-lived and Goethe had justification for saying, 'If people had followed the advice of Jungius as to methods of study the world would have reached a hundred years earlier that point at which it is today'. However, Jungius left Rostock for Hamburg where he became Rector of the Grammar School but devoted his time to scientific matters. His chief interest came to lie in Botany and Entomology and his attempts at classification and nomenclature were in advance of his time. (Sachs, *History of Botany 1530-1860*, p. 30.) Tassius informed Hartlib in 1640 that, although Jungius was forced to read Aristotle's notions, he did not hold them. (G. Turnbull, op. cit. p. 218.) In fact Jungius was accused, probably with justification, of being a Rosicrucian.

KOTTER, CHRISTOPHER, the tanner of Sprottau in Silesia, was one of the people whose prophecies had a profound effect upon the thinking of Comenius. Kotter received certain visions between 1616 and 1624 centring around the person of Frederick, Elector of the Palatinate, who was crowned King of Bohemia in 1619. They therefore covered the period in which Comenius passed from high hope to deep despair. In 1625 Comenius went to Poland to explore the possibility of a refuge for the scattered remnants of the Brethren and he visited Sprottau on the way. Kotter was then in Brandenburg with the exiled King Frederick but Comenius carefully examined his recorded prophecies and became convinced that it was the Word of the Lord to him. He translated them into Czech and copies were printed and widely circulated in Bohemia. In 1627 Kotter was thrown into prison but later released and exiled into Saxony where he lived peacefully until his death in 1647.

The fact that Kotter's prophecies were proved wrong by the course of events did not shake the conviction of Comenius that they were genuine. He regarded prophecy as being dependent upon man's response to God's will and therefore believed that particular events must be interpreted in the light of the ultimate purpose of God to establish his rule on earth. It was necessary to distinguish between things fundamental, instrumental and accidental.

LAUREMBERG, PETER (1585-1639) was the author of a book, *Pansophia sive Paedia philosophica*, published in 1633 which Comenius 'eagerly compared' but found nothing 'appertaining to divine wisdom'. Nevertheless he adopted the term 'Pansophia' to define his search for 'the very marrow of eternal truth' (*Via Lucis* XVI.4).

Peter Lauremberg was born at Rostock and studied in France at Montauban and then at Leyden where he published a work on Astronomy. Though he became Professor of Poetry at Rostock in 1620 his main interests continued to be in natural science and especially botany and medicine. In one of his works he describes the circulation of the blood but without any acknowledgement to Harvey. He was at Rostock at the time when Jungius made the abortive attempt to establish the Societas Ereunetica but may not have been concerned with it. The *Dictionnaire Universelle* describes him as 'plein de vanité'.

LUBINUS, EILHARD (1565-1621) was another of the Rostock professors who had influence on Comenius especially through a Prefatory Epistle to a tri-lingual New Testament which Comenius refers to as a 'Didactic' (Jelínek, *Analytical Didactic*, p. 45). Lubinus also influenced Comenius towards the use of illustrations in text-books. (Methodus VIII.) In 1654 Hartlib published a translation of an Epistolary Discourse by Lubinus entitled 'The True and Ready Way to Learne the Latin Tongue' in which the argument against a grammatical approach is put. Comenius, however, found his direct method not acceptable.

Lubinus was born at Oldenburg and at an early age showed great gifts in the ancient languages but he covered a wide field of knowledge including Mathematics, Literature and Theology. In 1601 he was Professor of Theology at Rostock. He was best known as a linguist and philologue and his *Clavis Graecae linguae* may be looked upon as a fore-runner of Comenius' Janua. Like others of his time he gave his attention to the metaphysical problem of the fundamental principles underlying the physical universe and suggested that evil was the tendency towards emptiness rather than towards God.

INDEX OF PERSONS

311

INDEX OF PERSONS

INDEX OF SUBJECTS

INDEX OF SUBJECTS

315

INDEX OF SUBJECTS

GEORGE ALLEN & UNWIN LTD

London: 40 Museum Street, WC1
Auckland: PO Box 36013, Northcote Central, Auckland N4
Bombay: 15 Graham Road, Ballard Estate, Bombay 1
Barbados: PO Box 222, Bridgetown
Buenos Aires: Escritorio 454-459, Florida 165
Calcutta: 17 Chittaranjan Avenue, Calcutta 13
Cape Town: 68 Shortmarket Street
Hong Kong: 44 Mody Road, Kowloon
Ibadan: PO Box 62
Karachi: Karachi Chambers, McLeod Road
Madras: Mohan Mansions, 38c Mount Road, Madras 6
Mexico: Villalongin 32-10, Piso, Mexico 5, DF
Nairobi: PO Box 4536
New Delhi: 13-14 Asaf Ali Road, New Delhi 1
Ontario: 81 Curlew Drive, Don Mills
Sao Paulo: Caixa Postal 8675
Singapore: 36c Prinsep Street, Singapore 7
Sydney, NSW: Bradbury House, 55 York Street
Tokyo: 10 Kanda-Ogawamachi, 3-Chome, Chiyoda-Ku

BERTRAND RUSSELL ON EDUCATION

JOE PARK

As one of the truly vigorous and creative thinkers of the twentieth century, Bertrand Russell has dared to raise and pursue questions that have been avoided by more timid and circumspect men; but although scholars from many disciplines have turned their attention to his work and appraised its significance for a number of fields, no thorough study of Russell's contribution to education – and area to which he devoted no small part of his energies – has appeared. Based as it is on interviews with Russell as well as diligent research in his writings and the sources of his thought, Mr. Parks' book will do much to remedy this deficiency. He offers a comprehensive treatment of Russell's unconventional educational theories and their application at Russell's own school, Beacon Hill, that will enlighten all who think seriously about contemporary education.

Demy 8vo.   25s. *net*

THE BURNING BOW

A *Selection from the Papers of*

T. F. COADE OF BRYANSTON

Thorold Coade was one of the great headmasters. He took up the appointment as Headmaster of Bryanston in 1932, four years after its opening, and while it was still beset with the teething troubles inherent in a new foundation. The magnitude of the task might have seemed too daunting for one of his unassuming nature, but he was a man with the inflexibility of purpose that enabled him to turn his ideals into reality. Crises of war and finance broke over him, but left him steadfast, while slowly the school grew around him, alive and sensitive.

For him education was a unity, the awakening of mind and body and spirit, and the harnessing of their energies to the purposes of God. Bryanston was a way of life; a place where all were educated – men and boys. The school was the place of the Individual in the Community, not of a set of individualists each fighting to get his own way. At Bryanston Thorold Coade reigned and not ruled. He was wise, understanding, and compassionate. His wit was a delight, and it sustained and decorated his talk. He spoke always with wisdom and imagination, and never without humour. When addressing the school he had the ability to put aside his serious subject and capture them with an amusing story, and returning to his theme, drive it home securely. He evoked enormous affection from both boys and men, many of whom held views widely differing from his own, perhaps because he was a compassionate man who could penetrate the superficial barriers which divide, so that those of each generation could find understanding.

Three of his colleagues have made a selection of the words and writings of his working life, which have been collected together in this book.

Demy 8vo.   42s. *net*

GEORGE ALLEN & UNWIN LTD